Photoshop 6 Visual JumpStart

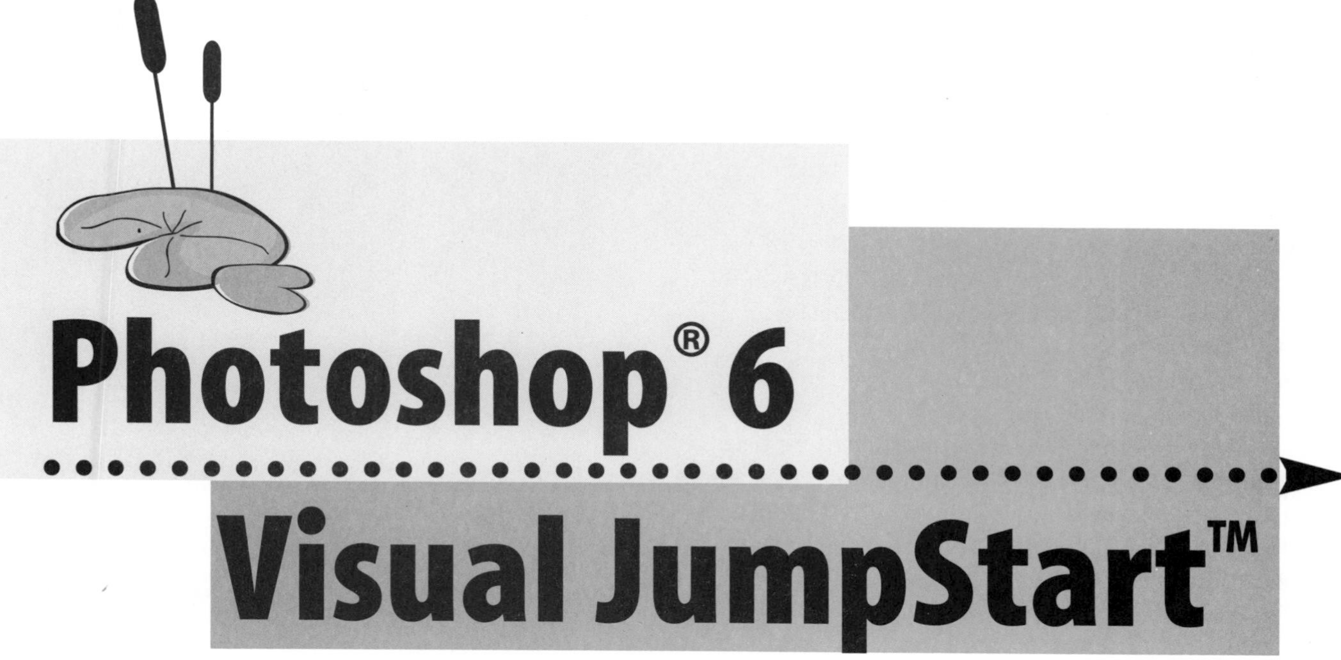

Photoshop® 6 Visual JumpStart™

Richard Schrand

SYBEX®

San Francisco • Paris • Düsseldorf • Soest • London

Associate Publisher: Cheryl Applewood
Contracts and Licensing Manager: Kristine O'Callaghan
Acquisitions and Developmental Editor: Mariann Barsolo
Editor: Marilyn Smith
Production Editor: Kylie Johnston
Technical Editor: Susan Glinert
Book Designer: Maureen Forys, Happenstance Type-O-Rama
Electronic Publishing Specialist: Maureen Forys, Happenstance Type-O-Rama
Proofreaders: Elizabeth Campbell, Andrea Fox, Nelson Kim, Nancy Riddiough, Nathan Whiteside
Indexer: Ted Laux
Cover Designer: Daniel Ziegler
Cover Illustrator: Ziegler Design

Library of Congress Card Number: 01-086077

ISBN: 0-7821-2866-1

Manufactured in the United States of America

10 9 8 7 6 5 4 3 2 1

To Jim Owens, Lorianne Crook, and Charlie Chase

Acknowledgments

This book has been a labor of love in many ways. And, as with all projects, it takes a lot of people to bring it through the various phases to become the product you have in your hands.

I'd like to thank Mariann Barsolo, Kylie Johnston, and Marilyn Smith for putting up with me as this book went from idea to publication. We went through a lot of ups and downs, and you stuck with me through all of it. I also appreciate Susan Glinert's work in checking this book's technical accuracy. Thanks go to Maureen Forys for her excellent job of laying out the book. Thanks also go to the proofreaders Elizabeth Campbell, Andrea Fox, Nelson Kim, Nancy Riddiough, and Nathan Whiteside and the indexer Ted Laux.

For all of their help and support, I wish to acknowledge:

- My agent, David Fugate, and his assistant, Maureen
- Everyone at Adobe involved with programming and producing the fantastic upgrades that have lead to Photoshop 6, the best in a long line of bests
- My parents, Ed and Jane
- My daughter Courtney, who will never let me forget that I put her brother's face onto her head within the pages of this book
- My sons Richard and Brandon, who had no say in my using them as guinea pigs on the various projects throughout these pages
- My daughter, Cyndi, her husband, Sam, and my grandchildren, Samantha and Joseph
- My wife, Sharon, who continues to stick by me through the ups and downs

Contents

Introduction

Photoshop is an awesome program. It's one of those rare applications that continues to astound, amaze, and fan the fires of creativity, no matter how long you have been using it. Its power lies in its almost limitless tools and effects, which allow you to create world-class images that jump off the computer screen or the printed page. Photoshop is more than a photograph-manipulation application. You can draw and paint, create seamless backgrounds for Web sites, and build effects to add to other images.

It's no wonder that Photoshop has become the image-manipulation program of choice for nearly all of the professional designers around the world. You literally cannot pick up a magazine without seeing something that has been created with the program. From *Time* to *Sports Illustrated* to *Newsweek*, almost every cover you see has been created in the program, not to mention the ads and images throughout the publications' pages. It's also pretty safe to say that even your local newspaper uses Photoshop as part of its design software. There are other programs out there, but none have the following of Adobe's premier application.

There is also no other program that has as many how-to books about it on the market. This is because Photoshop is filled with so many fantastic tools and effect generators that it can be very intimidating. Even the most seasoned "power users" won't claim to know this program inside and out. People are constantly finding new and exciting ways to create effects that are both eye-catching and cutting edge. Through the creative use of filters, layers, blending modes, and tools, you have virtually limitless design potential.

It may sound as if Photoshop is an extremely difficult program. Not really—it's only difficult if you don't have the information you need to help with the basics. The user's guide is a great place to start, and you should keep it close at hand to get the low-down on tools you haven't used before. But you also need something that gives you a real-world feel for what this fantastic program can do for you. That's where *Photoshop 6 Visual JumpStart* comes in. This book takes a highly visual, step-by-step approach to get you off to a quick start with Photoshop 6.

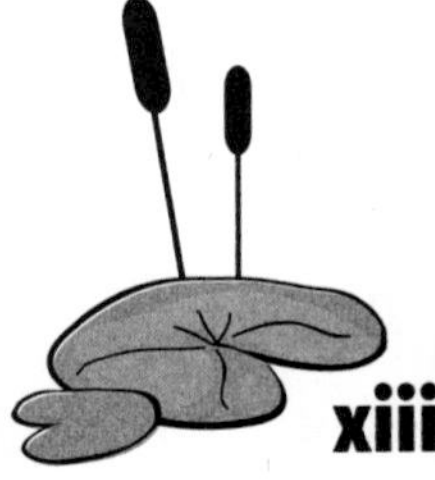

Image Sampler

The background banner in the image shown below was created entirely in Photoshop, using fills and the Airbrush tool for shading. You can also see other Photoshop effects in this image, such as drop shadows behind the logos to make them look as if they are positioned above the page, raised blocks, and slightly glowing text. These effects were built using layers and various filters.

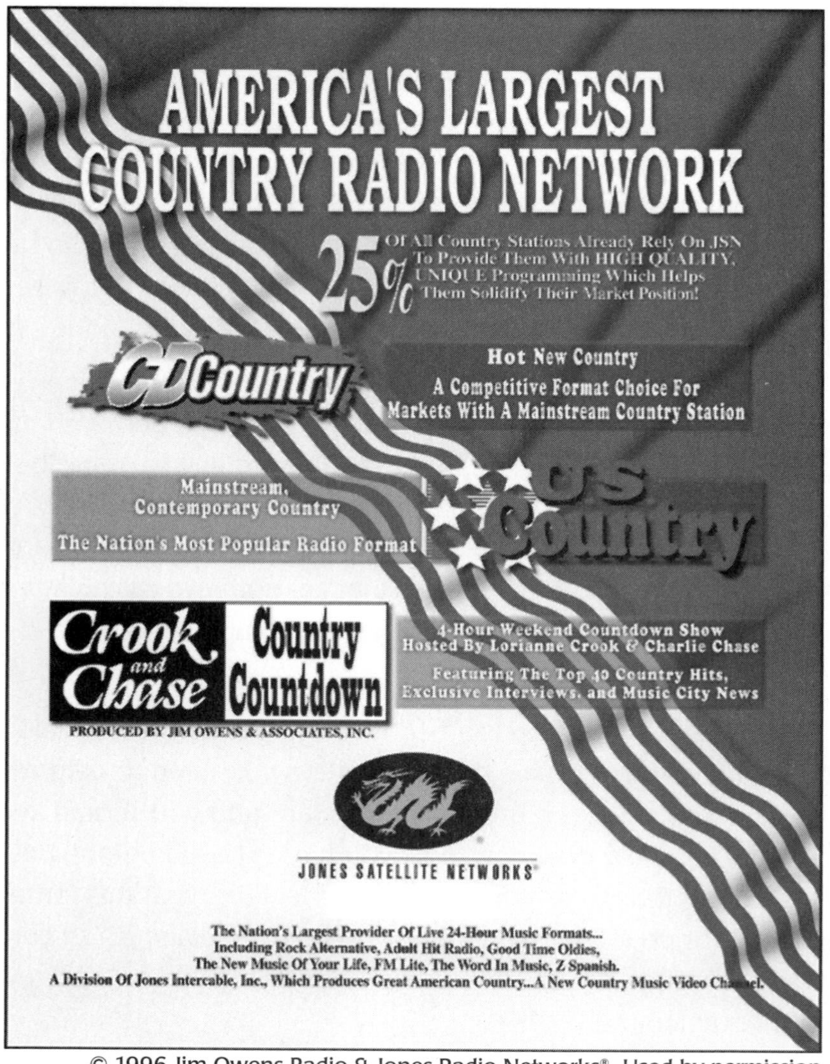

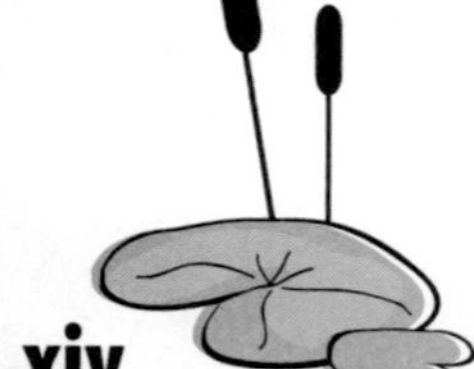

In the next image, the swirls behind the subjects were created using a filter and the Paintbrush tool. What you don't see in this image are sharp edges around the subjects. Through the use of the Blur filter, you can soften the edges of cutouts, giving them a more natural appearance.

©1996 Jim Owens Radio Used by permission

Along with projects designed for printed output, such as the magazine and newspaper advertisements, shown in these examples, Photoshop can also be used to build graphics for the Internet. To make Web design even easier, Photoshop 6 comes bundled with ImageReady 3.

What You'll Find in This Book

Photoshop 6 Visual JumpStart was designed with you, the beginning user, in mind. This book takes you through various projects that are designed to teach you the basics of the program, giving you the foundation to move onto more sophisticated work. You'll also get a feel for ImageReady 3 and how it works in unison with Photoshop to let you build elements for Web sites.

Here's a quick rundown on each of the chapters:

Chapter 1: Discovering the Features in Photoshop 6 Photoshop 6 has many new features that help expedite your workflow. In Chapter 1, you'll discover some of the more intriguing changes and additions to the program.

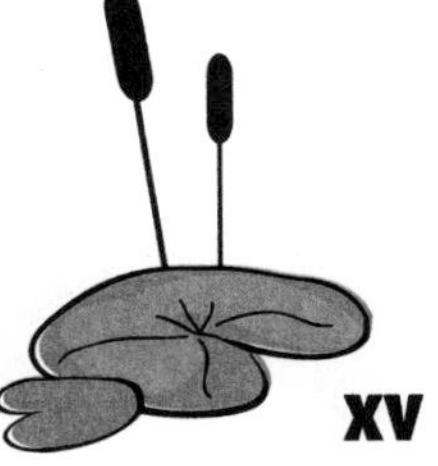

Chapter 2: Using the Editing Tools The Lasso, Magic Wand, Clone Stamp, Pattern Stamp, and Paintbrush are some of the tools that you'll employ almost every time you work with an image. In Chapter 2, you'll learn how to use these tools.

Chapter 3: Working with Layers, Channels, and Paths The Layers, Channels, and Paths palettes are three Photoshop features that give you the ability to build exciting images that combine text, elements from other images, and much more. In Chapter 3, you'll get hands-on experience with these palettes.

Chapter 4: Using Image-Modification Tools After you've had some experience working with layers, you'll want to explore the other image-modification tools in Photoshop's toolset. In Chapter 4, you'll learn how to use the Eraser tools, the History and Art History Brushes, the Blur/Sharpen/Smudge tools, and the Dodge/Burn tools.

Chapter 5: Working with Text Photoshop 6 includes many exciting features for working with text, including a new Text Warp option. In Chapter 5, you'll learn how to add text and create interesting text effects to enhance your images.

Chapter 6: Working with History States and Actions Using History states, you can correct errors and create special effects. Actions can speed you through repetitive tasks. In Chapter 6, you'll learn how to use the History and Actions palettes, which provide these features.

Chapter 7: Adjusting Images No matter how good a photographer you are or how good a scanner you have, you will frequently find that your images still need some adjustments for the best reproduction. In Chapter 7, you'll learn how to use the Photoshop features for controlling contrast, coloring, sizing, and other aspects of your images.

Chapter 8: Designing Images for the Web After you've worked with the main Photoshop tools, you'll want to discover how to get your images ready for the Web. In Chapter 8, you'll learn how to use Photoshop tools to design Web graphics.

Chapter 9: Using ImageReady ImageReady, which comes bundled with Photoshop 6, gives you added features for the creation of Web graphics. In Chapter 9, you'll learn the basics of using this program and how it interacts with Photoshop.

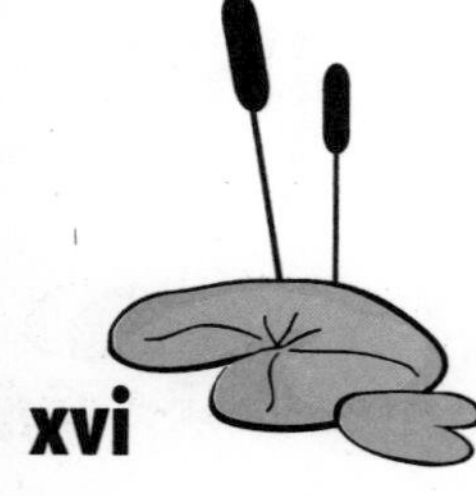

Chapter 10: Saving Images Saving your images in the most suitable format for their intended use is crucial to successful projects. In Chapter 10, you'll learn about the different formats in which your files can be saved, as well as how to use some Photoshop features for automating page layout.

As you can see, by the time you have worked your way through the book, you'll have a strong base from which your expertise can grow.

Making the Most of This Book

In each chapter of *Photoshop 6 Visual JumpStart* you will find a list of topics that you will learn in that chapter.

To enhance your knowledge of Photoshop design and animation, there are terms that are highlighted in the text and also defined in the margins of the book. Text that you are asked to type will appear in **bold font**.

You will also find other elements in the text to help you:

Note

Notes provide extra information and references to related information.

Tip

Tips are insights that help you perform tasks more easily and effectively.

Warning

Warnings let you know about things you should do, or shouldn't do.

Finally, when an operation requires a series of choices from menus or dialog boxes, the ➢ symbol is used to guide you through the instructions, like this: "Select Programs ➢ Accessories ➢ System Tools ➢ System Information." The items the ➢ symbol separates may be menu items, toolbar icons, check boxes, or other elements of the Windows interface—any place you can make a selection.

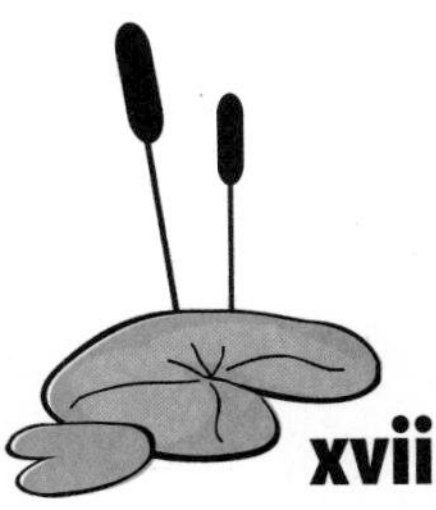

Revving Up

There is a lot to cover, and I know you want to get started. Before you do, though, I'd like to take a moment to thank you for purchasing this book. I hope you'll find it useful as you begin your exploration of Photoshop 6. And let me be the first to say:

Welcome to the Photoshop fold!

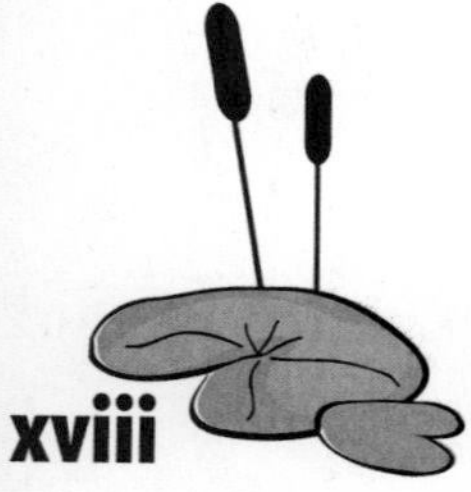

Part 1

Familiarizing Yourself with Photoshop

Using Photoshop 6 and mastering its myriad controls and functions can be a lifelong endeavor. Power users—those people who have learned the intricacies of the program over the years and who push the program to its limits—are still finding new and intriguing ways to create eye-catching and award-winning images using the program. But, before you can win your own awards with your Photoshop images, you need to start with the basics, and that's what will happen in this part.

Familiarizing Yourself with Photoshop

Chapter 1

Discovering the Features in Photoshop 6

In this chapter, you'll get acquainted with some of Photoshop's basic controls and tools, as well as experiment with some of the new tools that come with Photoshop 6:

- Photoshop Preferences settings
- The Photoshop toolbox
- Photoshop palettes
- The Background Eraser tool
- The Magic Eraser tool
- The Magnetic Lasso tool
- The Notes tool
- File tools

Setting Up Photoshop

Before you begin working with Photoshop, you may want to choose options to control certain ways that Photoshop behaves and the appearance of some Photoshop elements. If you have extra plug-ins or more than one hard drive, you also can set up Photoshop to use these resources.

Setting Preferences

You can set up Photoshop so that you are most comfortable with the workspace. This is accomplished via the Preferences dialog box.

1. Start up Photoshop 6. From the menu bar, select Edit ➢ Preferences ➢ General.

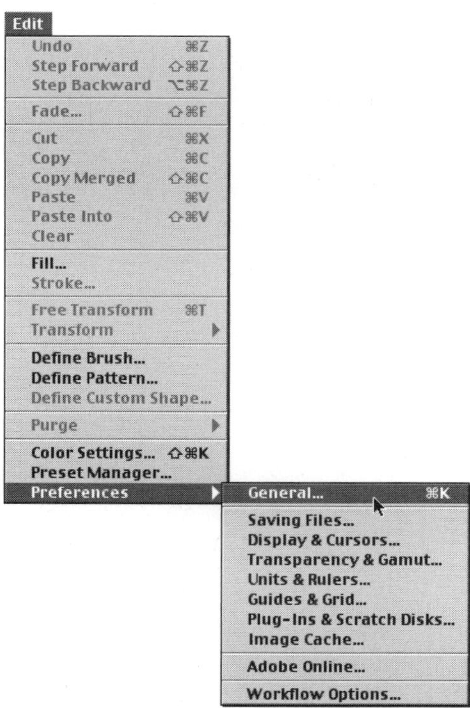

2. Select the options you want for the general layout of the program. For example, the Show Tool Tips option will help you with tool selection. You should keep this option active until you are familiar with the

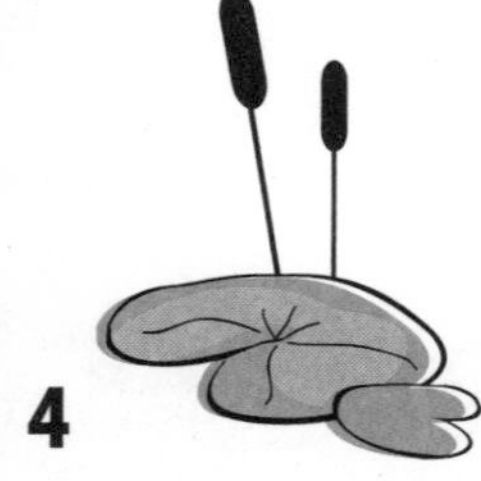

Photoshop tools and their position in the toolbox. Click the Next button located on the right side of the Preferences dialog box.

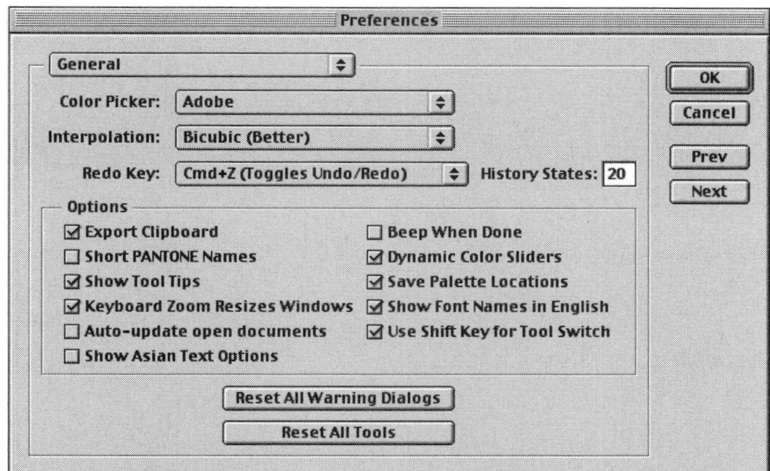

3. The Saving Files options relate to how your image files will be saved. For example, for ease of file identification, you should select Always Save for Image Previews. This way, you have a small visual representation of your file. The setup you see here (with some changes to the defaults) is a good starting point. After you've chosen your preferred options, click Next.

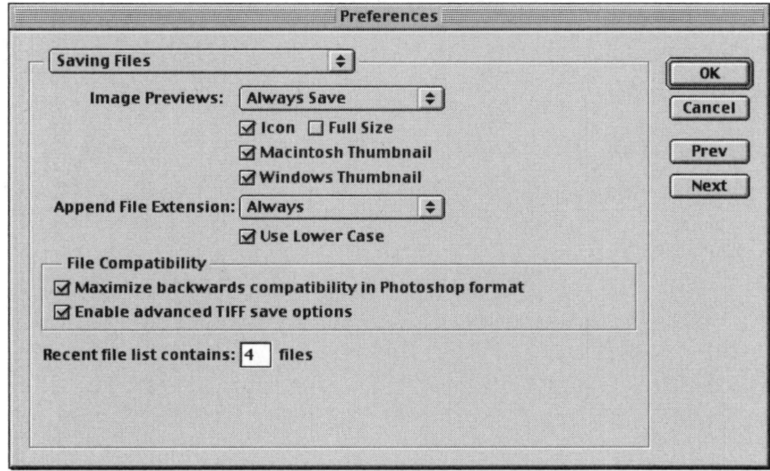

4. The Display & Cursors options let you choose how your image will appear, as well as the cursor icon that will be displayed when you choose various paint tools. For example, choosing Precise for both the

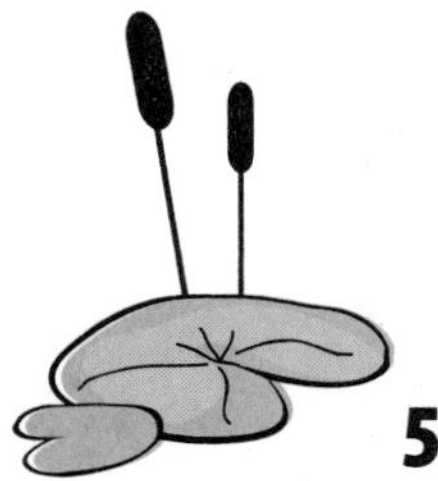

painting and other cursors makes the pointer appear as cross-hairs, which is helpful for working with your images. Click Next after you've set these options.

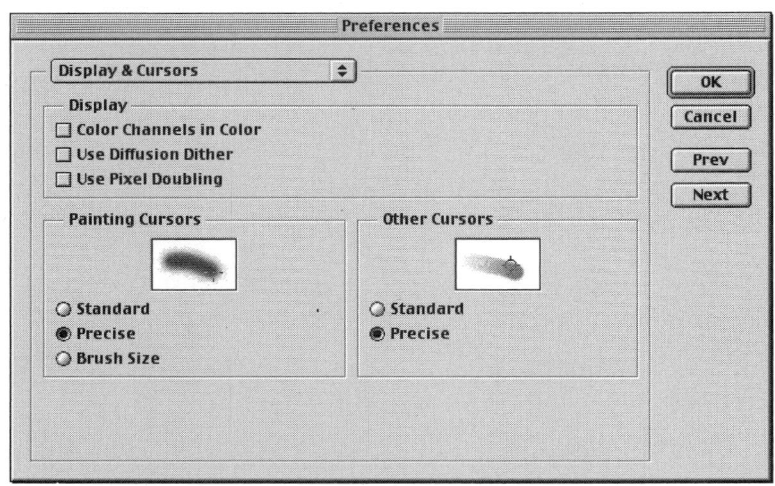

gamut
The range of viewable and printable colors for a particular color model, such as RGB (used for monitors) or CMYK (used for printing). When a color cannot be displayed or printed, Photoshop can warn you that it is out of gamut.

column
The vertical division of a page. Newspapers and many text books are printed using columns, so that more text can fit onto a page.

gutter
The blank space separating columns.

5. The Transparency & Gamut options let you determine how transparent (or invisible) areas of your image's background will be displayed, as well as how colors that are out of **gamut** will be shown. Use the pop-up menus to change the settings to suit your preferences. Click Next when you're finished.

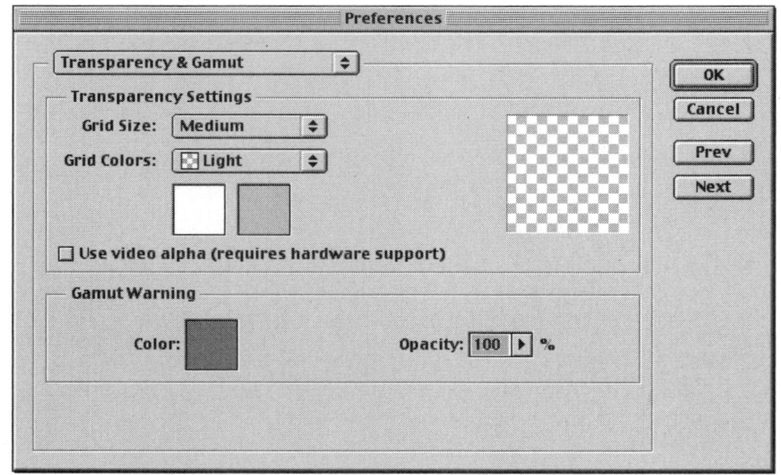

6. The Units & Rulers options let you select how your image is measured, how the rulers will be displayed, how **columns** and **gutter** widths are measured, and how text size will be displayed. Unless you're working on

a file that will be sent to a professional printer, it's best to change Rulers to Inches, since this is the most common form of measurement in the U.S. Click Next after choosing options.

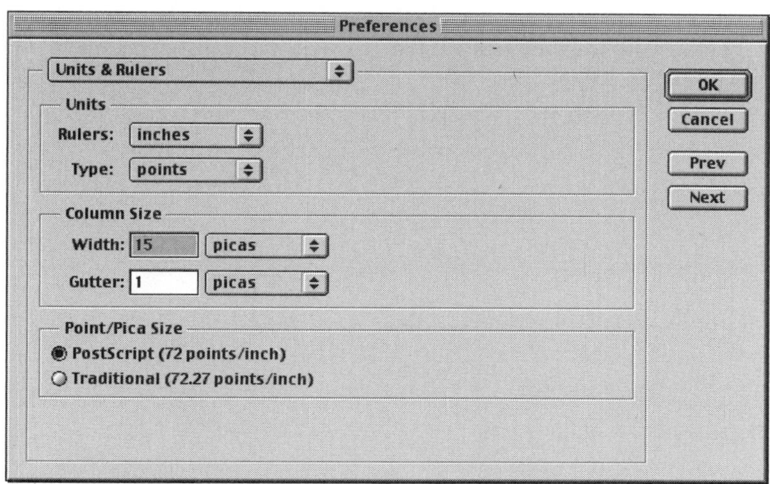

7. The Guides & Grid options allow you to select colors and styles for the nonprinting guides and grids that Photoshop displays to help with exact placement of elements. You can also choose the spacing of the grid. For now, leave the default settings.

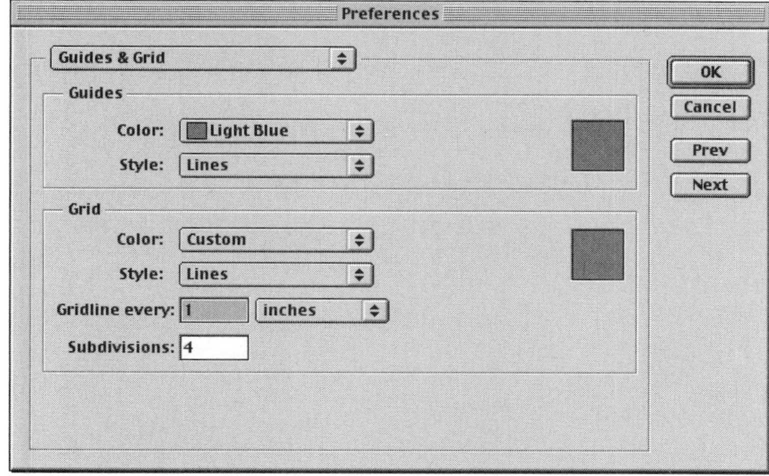

8. The Image Cache options are for cache levels and histograms. Image caching helps to speed up screen redrawing when you make changes to images. You can choose to use the cache for histograms, which are

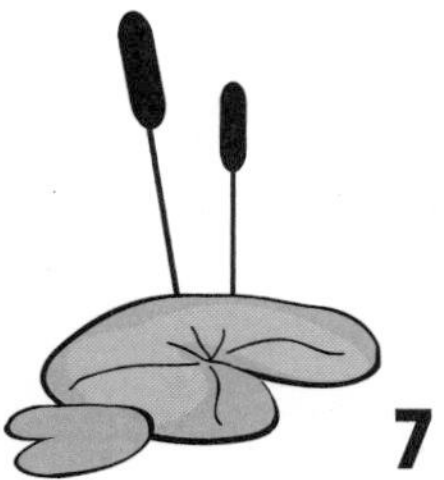

graphs of the brightness values of images. For now, leave these options at their default settings.

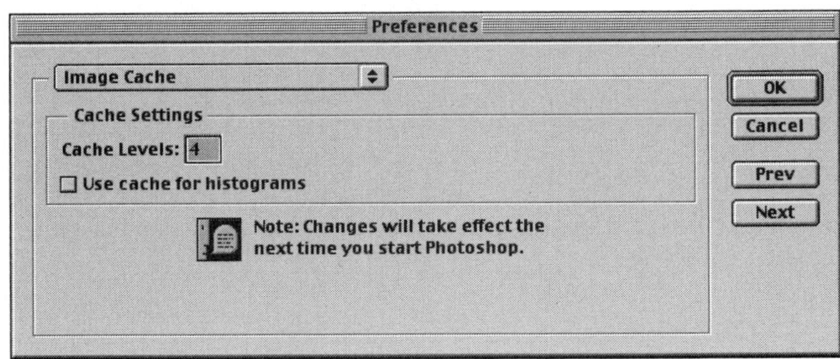

9. Click OK to close the Preferences dialog box.

The Preferences dialog box also includes Plug-ins & Scratch Disks options, which you'll set in the next sections.

Adding Plug-ins

plug-in
Software that adds functionality to Photoshop. Plug-ins generally give you the ability to add special effects to your image.

Plug-ins extend the creative options of Photoshop. There are numerous companies and individuals who have created plug-ins for the program. Photoshop automatically recognizes the plug-ins in its main plug-ins folder, but if you have extra Photoshop-compatible plug-ins stored with other programs (such as Adobe Illustrator), you need to set up Photoshop to recognize them.

1. Select Edit ➢ Preferences ➢ Plug-Ins & Scratch Disks.
2. Click the Additional Plug-Ins Folder check box and click the Choose button,

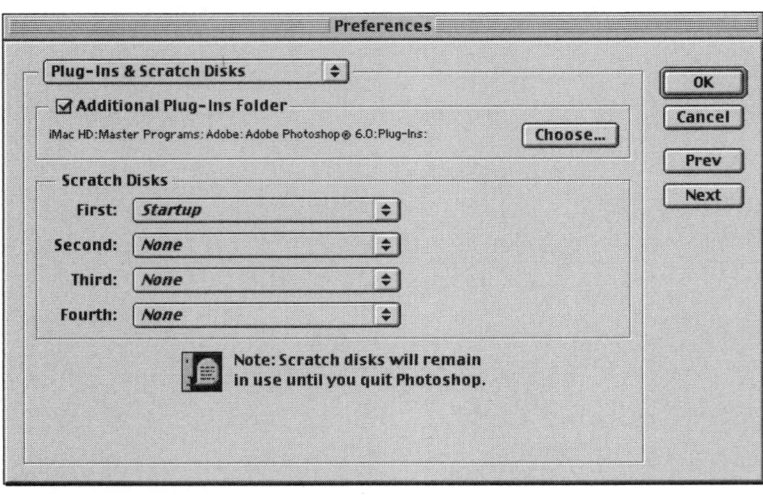

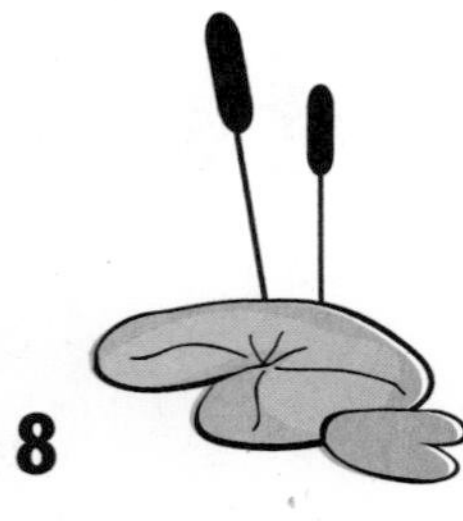

3. An Additional Plug-Ins Folder dialog box appears. Navigate to the additional plug-ins folder you want to use, and then click the OK button.

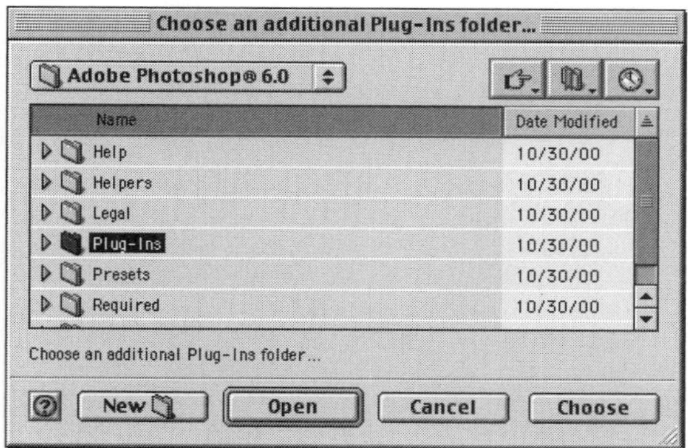

4. Click OK to save your settings and close the dialog box.

After you select an additional plug-ins folder, you will need to restart Photoshop for any of the plug-ins in that folder to appear in the Filter menu on the menu bar.

Note

If the plug-ins folder you selected does not have Photoshop-compatible plug-ins, they will not show up in the Filters menu.

Managing Memory

Photoshop likes to have as much memory as is possible to do its job more efficiently. To figure out memory requirements for the program, use a three-to-one ratio; in other words, the amount of RAM available should be triple the size of the image file you're working on. For example, if you have a file that is 50MB, you should have 150MB of RAM. For a 100MB file (which is not unusual when dealing with high-resolution images), you should have 300MB of RAM installed on your system.

Unfortunately, it's not always possible (financially or otherwise) to buy the maximum amount of RAM for your computer. But if you have a large hard drive or, even better, more than one hard drive on your system, you have some options for managing Photoshop's memory requirements: You can set up free space on

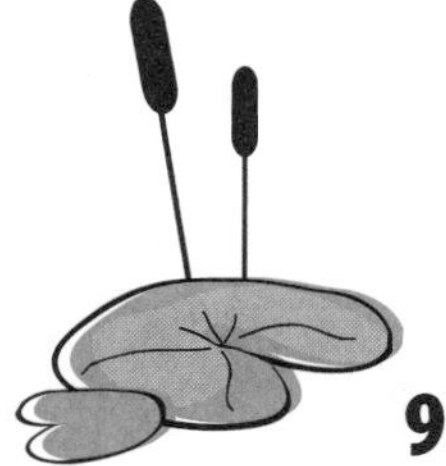

scratch disk
A hard drive with unused space that Photoshop can turn into memory that it will use if necessary.

your main hard driveor you can assign space from your second hard drive, through scratch disks, to handle the extra memory requirements.

1. Select Edit ➢ Preferences ➢ Plug-Ins & Scratch Disks.
2. In the Scratch Disks section of the dialog box, Startup should already be selected in the First box. If you have a second hard disk, select that disk from the Second pop-up menu.

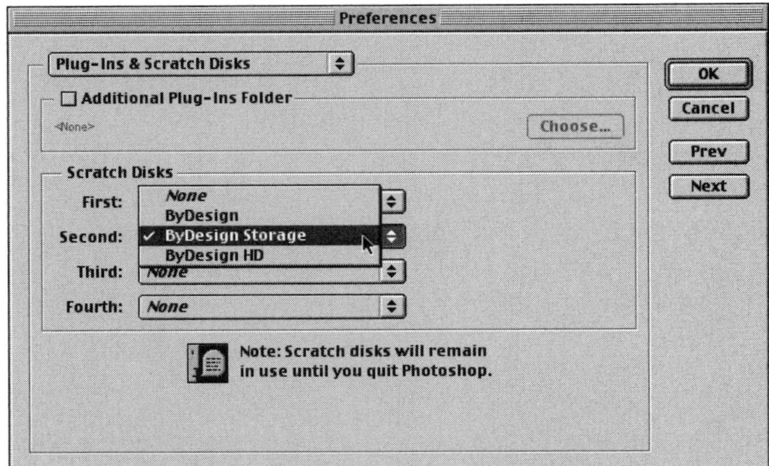

Note

With scratch disks assigned, Photoshop will use open space on your hard drive(s) and use that open space as extra memory when necessary.

3. In the Third and Fourth boxes, select other disks if you have more drives attached to your system.
4. Click OK to save your settings and close the dialog box.

Getting to Know the Photoshop Tools

After you've set up Photoshop, you can start to spend some time learning where the various tools are and what they are used for. All of the tools are

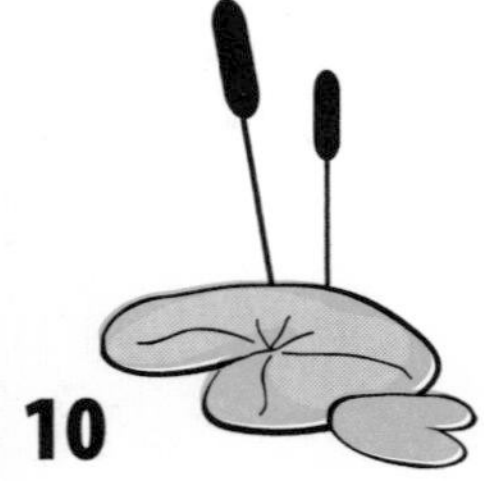

located in the toolbox on the left side of your screen. The toolbox also offers other controls for working with your images and getting online.

Introducing the Tools

The toolbox holds the Photoshop tools you will use to create and modify images. In many cases, the space occupied by an icon you see actually holds several tools. To switch to another tool in the same area, press and hold down the mouse button over the tool icon in the toolbox to see the other tools, and then click to select the tool you want to use.

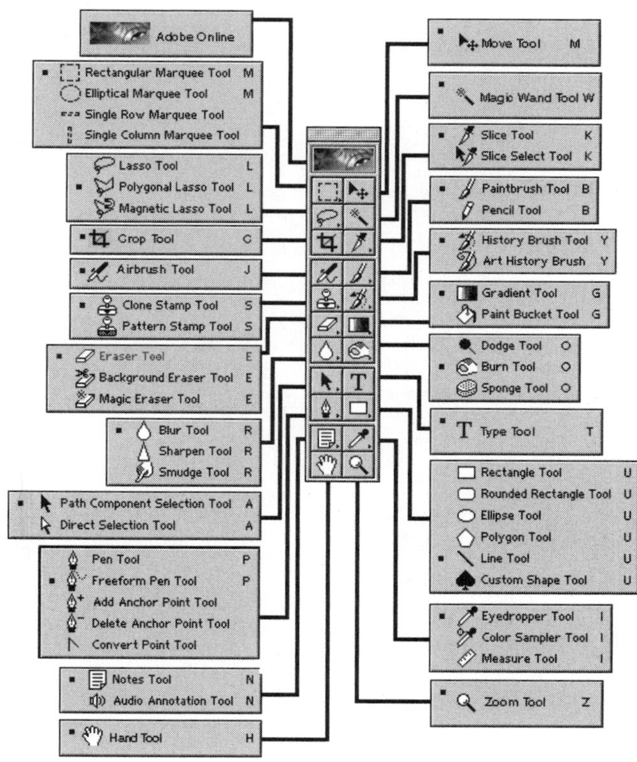

Here's an overview of the main tools that are shown when you first start the program, starting with the top-left tool and moving from left to right, row to row:

Rectangular Marquee Allows you to select a rectangular portion of an image so you can move it to another location or modify what is inside the selected area

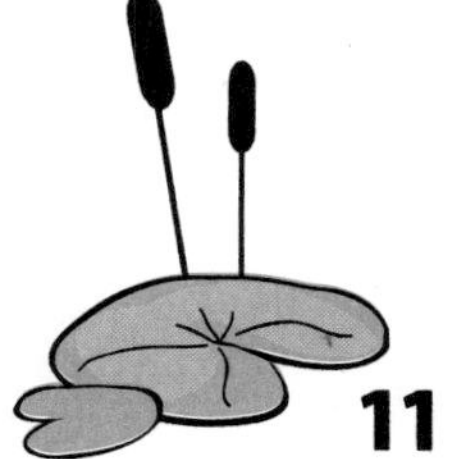

Move Allows you to move image elements

Lasso Allows you to draw around a particular element in your image to select it

Magic Wand Gives you the ability to select specific colors

Crop Allows you to select an area of an image and crop the image to that specified area

Slice Lets you cut the image into sections, which is handy for creating Web graphics

Airbrush Just like its real-world counterpart, gives you the ability to paint onto the image with an airbrush effect

Paintbrush Again, like its real-world counterpart, lets you paint onto the image with a painting effect

Clone Stamp Lets you copy a portion of an image and recreate it in another area of the image

History Brush Allows you to paint a copy of an image (in this case, called a state or snapshot) onto the current version of the image

Eraser Gives you the ability to erase portions of your image

Gradient Gives you the ability to assign a gradient to a background or a selection in your image

Smudge Lets you smudge areas of the image, much like when you color with a crayon or chalk and then rub your finger over colors next to each other, smudging them together

Dodge Lets you lighten image areas

Path Component Selection Lets you work with and modify paths you create in your files

Type Gives you the ability to add text to your image

Pen Allows you to create a path by laying down points

Rectangle Lets you create a rectangular element in your image

Notes Lets you add textual notes to the image

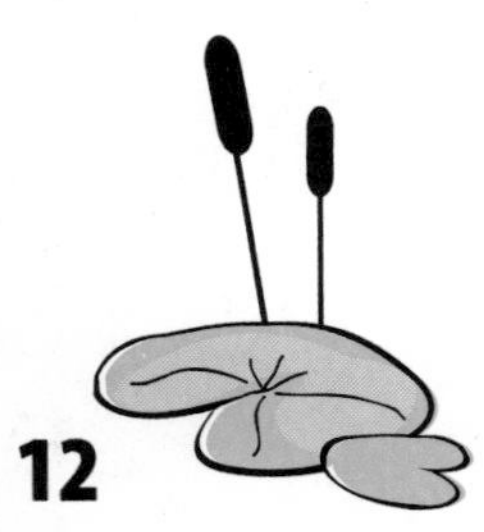

Eyedropper Lets you select a specific color in an image for use in another part of your image

Hand Gives you the ability to pan across your image on the screen

Zoom Zooms in on an image

zoom
To magnify an image or specific area of an image so you can see fine details better.

When you select a tool, the information in Photoshop's options bar changes to reflect that tool's settings. You can modify how the tool reacts to an image by changing the settings in the options bar.

Tip

When you first start Photoshop, the options bar appears at the top of the screen, but you can move it anywhere in the workspace. To move the options bar, drag it by its left edge.

Using Other Toolbox Controls

At the bottom of the toolbox, you'll find a set of controls that provide easy access to common Photoshop functions.

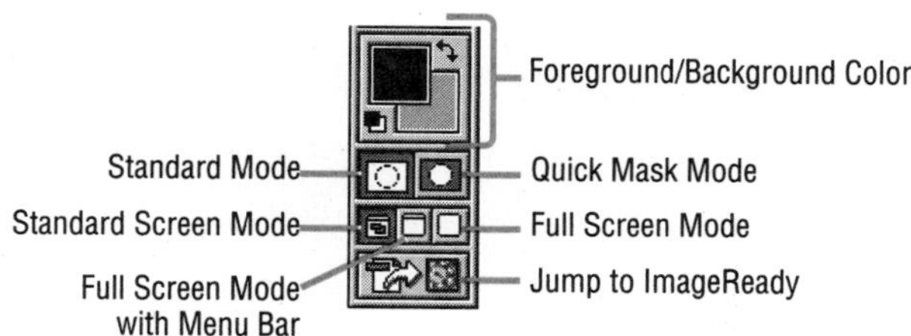

These seven controls work as follows:

Foreground/Background Color Opens the Color Picker so you can choose a color, or swaps the foreground and background colors (when you click the arrow on the upper-right side of the control)

Standard Mode Switches to Standard mode, which is the mode most often used to build images

Quick Mask Mode Switches to Quick Mask mode, which is the mode used to add or create a mask (which helps you delineate between the areas that will be affected by an operation and those that won't)

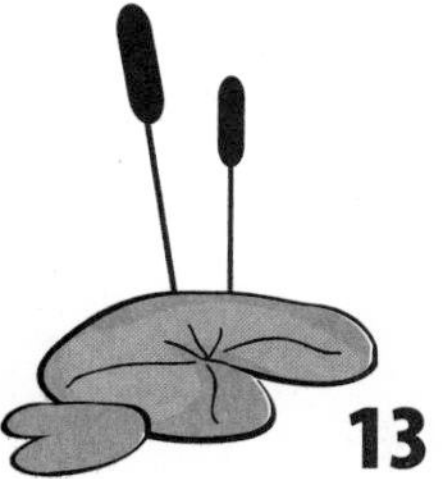

Standard Screen Mode Shows all of the controls and your workspace in the default window setup

Full Screen Mode with Menu Bar Displays a full-screen window with a menu bar and all open palettes and windows

Full Screen Mode Displays a full-screen window without a menu bar and all open palettes and windows

Jump to ImageReady Opens ImageReady, the companion program to Photoshop

Getting Online

The Go to Adobe Online button (the one with the picture icon) is located at the very top of the toolbox. Clicking it takes you to Adobe's Photoshop Web site, which can be valuable to even the most experienced Photoshop users.

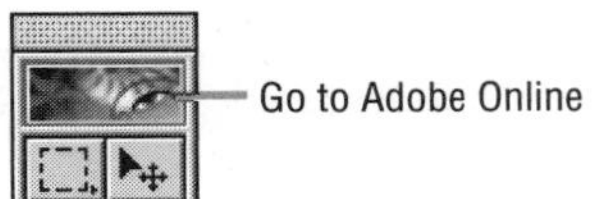

Click the Go to Adobe Online button to see a screen with numerous informational links. Click the link that you would like to follow. For example, click the Support link if you need to access online support for Photoshop. You will be connected to the Internet and taken to the area you selected.

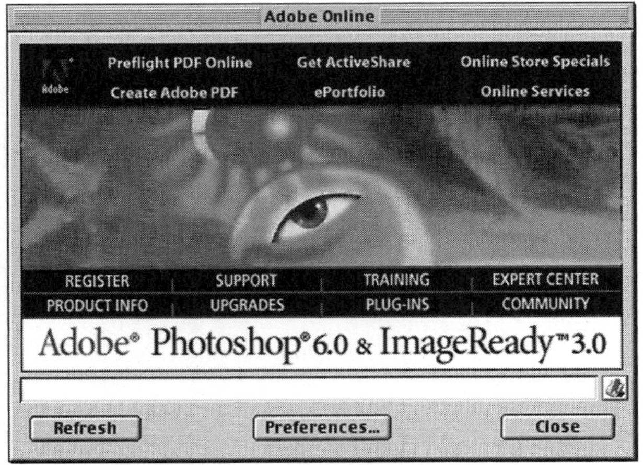

Working with Palettes

Photoshop 6 makes it easy for you to create a work area that contains the program elements that you use most often in a way that is most conducive to your work habits.

Accessing and Arranging Palettes

You can show and hide Photoshop elements and change the way that they are grouped. For instance, you can arrange different windows into groups to help you save screen real estate if you're working on a smaller monitor.

palette A Photoshop window that contains controls or options for specific program areas.

1. Click Window in the menu bar to open the Window menu. This menu lists choices for hiding and showing the various windows, called **palettes** in Photoshop. This list is divided into groups, so when you choose one in the group, the others in the set will also appear.

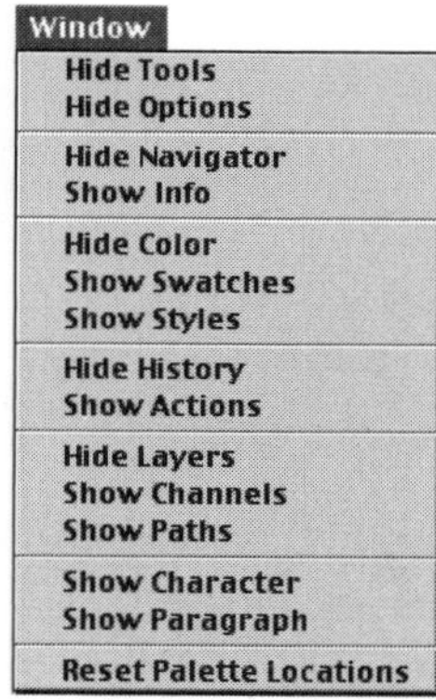

2. Select Show Character. You will see the Character palette. Notice that this palette has a Paragraph tab, which you can click to access the Paragraph palette.

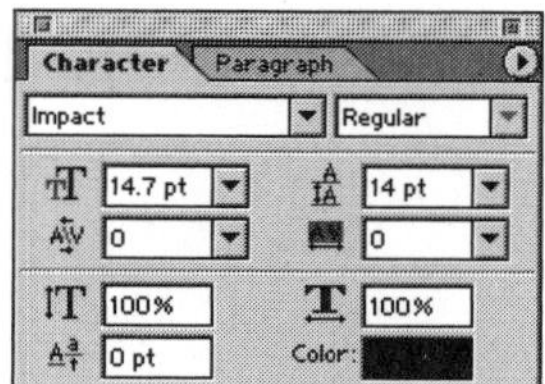

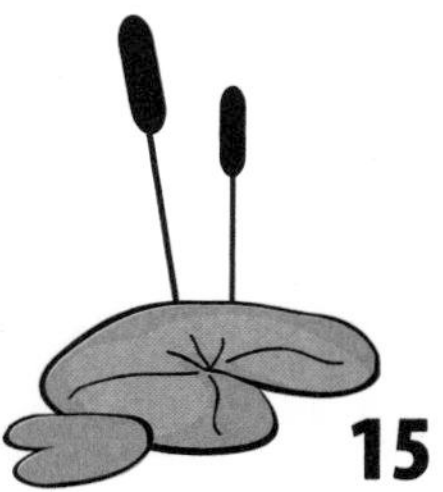

3. If the Layers palette isn't already displayed, select Window ➢ Show Layers. Notice that the Layers palette has Channels and Paths tabs. Each of the tabbed palettes can be "torn away" from the group. Click the Layers tab, hold down the mouse button, and drag the palette to another location on the screen, away from its group.

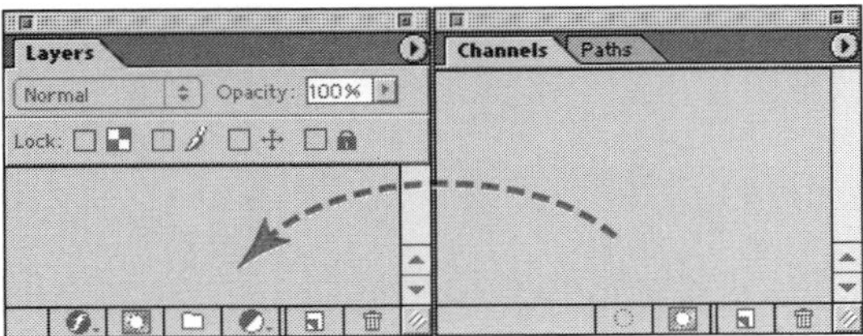

4. Select Window ➢ Reset Palette Locations to return the palettes to their original arrangement.

Grouping Palettes

As well as separating palettes, you can group them, as follows:

- Group different palettes together by dragging the appropriate tab onto another tab in a different palette, creating a new group that will remain together until you rearrange the palettes again.

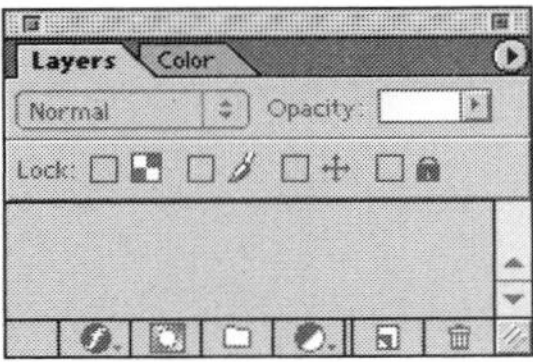

- Create multiple groups in one palette by dragging a tab from one palette onto another palette.

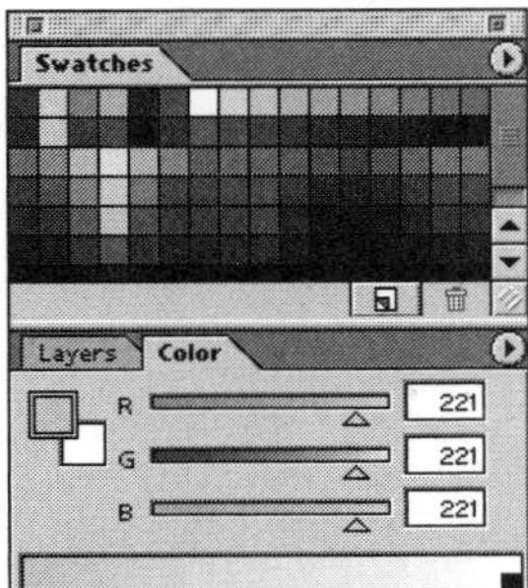

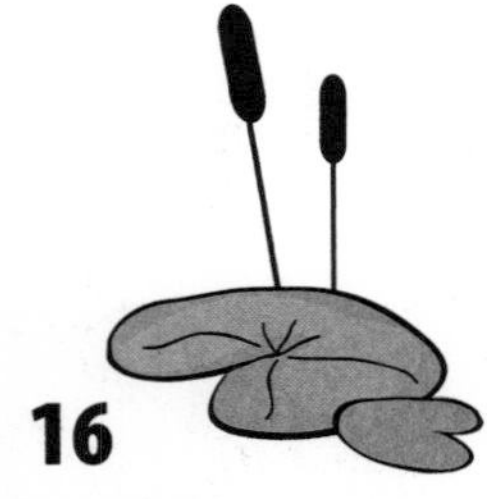

- Collapse a section of multiple palettes or an entire palette (so all that appears are the tabs and their names), by double-clicking a tab in the section or the palette group. Double-clicking a tab again opens the section or palette.

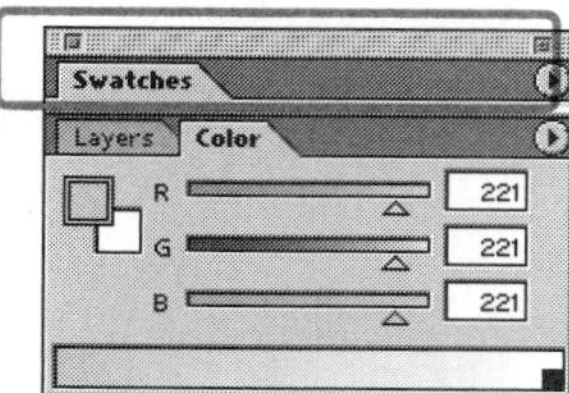

When you become more familiar with Photoshop, you can set up the palettes as you like.

Choosing Palette Options

Notice the circular button with an arrow inside it to the right of the tabs in any of the Photoshop palettes. Clicking this button displays a pop-up menu with more choices for that palette. Let's work with the Swatches palette as an example.

1. If the Color palette is on your screen, click the Swatches tab. Otherwise, select Window ➢ Show Swatches. Click the arrow button to see the palette's options menu.

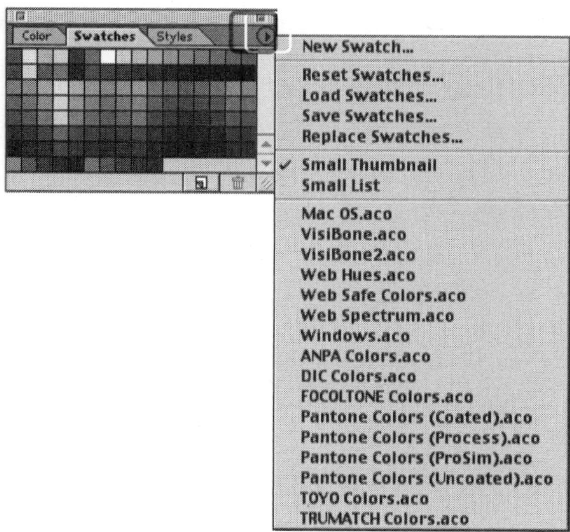

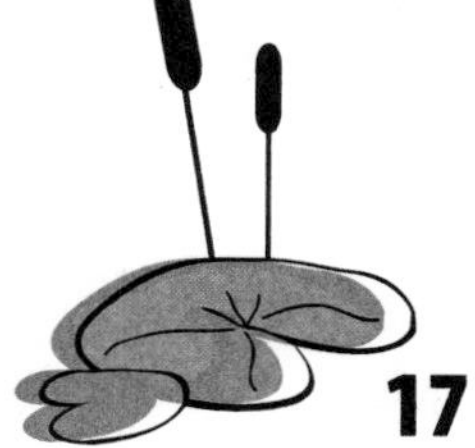

2. Select Pantone Colors (Process).aco. Then resize the window to show more of the color swatches available to you.

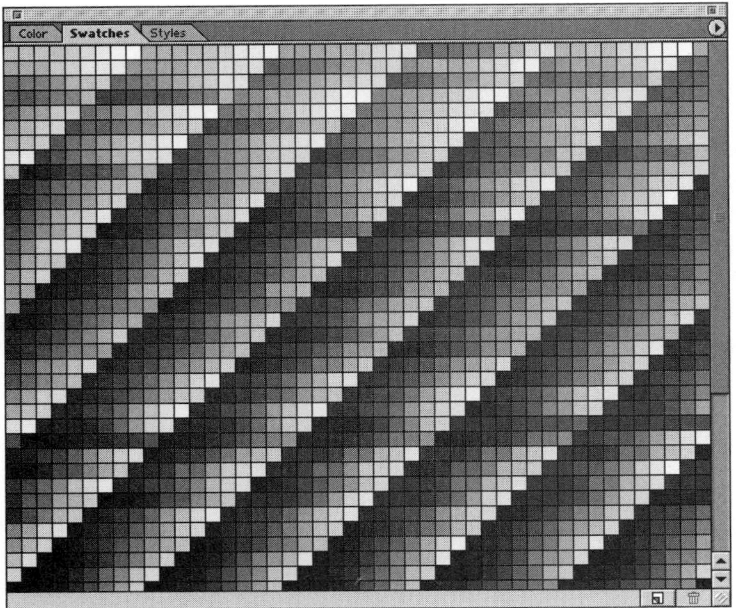

3. To return to the default color set, click the palette options menu button and choose Reset Swatches.

Using Power Tools

There are some wonderful tools included in Photoshop that can make your life a lot easier, especially when modifying photographs. To experiment with them, download the `MugShot.jpg` image from this book's Web site at `www.sybex.com`, or use a photographic image of your own that has a lot of elements.

Getting Rid of the Background with the Background Eraser

It's not unusual to have a picture in which the background is too distracting or has unwanted elements. For example, suppose that in the `MugShot.jpg` example, all you really want is that guy, without any of the things behind him.

This is when you want to use the Background Eraser tool, which erases similar colors.

1. To open an image file, select File ➢ Open. In the Open dialog box, navigate to the file you want to use. If you downloaded the `MugShot.jpg` image from this book's Web site, open the folder where you stored the image, select `MugShot.jpg`, and click Open to open the file.

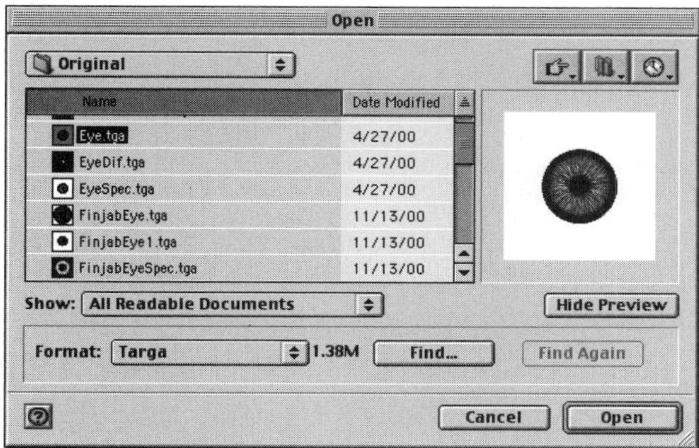

Note

Click the Show Preview button on the Open dialog box to see a preview of the selected image. Click Hide Preview to turn off the preview display.

2. Click the Eraser tool in the toolbox and hold down the mouse button. This reveals the expanded list of tools. Click Background Eraser Tool to select it.

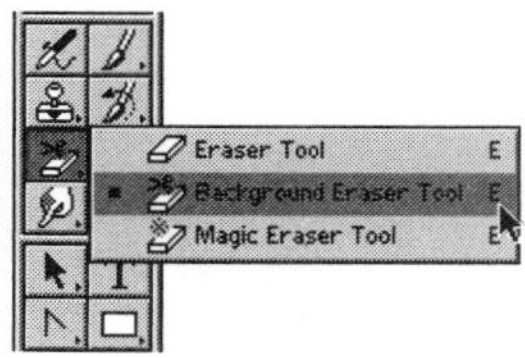

3. You should now see the Background Eraser's options bar at the top of the screen. In the options bar, click Brush and choose the Hard Round, 19 **pixels** brush.

pixel
A tiny block of colored light, which is the smallest editable unit in a digital image.

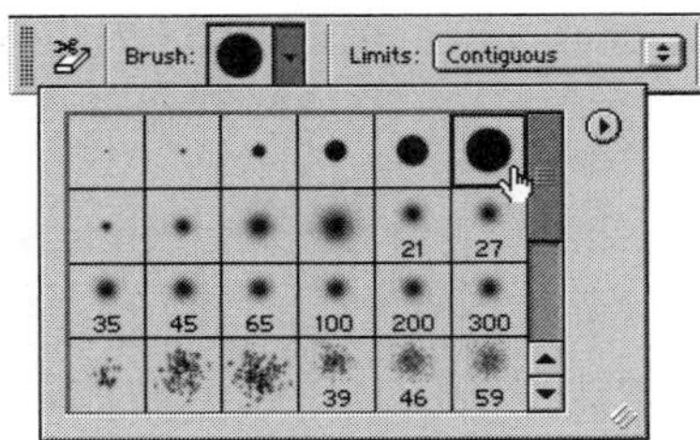

Tip

By double-clicking a brush icon, you can open a dialog box that lets you rename the brush and create new brush sizes.

4. In the options bar, click the button adjacent to the Tolerance text box. This opens a slider bar. Use this slider to change the Tolerance setting to 50% by dragging the triangle along the slider bar. The higher the number, the more accurate the Background Eraser tool will be in erasing similar colors.

5. Choose a section of the photo that you want to erase and click it. In the `MugShot.jpg` example, click the wall in the background. While holding down the mouse button, drag the cursor over the wall. Notice how it erases anything with a similar color.

6. As you drag the cursor along the image, take a look at the Foreground/Background Colors indicator in the toolbox. Notice how the colors change.

7. Place the cursor on the back wall next to the guy's hair and drag down, making sure not to move into the hair at all. If you do that, the color parameter set by the brush will change and erase the hair, too.

8. Because this is just a quick introduction to the Background Eraser tool, select File ➢ Revert to go back to the original image before moving on. If you continued using the Background Eraser tool, you could erase the entire background, while leaving the subject alone.

Erasing Similar Colors with the Magic Eraser

Like the Background Eraser tool, the Magic Eraser tool shares the Eraser tool location in the toolbox. The Magic Eraser tool works differently from the Background Eraser tool, in that it will erase all colors in a picture that are similar (based on the Tolerance setting) to the one you select. With your practice image still on the screen, let's see how this tool works.

1. Click the Eraser tool in the toolbox and hold down the mouse button. In the expanded list of tools, click Magic Eraser Tool to select it.
2. In the Magic Eraser tool's option bar, change the Tolerance setting to 25% by typing **25** in the text field, and deselect the Contiguous check box. Make sure Anti-aliased is checked. (You'll learn more about how these options work in Chapter 2.)

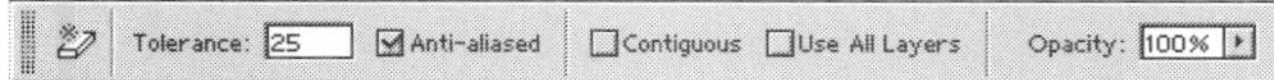

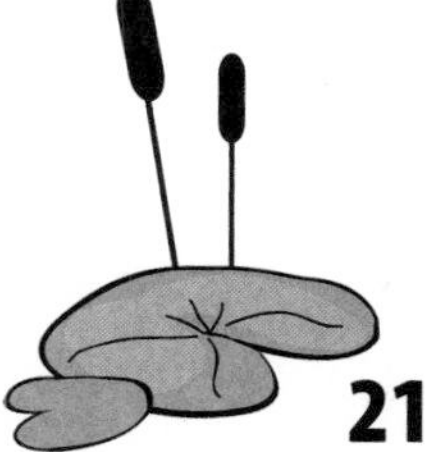

3. Click the wall behind that guy in the picture. All similar colors in the image will be erased.

4. Choose Edit ➢ Undo Magic Eraser to undo what you just did.

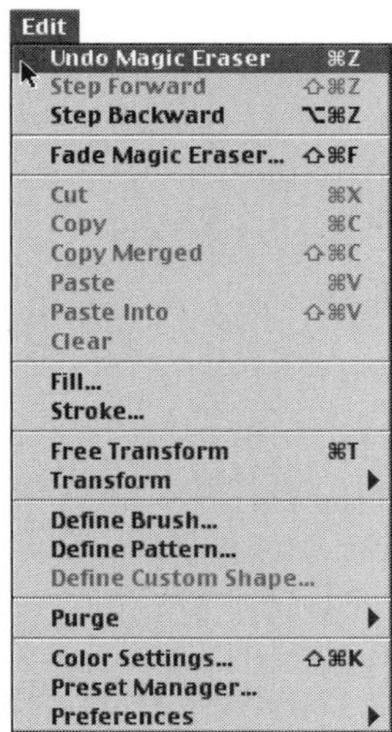

5. In the options bar, select the Contiguous check box.

6. Click the same spot as you just did in step 3. Notice that the Magic Eraser tool now only erases the color that is within a boundary set

by the image colors. Once a color change is recognized, erasing is stopped.

7. Select File ➢ Revert to go back to the original image before continuing.

Selecting Similar Color Areas with the Magnetic Lasso

The Magnetic Lasso tool is one of the great discoveries of the twenty-first century. Okay, I'm overplaying it, but it really can be a massive lifesaver if you have an image with some difficult elements you want to select. The Magic Eraser tool works by sampling colors based on where the selector is. As you drag around the edge of the image element, it keeps the border of the selection even with that sampled color. Continuing with your practice image, see how the Magnetic Lasso works.

1. Click the Lasso tool in the toolbox and hold down the mouse button to display the pop-up list.

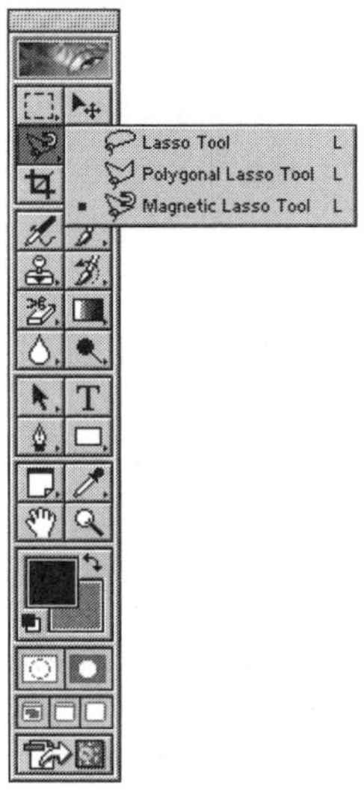

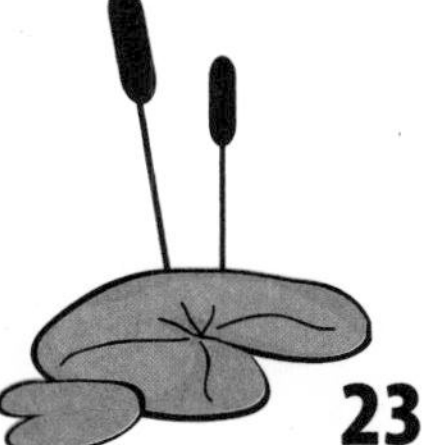

2. In the tool list, click Magnetic Lasso Tool to select it.
3. In the options bar, change the Feather setting to 5 pixels and the Width setting to 1 pixel.

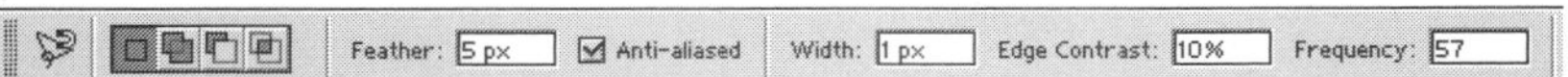

4. Click the edge of the shirt, and then begin dragging the mouse around it. Notice how the Magnetic Lasso tool follows the edge. Once you've worked your way back to the starting point, click the mouse button to connect the starting and ending points. The shirt will be outlined and selected.

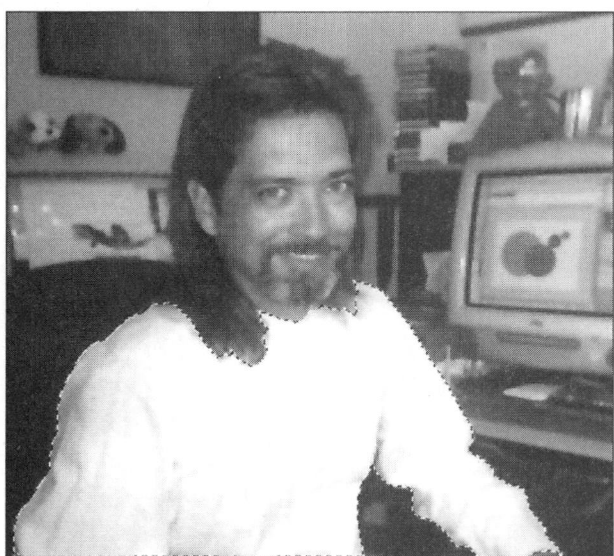

5. The outline indicates that that particular area is selected and can be modified. However, in this example, you want to get rid of everything except the shirt. To do that, choose Select ➢ Inverse. This reverses the selection, so that the selected area is everything in the picture *except* the shirt.

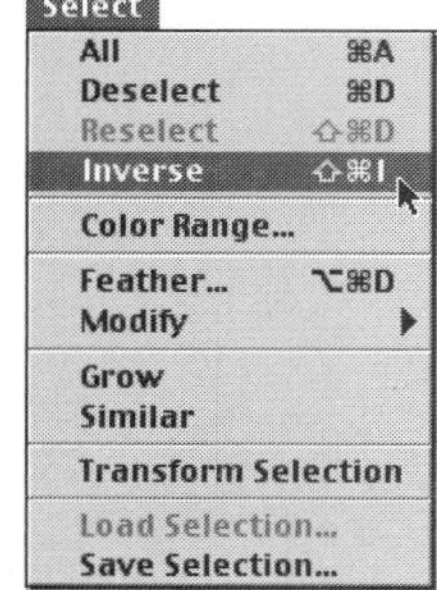

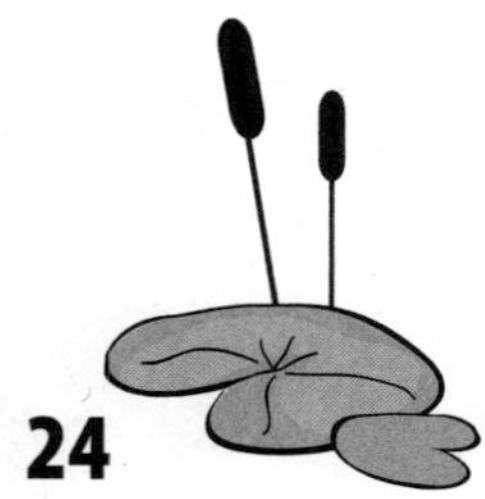

6. Choose the Eraser tool (not the Magic Eraser or Background Eraser tool). In the options bar, click Brush and set the Soft Round, 300 pixels brush.
7. Now erase everything, and don't worry about erasing over the shirt, because it won't be affected.

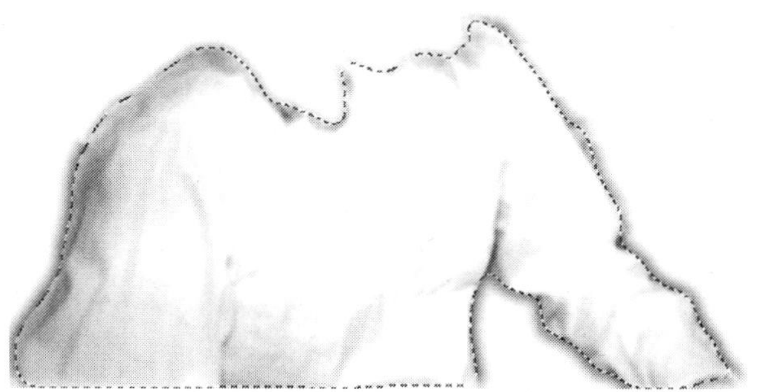

Creating Notes

The Notes tool is extremely handy item, which you definitely want to get used to using. If you have created a great effect, keeping notes about how you did it will help jog your memory when you want to recreate that effect. And, if you plan to send the image to someone else to show how you created the effect, the recipient can read the notes as well.

Photoshop provides tools for creating text notes as well as audio notes. You can add as many notes as you like to highlight particular areas of your work in a file.

Let's add some notes to an image. You can either continue with the practice image you used in the previous sections or open another image file.

1. Select the Notes tool.

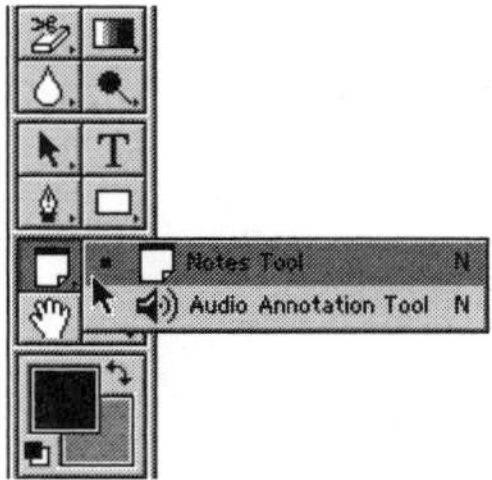

2. Click a spot on your image. A note window appears. Type your message in the window.

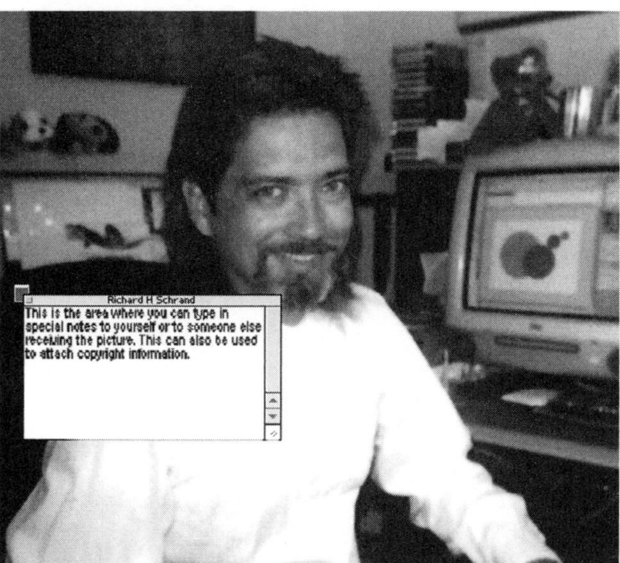

3. When you're finished, collapse the note by clicking the small box in the upper-left corner of the note window. All that is left is a small icon indicating a note is attached.

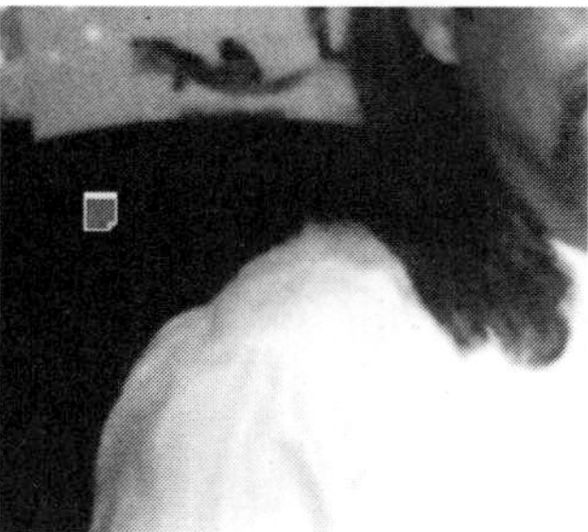

4. If you have a microphone attached to your computer, you can attach an audio note using the Audio Annotation tool. Click the Notes tool in the toolbox and hold down the mouse button. In the tool list, click Audio Annotation Tool to select it.
5. Click the image. A recording dialog box appears. Record your message.

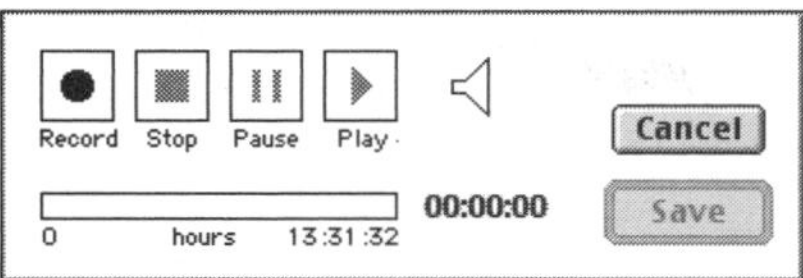

6. When you have finished your recording, click Save.
7. A speaker icon appears on the image to alert the recipient or yourself that an audio note has been attached. Double-clicking this icon plays back your recorded note.

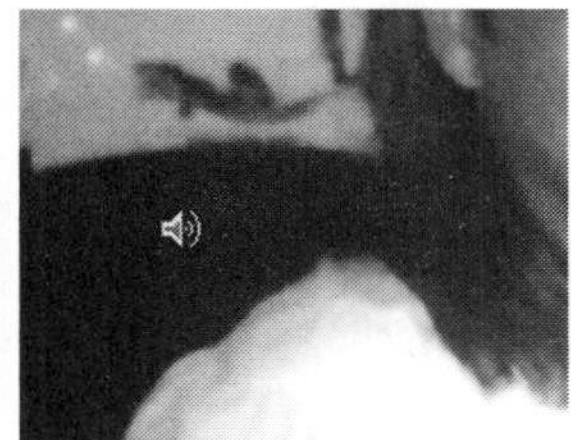

Using File Features

Photoshop includes features for setting up your files for viewing or storage. To access these features, select File ➢ Automate.

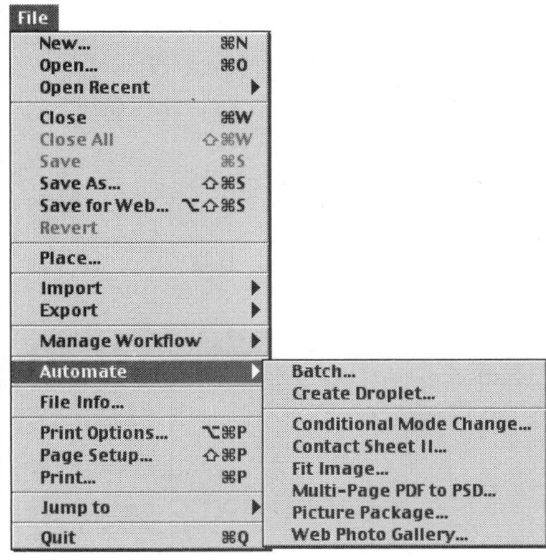

Contact Sheet

Contact Sheet II lets you create a contact sheet from a series of photographs or images stored in a common folder.

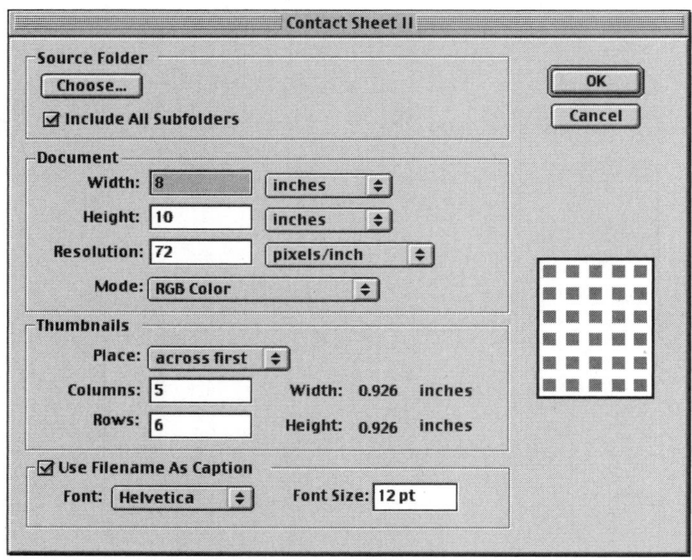

Picture Package

Picture Package lets you create a page with a photograph at various sizes. This is exactly like the photo sheets you get from a school photography package.

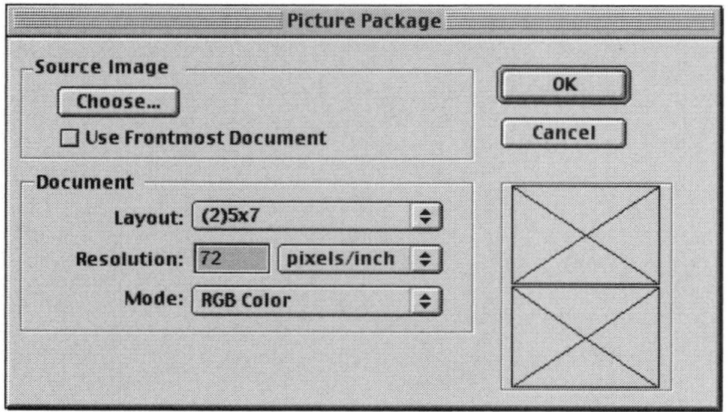

Web Photo Gallery

Web Photo Gallery allows you to set up a page for viewing on the Web. The small images (or thumbnails that are created) act as links to view the larger image.

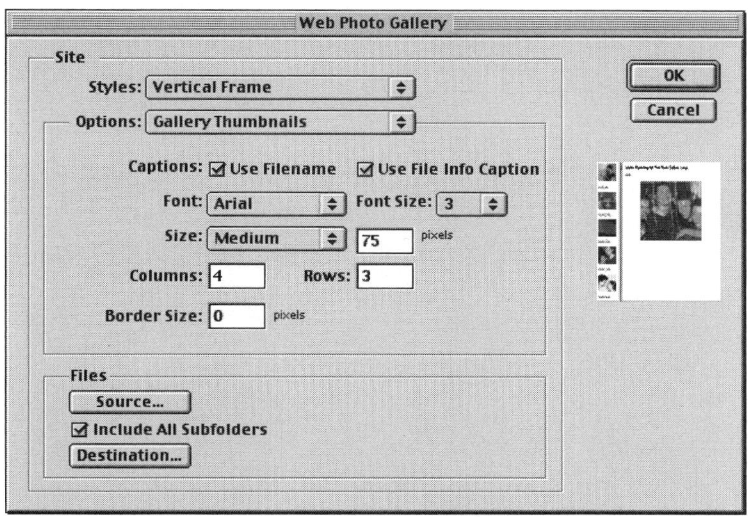

Convert Multi-Page PDF to PSD

Convert Multi-Page PDF to PSD is a very handy tool when you have a **PDF** form you want to use in a Photoshop document. This automatically turns each page of the PDF document into a Photoshop file that you can manipulate.

Convert Multi-Page PDF to PSD

Source PDF

Choose...

OK

Cancel

Page Range

All From: 1 To: 1

Output Options

Resolution: 72 pixels/inch

Mode: Grayscale Anti-aliased

Destination

Base Name:

Choose...

PDF

The Portable Document Format, which was developed by Adobe as a way to share files no matter what type of computer you use. PDFs can be created in Photoshop, Illustrator, Acrobat, and other programs.

Moving On

This chapter provided an overview of some of the tools that come with Photoshop 6 and gave you a feel for working with some of the new tools in this version. If you have used earlier versions of the program, you will definitely want to explore these new features further. If you are just getting started with Photoshop, this chapter gave you an idea of what can be accomplished with the Photoshop tools.

From this point on, it's time to discover the power that lies within this phenomenal program. So, let's head to Chapter 2 to begin understanding what has made Photoshop the professional image-manipulation program of choice for millions of people around the world.

Chapter 2

Using the Editing Tools

There are some basic Photoshop tools that you will use over and over again. These tools are literally the power behind the concept of Photoshop, so learning to work with them will be paramount to your success with the program. Photoshop 6 has added a number of powerful updates to the toolset. Here, you'll learn how to use some of the editing tools that let you change your images:

- The Lasso tools, for isolating parts of your images
- The Magic Wand tool, for selecting image areas by color
- The Clone Stamp and Pattern Stamp tools, for replacing parts of your image
- The Paintbrush tool and filters, for coloring and adding effects to your images

Selecting Areas with the Lasso Tools

The Lasso tools are some of the most useful tools in Photoshop. With them, you can select areas of a picture simply by drawing around those areas. In Chapter 1, you experimented with the Magnetic Lasso tool, which surrounds an element of an image based on the first pixel color assigned to it. Here, we will look at the Lasso and Polygonal Lasso tools.

Tip

I highly recommend purchasing a graphics tablet for use with Photoshop. Graphics or drawing tablets act like pencil and paper, allowing you to literally draw around an image. The leading vendor of graphics tablets is Wacom (`www.wacom.com`), but many other companies also produce them.

Selecting Free-Form Shapes

Of the three choices you have in the Lasso tools area, the Lasso tool is the main one. It is a free-form tool, meaning that it is not limited to straight lines or working on certain planes, such as horizontal and vertical. To get a feel for working with the Lasso tool and selections, do the following:

1. Open an image file and select the main Lasso tool from the toolbox.

Tip

If you don't like the way the cursor appears on the screen, you can change it through the Display & Cursors page of the Preferences dialog box (select Edit ➢ Preferences ➢ Display & Cursors). See Chapter 1 for more information about Preferences settings.

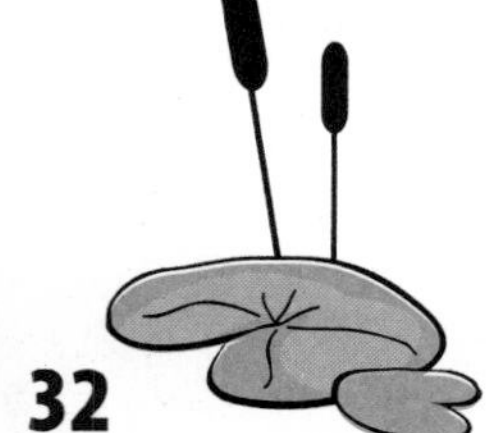

2. Zoom in on your subject by pressing the Ctrl+plus (Cmd+plus) key combination, so you can be more precise when tracing an image.

Note

Throughout this book, key combinations are shown for both Windows and Macintosh systems, in the format Windows keystrokes (Mac keystrokes).

3. Begin drawing around the area you want to select, keeping as close as you possibly can to the subject. Notice how a line appears as you are tracing the edge of the subject.

Tip

If you are using a mouse rather than a drawing tablet, don't worry about tracing around an entire subject. In the options bar, choose Add To or Subtract From to extend the selected area or deselect portions of a selected area, respectively.

4. When you're finished, you will see your subject surrounded by a moving dotted line (called **marching ants**).

marching ants
Describes the movement of the outline created around an object when using a Photoshop selection tool such as the Magic Wand, Lasso, or Marquee tools.

5. To delete the selected image, press the Delete key. To cut the selection to the Clipboard, select Edit ➢ Cut (notice the shortcut is Ctrl+X or Cmd+X).

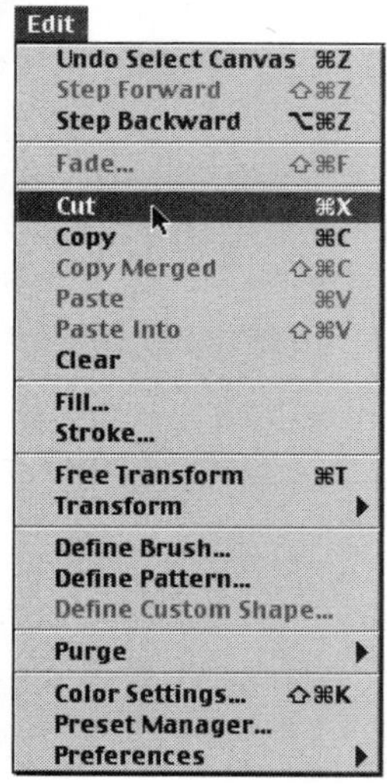

invert
Changing the area of the selection by reversing the area you selected.

6. To **invert** your selection, so that everything except what you traced is deleted, choose Select ➢ Inverse (notice the shortcut is Shift+Ctrl+I or Shift+Cmd+I), and then delete the selected portion.

Selecting Straight Edges

Unlike the main Lasso tool, the Polygonal Lasso tool creates straight lines in horizontal, vertical, or angled planes. You can use this tool in conjunction with the other selection tools to select complex image elements. Here's how:

1. Open an image file that contains elements with straight edges.

2. Press and hold down the mouse button over the Lasso tool icon in the toolbox to reveal the other sections, and then choose the Polygonal Lasso tool.

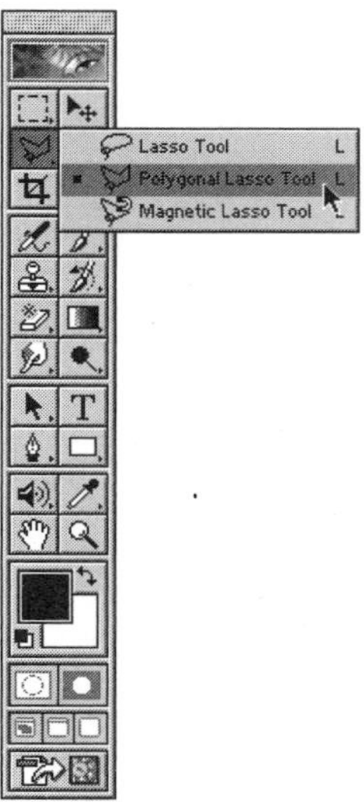

3. Click to set the first point. Move the mouse to the next point in the image and click again. Repeat this process until the portion you want to select is completely surrounded.

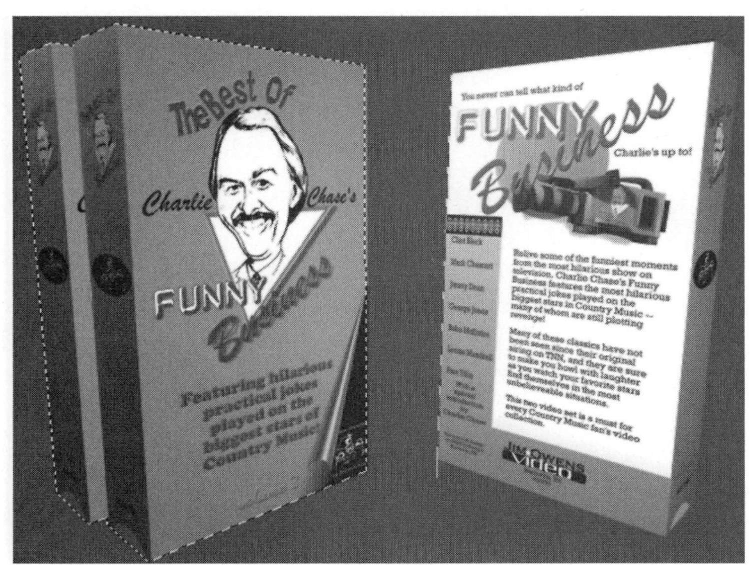

Modifying the Lasso Tool Settings

The settings for the Lasso tools make them more or less sensitive. The controls for the Lasso tools are located in the Lasso tool's options bar.

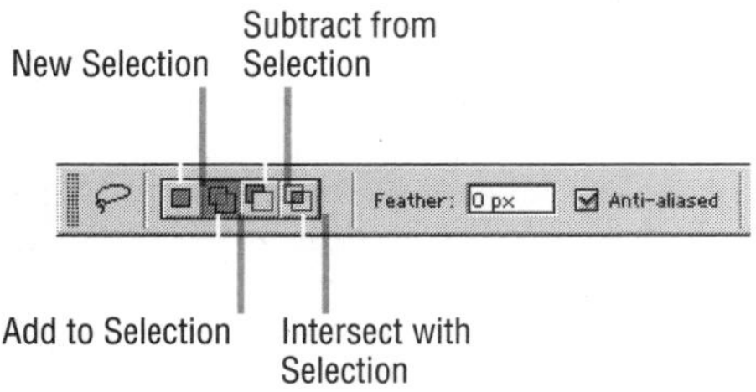

From left to right, these tool-modification controls work as follows:

- The New Selection option allows you to create a new selected area with the tool. If you have already traced around a portion of the image and want to keep that as a selection, hold down the Shift key while tracing around the new area.
- The Add to Selection option works the same as holding down the Shift key when New Selection is active.
- The Subtract from Selection option allows you to trace around a portion of a selected area, deselecting that portion of the image.
- The Intersect with Selection option removes all of the selected areas except for those included in your new selection.
- The Feather setting determines whether the edges of the selected area are sharp or blurred. **Feathering** is set in pixel increments.
- The Anti-aliased option determines whether the edge of the selected area is smooth or jagged. **Anti-aliasing** adds a small border around edges to blend into the surrounding area.

feathering
Blurring the edges of a selection, making the edges appear to fade out into the background.

anti-aliasing
Smoothing out of the pixels that make up the edges of the image. When you select the Anti-aliased option for a tool, Photoshop creates a subtle transition between pixels to make the edges appear smooth, rather than jagged.

Let's see how some of the modification tools work.

1. Using the Lasso tool (the main one), select a portion of your image.

2. Click the Add to Selection button. Draw around another area of the picture. Both areas are now selected.

3. Select Subtract from Selection. Use the Lasso tool inside one of the selected areas. That area is no longer a part of your selection.

4. Select Intersect with Selection and draw an area between your two selections. The areas within your selection are the only portions left selected.

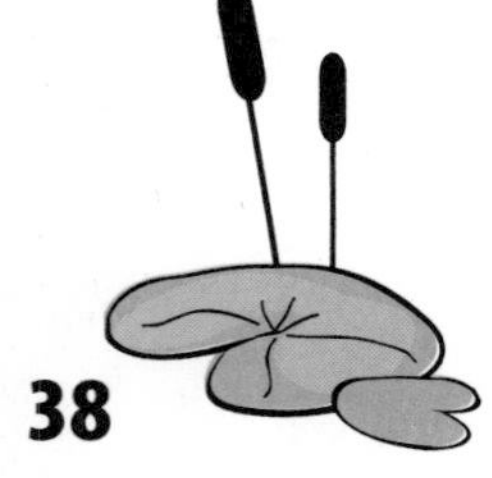

Tip

To be more precise when outlining objects with many of Photoshop's tools, zoom in as close as you can without losing sense of what you are looking at. You can zoom in up to 1600 percent of the image size.

Selecting Colors with the Magic Wand

The Magic Wand is an indispensable tool you will use often. With it, you can choose specific colors or shades of gray for modification within your image.

The Magic Wand's option bar contains settings that let you control how the tool selects colors. The New Selection, Add to Selection, Subtract from Selection, Intersect with Selection, and Anti-aliased options work the same as they do with the Lasso tools, as described in the previous section. The Magic Wand also offers the following modifiers:

- The Tolerance setting controls the sensitivity of the Magic Wand; the higher the number, the more variations of the color you are selecting are included.
- The Contiguous option selects only the colors that are touching the area you click. When this is deselected, all instances of the selected color in the entire image are chosen.
- The Use All Layers option chooses all instances of the selected color simultaneously in all open layers (when you have more than one layer with image information).

Let's see how the Magic Wand and some of its controls work.

1. Open an image file and select the Magic Wand.

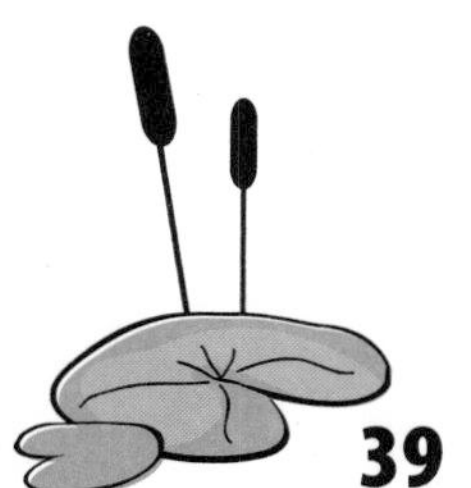

2. Place the Magic Wand cursor over a color in your image. In the options bar, change the Tolerance to **15** and make sure that the Contiguous and Anti-aliased check boxes are checked.

3. Click the color you want to select. It becomes outlined with the marching ants.

4. Press Ctrl+D (Cmd+D) to deselect the selection. Change the Tolerance to **50**. Now click in the same area as before. Notice how much more of the color is selected this time.

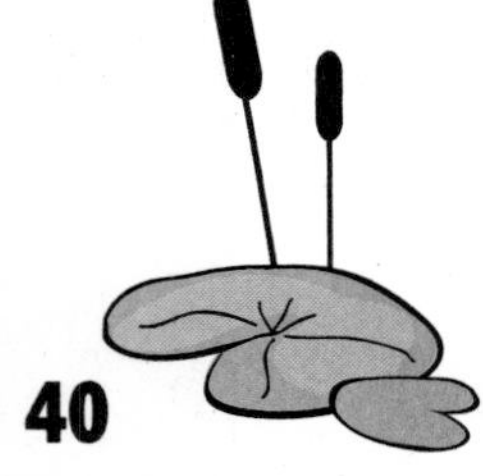

5. Deselect the selected color. Change the Tolerance back to **15** and turn off Contiguous. Click the color you want to select. Notice how all similar colors are outlined by the marching ants.

Cloning with the Stamp Tools

Two other tools that will become part of your most-used toolset are the Clone Stamp and Pattern Stamp tools. The Clone Stamp tool is particularly useful. You will find that it is invaluable for fixing blemishes in photographs, changing the look of an image, and creating and applying new patterns to your images.

Working with the Clone Stamp Tool

Now you will get a feel for what can be accomplished by using the Clone Stamp tool.

1. Open an image file. (I chose a picture of three of my children, so that I can play mad scientist and clone my son's face onto my daughter's head.)

2. Select the Clone Stamp tool. You'll see that the Clone Stamp's option bar has several interesting settings. We'll examine these more closely later, after we've experimented with the Stamp tools. For now, just make sure that the following settings are selected:

   Brush: 21 Soft-edged

   Mode: Normal

   Opacity: 100%

   Aligned: Selected

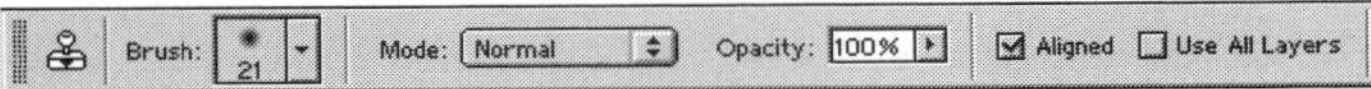

3. Place the cursor over the part of the image you want to clone and, while holding down the Alt key (Option key), click the area.

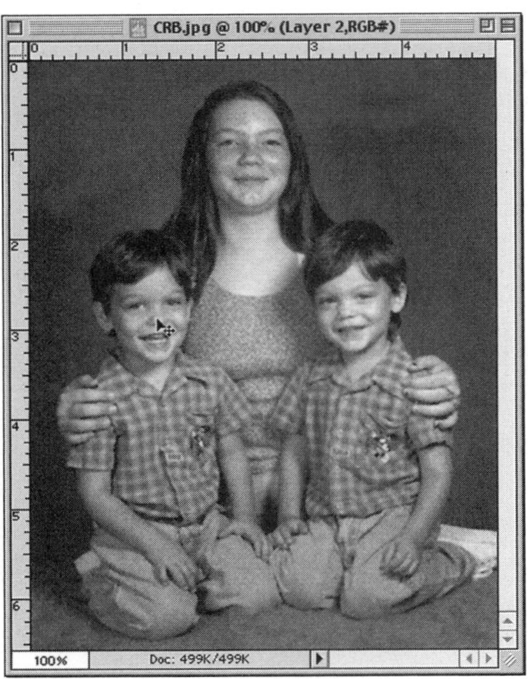

4. Place the Clone Stamp brush over the area you want replaced. Hold down the mouse button, and the cloning process begins. (Oh, the things you could do to photos of your boss; that is, unless you're the boss.)

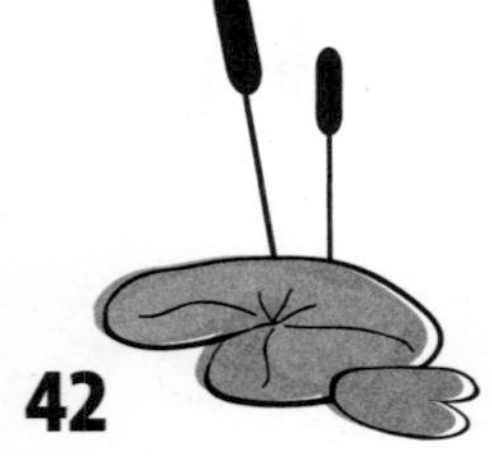

5. Move the Clone Stamp tool over another part of the image. Notice that, with the Aligned option turned on, the clone area remains constant with the placement of the brush.

6. Select File ➢ Revert to return your image to its original state.
7. Turn Aligned off. Repeat steps 3 and 4.
8. Move the cursor to another area. Hold down the mouse button and clone the image into this new area. Notice that with Aligned off, you cloned the original selection again.

Cloning Patterns with the Pattern Stamp Tool

The Pattern Stamp tool has one major difference from the Clone Stamp tool: a Pattern option that allows you to clone using a pattern. Let's try it out.

1. Select an area of your image by encircling it with the Lasso tool (the main one). This provides you with an area where the change will take place and, even if you go out of the lines, the other parts of the picture won't be affected.

2. Select the Pattern Stamp tool. Notice that the modifiers now include a Pattern option. Photoshop comes with a number of preset patterns that you can use.

3. For this example, choose the brick pattern. Move the Pattern Stamp tool into the selected area and paint in the new pattern.

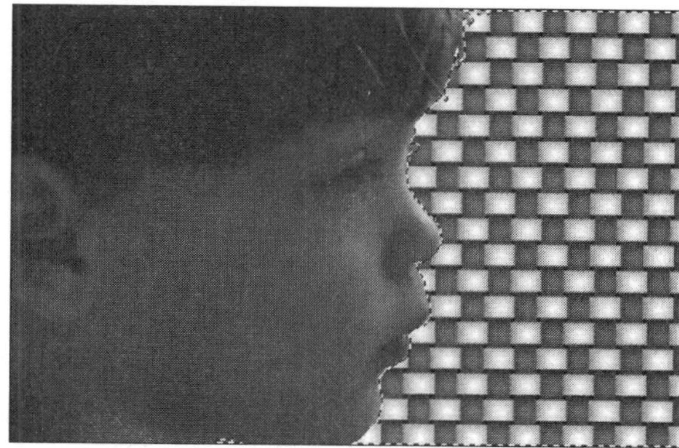

Notice that all of the detail in the selected area has been lost. This is because you are simply replacing the one image with your new one. You can modify how the Pattern Stamp and the Clone Stamp tools blend images by adjusting the settings on the options bar, which are discussed next.

Modifying the Stamp Tool Settings

The options bar for the Clone Stamp tool contains settings for painting cloned areas. The Use All Layers option works similarly to how it does with the Magic Wand tool, giving you the ability to sample an area to be cloned from one layer and painted onto another layer. The other options are described in the following sections.

Brush Options

The Brush setting gives you access to various styles and sizes of brushes that paint the cloned information onto other parts of the image. The predefined brushes range in size and edge softness. There are also some fancy brush styles for more artistic use. Click the down arrow to the right of the current brush setting to see the Brush menu.

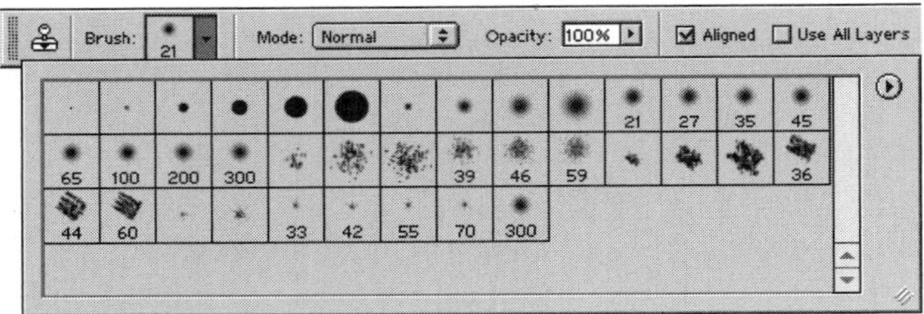

For more control over the Brush setting, click the right-pointing arrow at the top-right side of the Brush menu. This opens a pop-up menu that offers options for modifying the brushes, opening other stored brush sets, and changing how the brush icons appear on the screen.

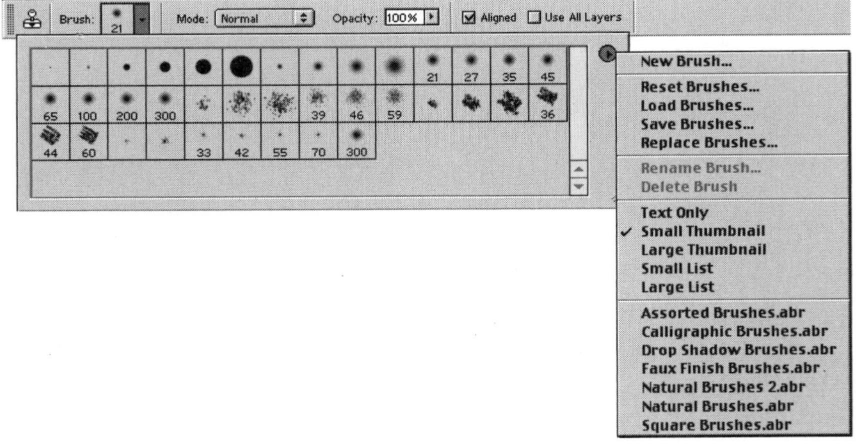

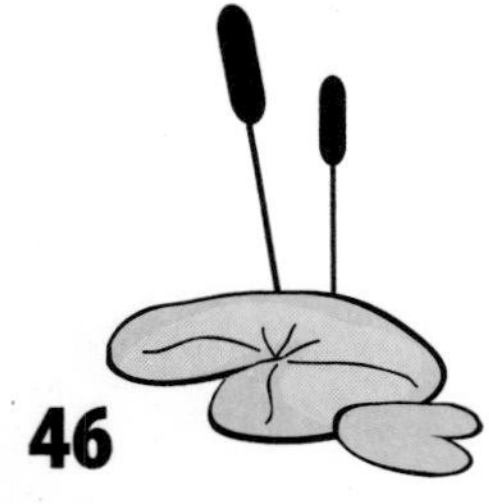

Mode Options

The Mode setting controls the blending mode, or the way that a brush paints the cloned area over the new area. Click the Mode drop-down arrow to see the available blending modes. If you want to experiment with these modes, undo the pattern change (Edit ➢ Undo Pattern Stamp) from the last exercise, and then use the Clone Pattern Stamp tool over a small region of the selected area. You can undo each change before working with the next effect.

- Dissolve gives the edges of the image a rough, uneven edge that makes it appear to look like it's dissolving the further out it goes.
- Multiply blends the upper and lower layers, multiplying the brightness values, and darkening anything in the lower layer.
- Screen adds brightness to the area by blending the top and bottom images. Technically, this and the other modes work on a pixel-by-pixel basis.
- Overlay blends the light and dark areas of the top layer with the light and dark areas of the bottom layer, effectively increasing the contrast and color intensity.
- Soft Light gives a nice, subtle look to the mixture of the original image and the cloned area or pattern.
- Hard Light is harsher version of Soft Light. It makes the lighter areas of the cloned area or pattern stand out more.
- Color Dodge acts much like Hard Light, but actually lightens the underlying cloned area or pattern.
- Color Burn uses the lighter areas of the cloned area or pattern to darken the underlying image's color.
- Darken looks for the darker areas of an image in the top and bottom layer and then uses the darkest area.
- Lighten is the same as Darken, only it uses the lightest areas.
- Difference blends the upper and lower layer, showing the difference between the two (easier seen than explained).
- Exclusion combines the colors together in a more muted way than Differences does. This is accomplished through inverting the light areas. Black (or dark) areas are not affected.
- Hue replaces the colors of the cloned area or pattern to affect the **hue** of the underlying color(s).

hue
The tonal quality of a color.

saturation
How intense or deep a color is.

- Saturation replaces the **saturation** of the bottom image with that of the top image.
- Color combines the hue and saturation of the top and bottom pixels.
- Luminosity changes the brightness of the image on the lower layer.

Note

Since many of these effects are very subtle, it is much easier to see them in color. All of the blending mode effects are illustrated in the color section of this book.

If you experiment, you will see that a lot of different effects can be generated simply by changing the Mode setting for the Clone Stamp and Pattern Stamp tools.

Opacity Setting

The Opacity percentage determines the transparency of the painted image. The range is 0%, which is totally transparent (and thus, useless for the purpose of the cloning), to 100%, which is completely opaque (does not allow any of the underlying image to show through).

Aligned Setting

As you saw in the exercise using the Clone Stamp tool, the Aligned option keeps the area that is being cloned constant. Using Aligned, when you select an area to act as the source, release the mouse button, and move to another area of the image, the sample area will be relative to the location of the new point. When the Aligned option is not active, no matter where you place the Clone brush on the document, that selected area will be used.

Painting with the Paintbrush Tool

Just as its name suggests, the Paintbrush tool gives you the ability to paint on your image, whether it's to create a background or to change the color of a portion of your image.

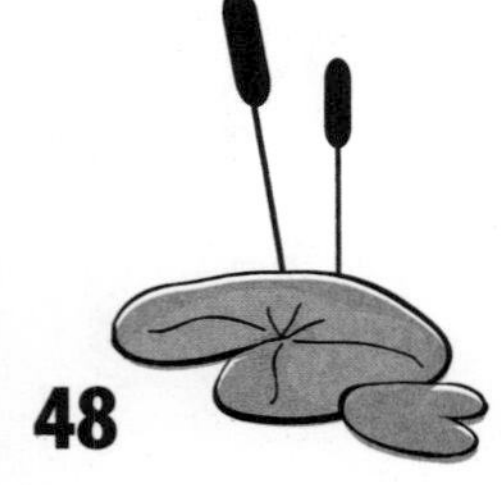

As with the other tools, you can change the tool options to create some interesting effects.

In the Paintbrush tool's options bar, the Brush, Mode, and Opacity settings work similarly to how they do with the Clone Stamp and Pattern Stamp tools, The Wet Edges option gives the effect of watercolor on the edge of the paint. The Brush Dynamics settings change the way that the brush applies "paint" to the workspace.

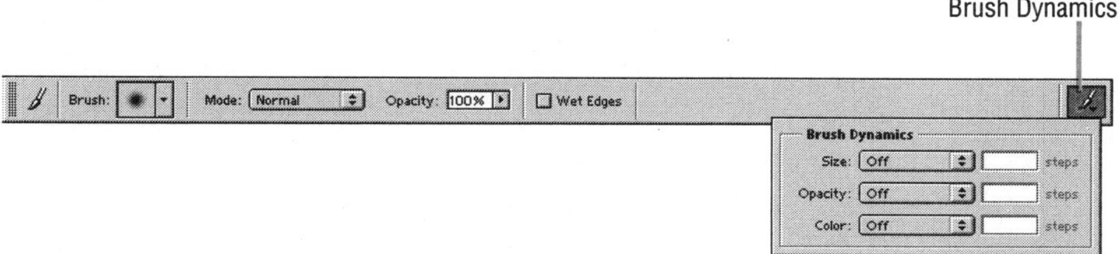

Setting Brush Dynamics

The Brush Dynamics settings can help you create some interesting looks when painting. For example, you can make your brush stroke fade or taper off at a designated distance. Let's experiment with some of the Brush Dynamics effects.

1. Select File ➢ New to create a new document. (Its size and resolution are not important for this example.)
2. Select the Paintbrush tool.

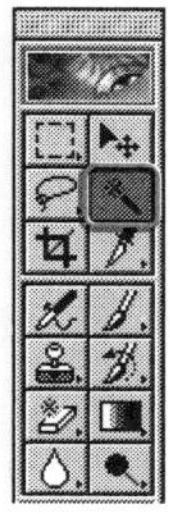

3. Leave the default settings for the other options and click the Brush Dynamics button (on the far right of the toolbar) to display the Brush Dynamics settings.

4. Click the Size pop-up menu and choose Fade. In the adjacent Steps text box, type **15**. Then click in the document window and drag with the Paintbrush tool to create a brush stroke. Notice how the stroke tapers off into nothingness.

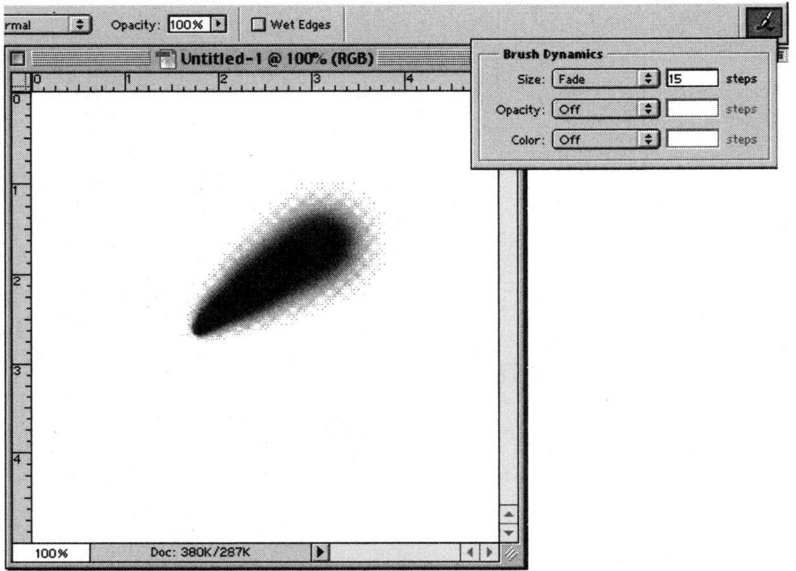

Note

The Stylus option will be available only if you have a drawing tablet (such as a Wacom tablet) attached to your computer. Stylus refers to the pen used to draw on a drawing tablet.

5. Press Ctrl+Z (Cmd+Z) to undo the brush stroke.

6. Select Fade from the Brush Dynamics Opacity pop-up menu. In the Steps text box next to Opacity, type **15**. Draw a second brush stroke. Notice how the stroke not only tapers off, but also fades out.

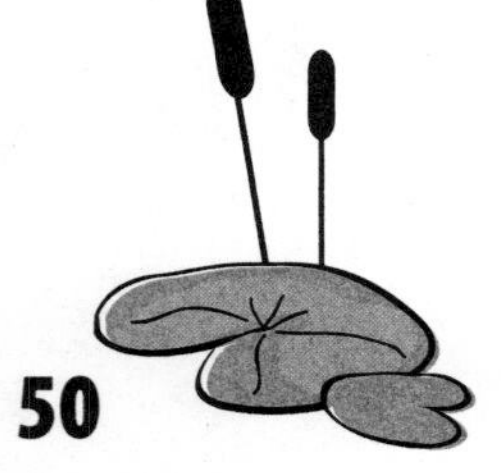

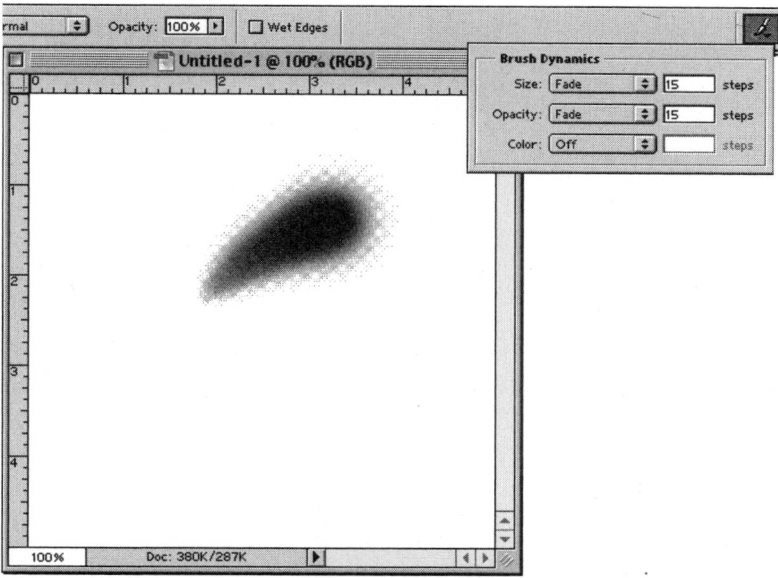

7. Press Ctrl+Z (Cmd+Z) to undo the brush stroke.
8. Select Fade from the Brush Dynamics Color pop-up menu. In its Steps text box, type **7**. Color Fade tells the program to fade from the foreground color to the background color over a certain amount of time.
9. Click the background color swatch in the toolbox and select a different background color. Then create another brush stroke on your document.

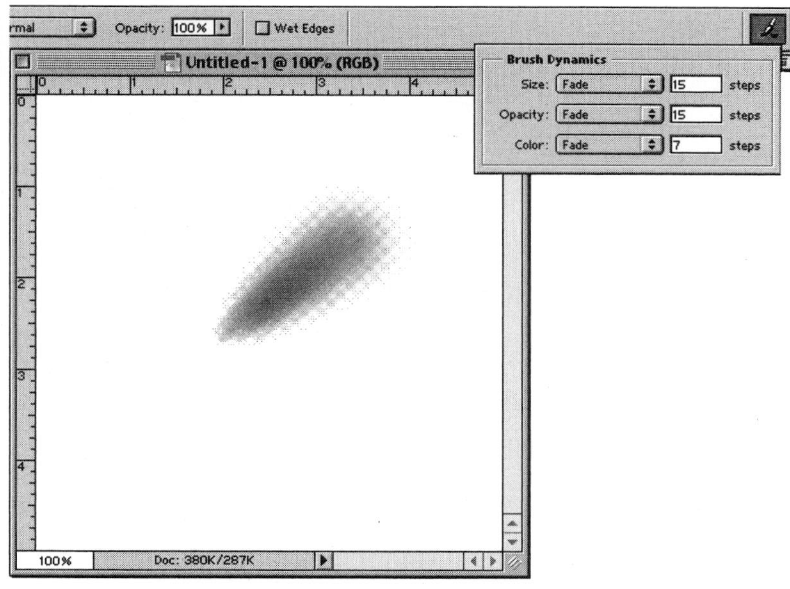

10. Turn off all of the Brush Dynamics settings and close the document.

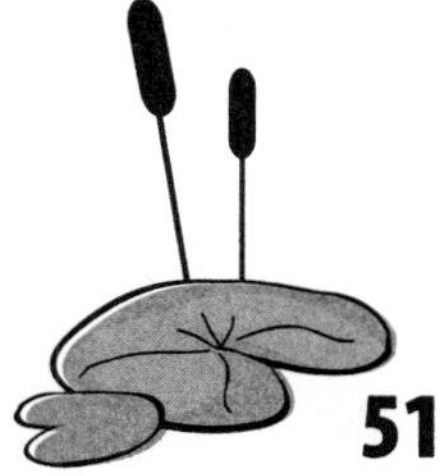

Using the Paintbrush Tool to Create a Background Image

Next, you will create a galaxy-like background using the Paintbrush tool and some of the filters included with Photoshop. This will give you a good idea of how this tool works, as well as the effects that you can achieve with filters.

1. Create a new document (select File ➢ New) that is 5 × 5 inches and 72 pixels dpi. Make sure the color swatches at the bottom of the toolbox are at the default Black/White setting by clicking the small squares.

2. Choose Edit ➢ Fill and fill the document with the foreground color.

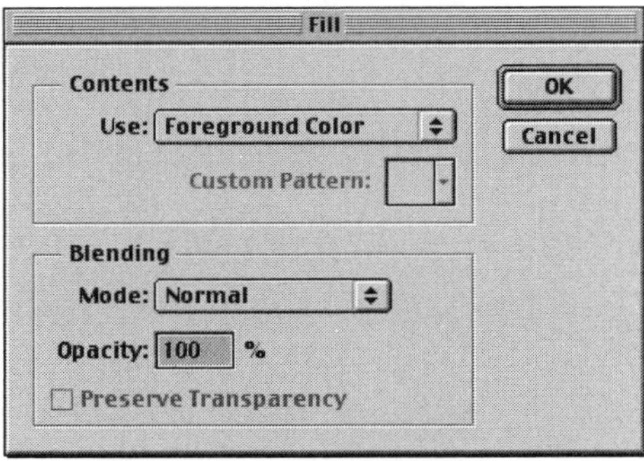

3. Select the Paintbrush tool.
4. If the Color palette isn't open, select Window ➢ Show Color to open it. Choose a nice shade of yellow.
5. Change the Brush setting to Soft Round, 65 pixels. Make sure all of the Brush Dynamics settings are set to Off.

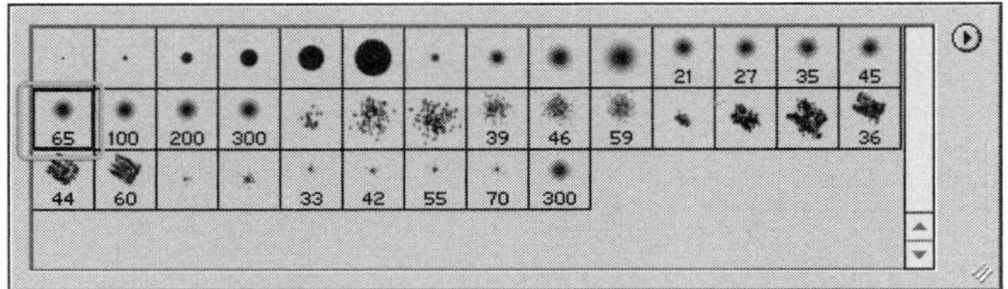

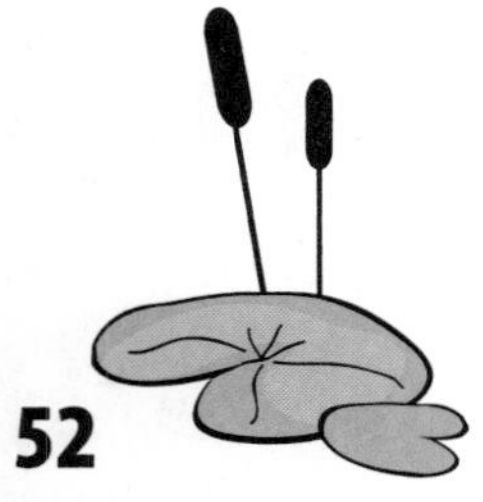

6. Create a diamond-like pattern on the workspace. Do this by painting on the workspace with the Paintbrush tool, overlapping the lines you create.

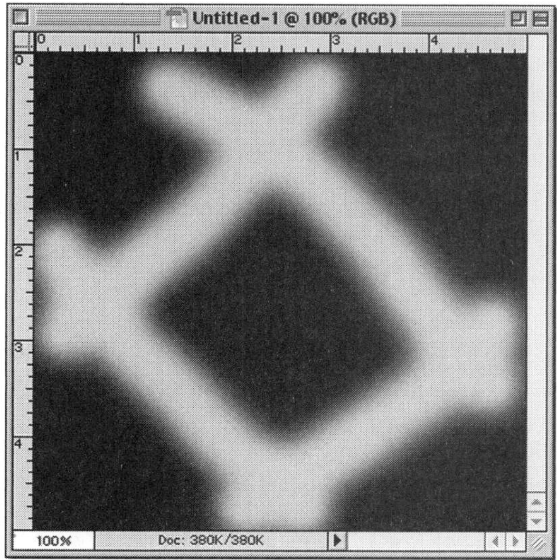

7. Change the Brush setting to Soft Round, 35 pixels and select a greenish color. Use the Paintbrush tool to create a checkerboard pattern over the pattern you just created.

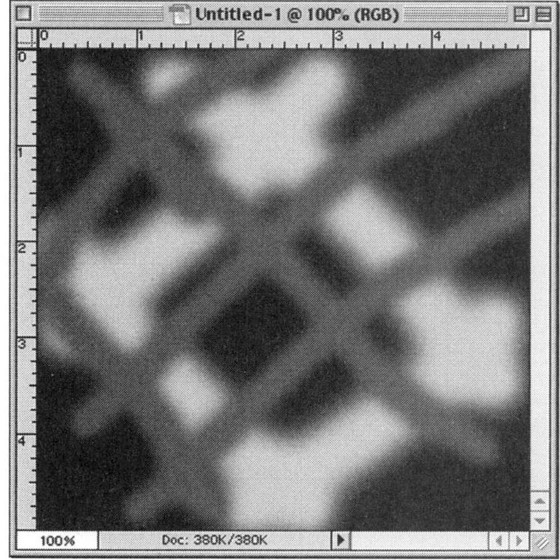

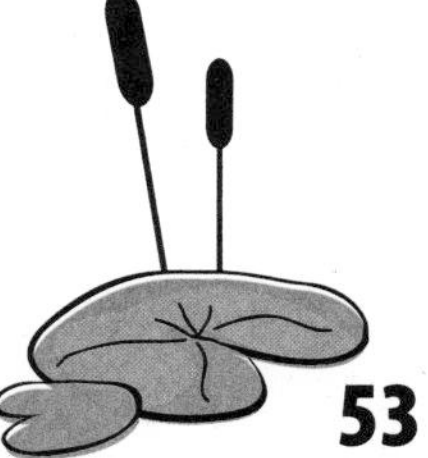

8. Select Filter ➢ Distort ➢ Twirl.

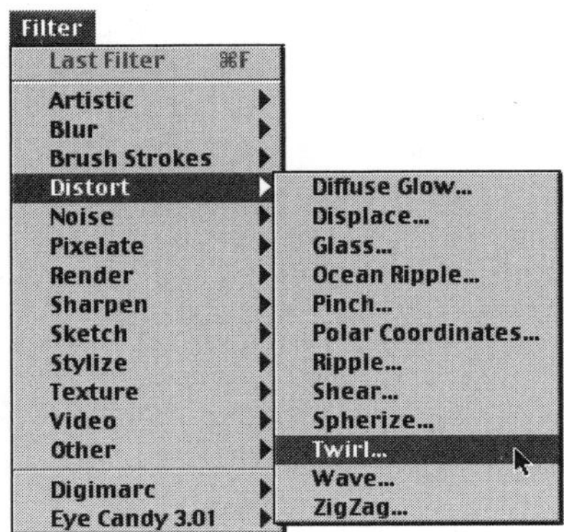

9. In the Twirl dialog box, set the Angle to its maximum level of 999 by either typing it into the text box or moving the slider all the way to the right.

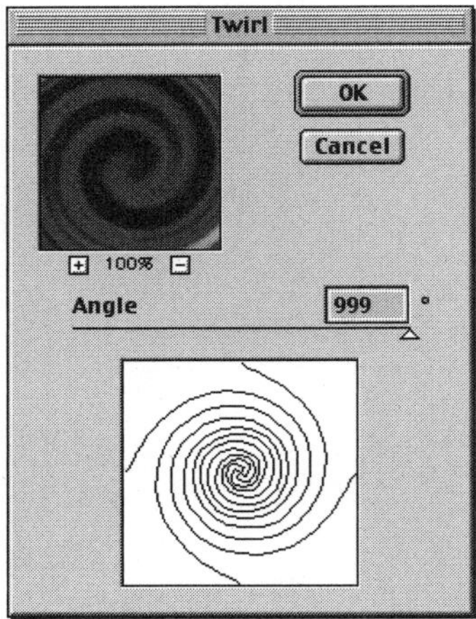

10. Select Filter ➢ Blur ➢ Gaussian Blur.

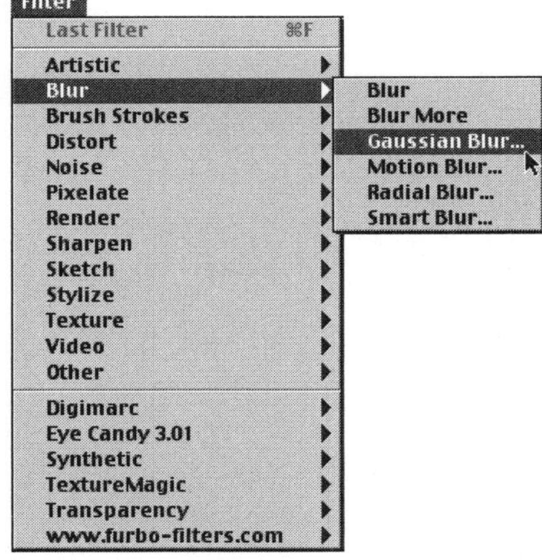

11. In the Gaussian Blur dialog box, set the Radius to **5** pixels. To see the effect before you click OK, select the Preview check box.

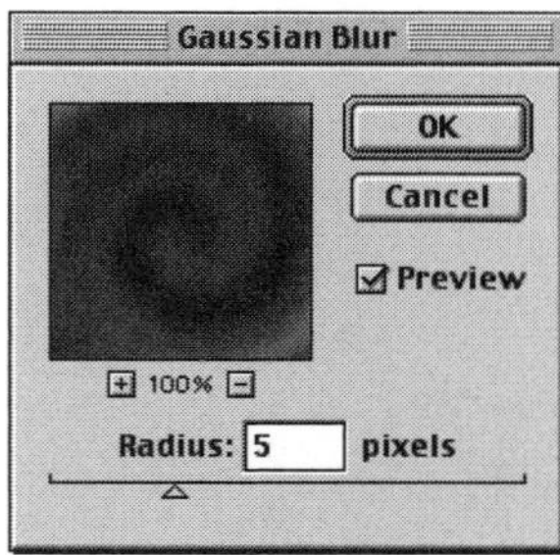

12. Choose Filter ➢ Render ➢ Lighting Effects.

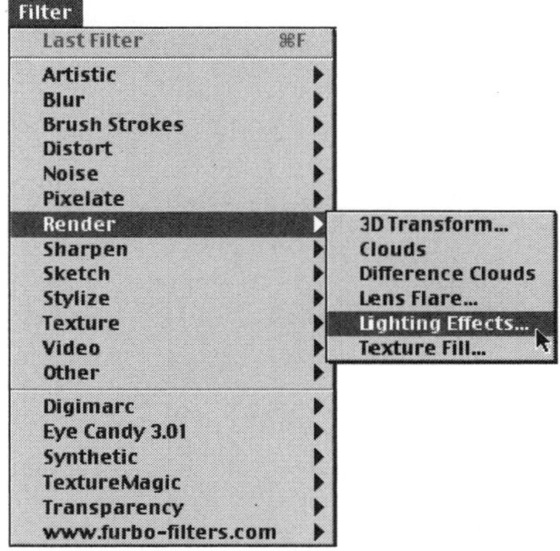

13. In the Lighting Effects dialog box, set the following parameters:

Style: 2 O'Clock Spotlight

Light Type: Spotlight

Intensity: 17

Focus: 91

Gloss: -67

Material: -58

Exposure: 0

Ambience: 20

Texture Channel: Red

White Is High: Selected

Height: 96

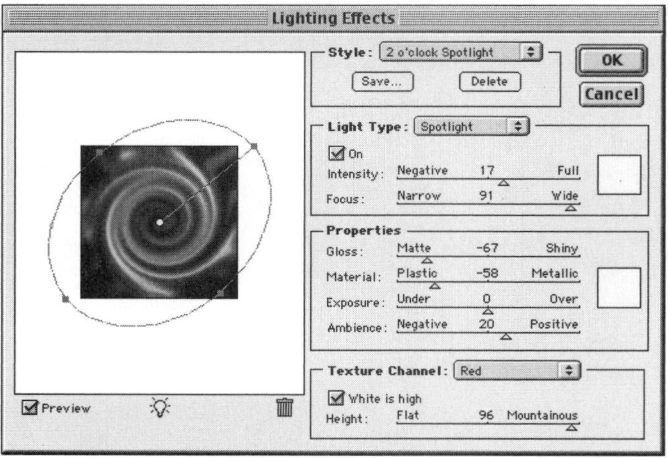

You now have a pattern that looks like a green-and-yellow galaxy.

Moving On

As you can see, the modification tools give great flexibility when it comes to working with your images. Before continuing with the next chapter and learning about some of Photoshop's other tools, take some time to experiment on your own with the tools covered in this chapter: the Lasso tools, Magic Wand tool, Clone Stamp tool, Pattern Stamp tool, and Paintbrush tool. You can also have fun trying out some of the other filters available on the Filter menu.

In the next chapter, you will learn about Photoshop layers, which allow you to work individually with different parts of a single image.

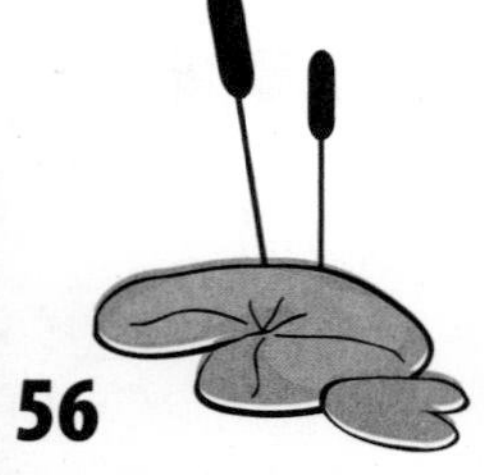

Chapter 3

Working with Layers, Channels, and Paths

When you work with Photoshop, even before you delve into its more esoteric power tools, you will quickly discover the usefulness of its layers feature. Layers help you build intricate pictures and change the appearance of your images, allowing you a large amount of creative freedom.

Along with layers, Photoshop provides controls for color channels and drawing paths. These tools provide great flexibility in image design.

In this chapter you'll learn how to use the following Photoshop features:

- Layers palette
- Channels palette
- Paths palette

Introducing the Layer Controls

layer

An additional level to your working file that allows you to place image information on it without affecting the layer beneath or above it. Think of a layer as a sheet of acetate through which you can see what is beneath it.

Layers provide a way for you to work with parts of an image independently. Photoshop allows you to have up to 99 layers associated with an image.

You can view and manipulate layers through the Layers palette. You should always have the Layers palette open—it's that important a tool. So, if it isn't open when you start Photoshop, select Windows ➢ Show Layers to display it on your screen.

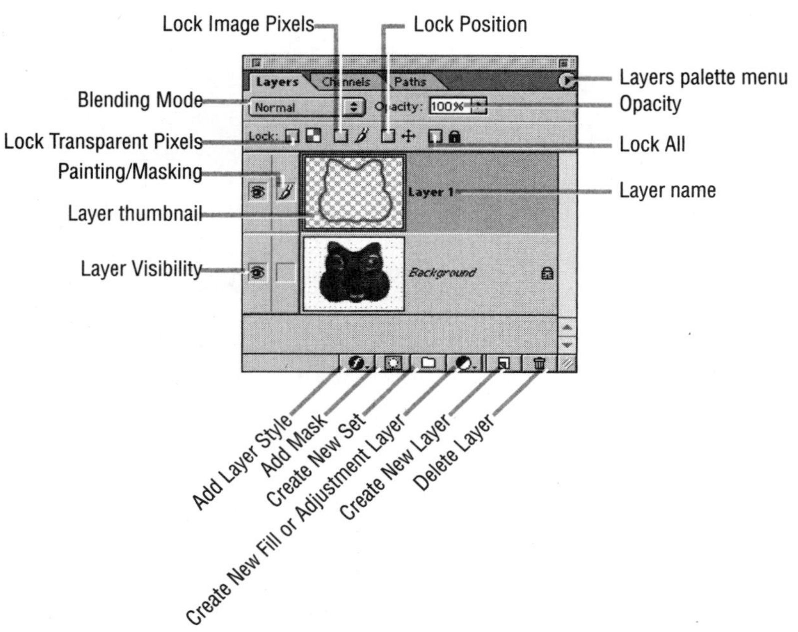

Note

Two other tabs are visible on the Layers palette: Channels and Paths. Both of these palettes are discussed later in this chapter.

The Layers palette consists of the following features:

- The Blending Mode pop-up menu contains the same mode controls as those discussed in Chapter 2. In this case, the blending affects the entire layer rather than a specific portion of it.

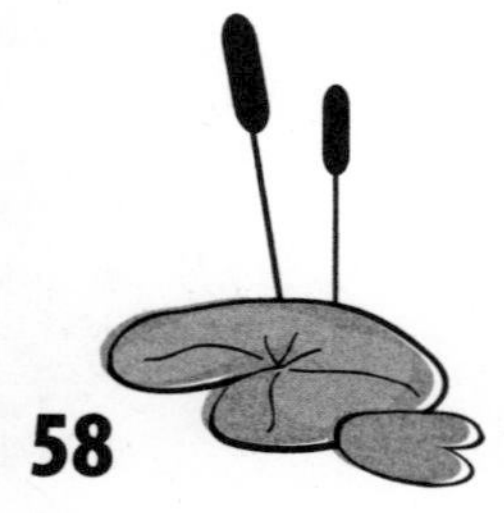

- The Opacity setting allows you to change the opacity of your layer from invisible (0%) to opaque (100%).
- The Lock Transparent Pixels option prevents any changes you make to the image content from affecting transparent areas.
- The Lock Image Pixels option prevents any changes you make to a layer from affecting whatever image content is present.
- The Lock Position option locks the layer into place so it can't be moved accidentally.
- The Lock All option prevents you from making any changes to that particular layer.
- The Layer Visibility indicator is the eye icon. When the eye icon appears, the layer can be seen on your main workspace. When it's deactivated, the layer becomes hidden on the main workspace (but is still there).
- The Painting/Masking indicator is the paintbrush icon. When this icon is present on a selected layer, it indicates that any modifications are made to that layer.
- The layer **thumbnail** shows a small image of the contents of the layer.
- The layer name appears next to its thumbnail. The default name for each new layer is Layer followed by the next number in order. Layers are numbered from the bottommost to the topmost.
- The Add Layer Style button lets you assign styles to the chosen layer.
- The Add Mask button lets you turn the layer into a **layer mask** to create different effects. (Masks are discussed in the "Creating a Path and Mask" section later in this chapter.)
- The Create New Set button gives you the ability to add sets to a particular layer. When selected, new layers are placed inside this set, giving you the ability to manipulate specific parts of your image as a single unit.
- The Create New Fill or Adjustment Layer button gives you the ability to add specific filter effects to the chosen layer.
- The Create New Layer button creates a new layer above the topmost or selected layer.

thumbnail
A small graphic representation of a larger image.

layer mask
An effect that removes a portion of an image to reveal the image behind (or underneath) it. In Photoshop, you can create layer masks using the Pen tool and the Paths palette.

- The Delete Layer button removes the selected layer from the Layers palette.
- The Layers palette menu button (the circular button with the triangle inside it, located in the top-right corner) provides access to a menu of layer-modification controls to help you manage the layers.

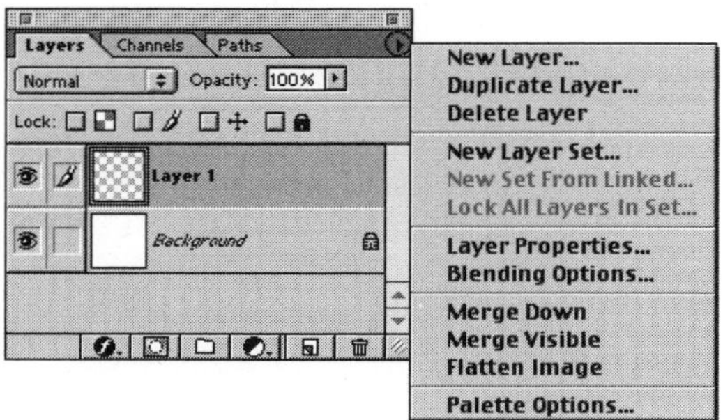

New Layer adds a new layer to the image.

Duplicate Layer duplicates the selected layer.

Delete Layer deletes the selected layer.

New Layer Set creates a folder inside the Layer palette.

New Set From Linked creates a set including all related layer groups when you create linked layers.

Lock All Layers in Set locks all layers within a group so they can't be modified.

Layer Properties brings up a dialog box where you can rename the layer and assign a color to the layer or layer set.

Blending Options allows you to assign specific blending modes to layers.

Merge Down combines the selected layer with the one immediately beneath it.

Merge Visible combines all visible layers into one.

Flatten Image combines all layers, along with the **Background**, into one.

Palette Options lets you change the size of the layer thumbnail.

When you open an image in Photoshop it will become the background. Every layer you add will be placed on top of the Background.

Background
The bottom level of the workspace. The Background is locked and content cannot be modified like other layers (although you can fill the Background with a color). To modify the Background, make a copy of it and work with the new layer.

Note

Most of the Layers palette controls do not work with the Background. For example, you cannot choose a blending mode, set the opacity, or lock pixels for the Background.

The thumbnails to the left of the layer names show you what is going on in each layer. Using larger thumbnails is useful, but it takes up more memory in Photoshop. If you don't have a lot of RAM installed on your computer, you may need to either set the smallest thumbnail size or turn thumbnails off altogether. To set the thumbnail size, choose Palette Options from the Layers palette menu and click a thumbnail size. To turn off the display of thumbnails, click None.

Creating Layers

You'll want to create layers when you need to edit different parts of a graphic separately and move parts independently of each other. You can also change the positions of graphic elements by rearranging the order of layers, stacking them to create the effects you desire.

Adding Layers

Let's get started by creating a couple of new layers and adding content to them.

1. Open an image file with a solid-color background, like the one shown below, if you have one (it's okay if you use one that has another kind of background).

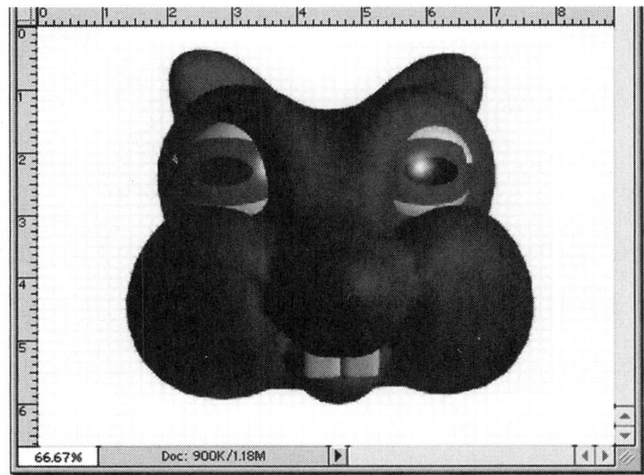

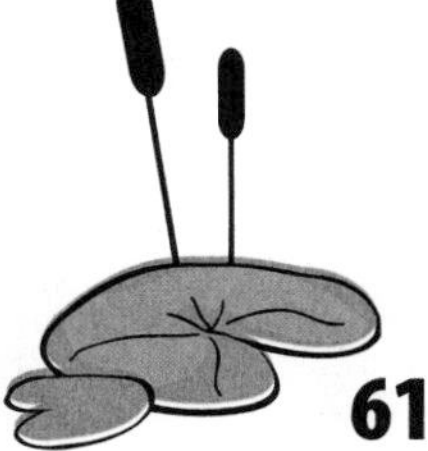

2. Click the Create a New Layer button at the bottom of the Layers palette. This creates a layer above your main image called Layer 1.

3. Select the Paintbrush tool. Open the Swatches palette and select a deep green color.
4. Change the Paintbrush brush size to Soft Round, 21 pixels.

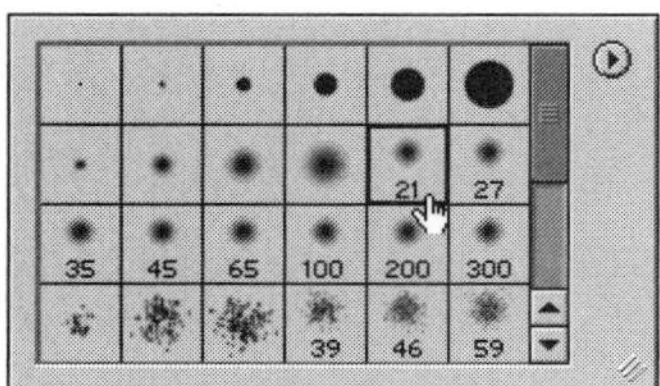

5. Begin roughly painting around the portion of the image you want to make the focus of the picture. Notice how the outline you created is now reflected in the Layer 1 thumbnail.

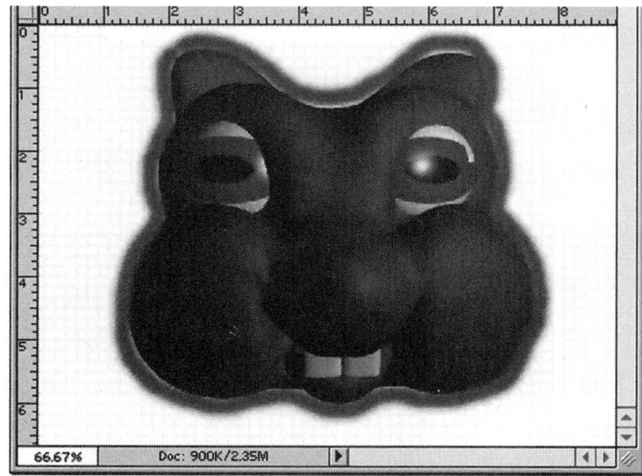

6. Click the Create a New Layer button to create another new layer.
7. Change the Paintbrush tool's color to a bright red and the brush size to Spatter, 39 pixels.

8. Create some squiggly lines around the image.

Note

The checkerboard pattern you see in the thumbnails of Layers 1 and 2 is Photoshop's way of showing a transparent background. If you prefer, you can choose another representation for transparency. To do this, select Edit ➢ Preferences ➢ Transparency & Gamut.

Congratulations, you have now created a multiple-layered image file.

Adding Content from Another File

Many times, you will want to combine elements from multiple images. This involves not only having two images open, but also using one of the selection tools to select elements. You select an element in one image that you want to use in another image and **drag and drop** it into the other image. Let's try this approach.

drag and drop
To move an image or selected area of an image from one workspace and place it onto another workspace. In the case of Adobe products, you can also drag and drop from one program to another, such as from Photoshop to Illustrator.

1. Open two image files. If you need to, press Ctrl+hyphen (Cmd+hyphen) to zoom out so you can see both images.

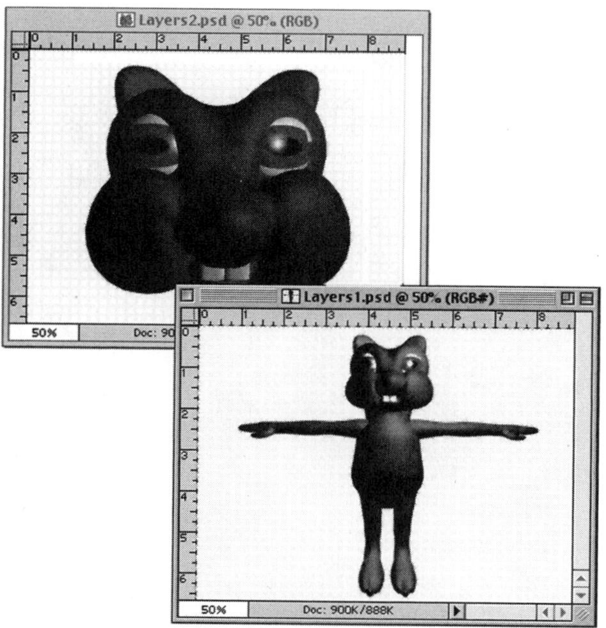

busy

Refers to an image that has a lot of visual information.

2. If your image has a plain background, use the Magic Wand tool to select the background of the image you want to transfer. If you have an image that is rather **busy**, use the Lasso tool to outline the area you want to transfer (selecting the element rather than the background) and skip to step 4.

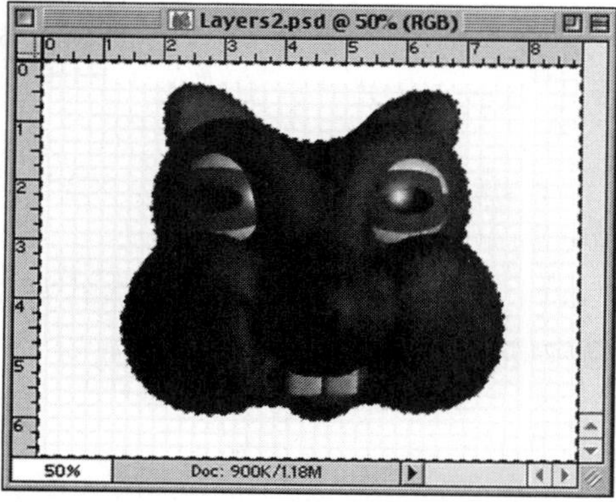

3. With the background selected, choose Select ➢ Inverse to invert the selected area so that the subject is outlined.
4. Select the Move tool, place it over the selected element, and drag and drop that element to the other image.

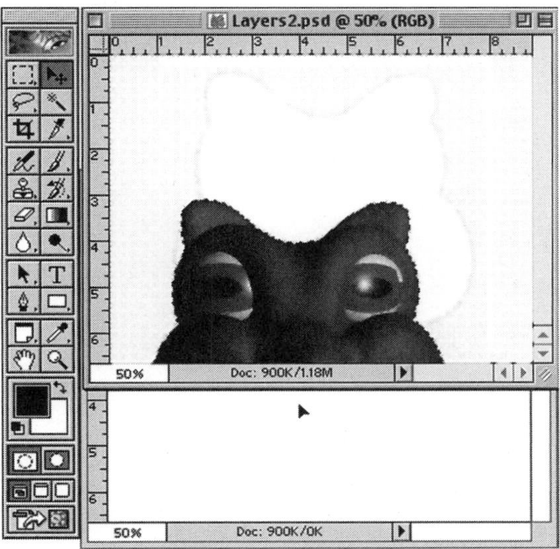

5. Notice a new layer was automatically created when you moved the selected element. In this example, the element (the squirrel's head) in the new layer is too large.

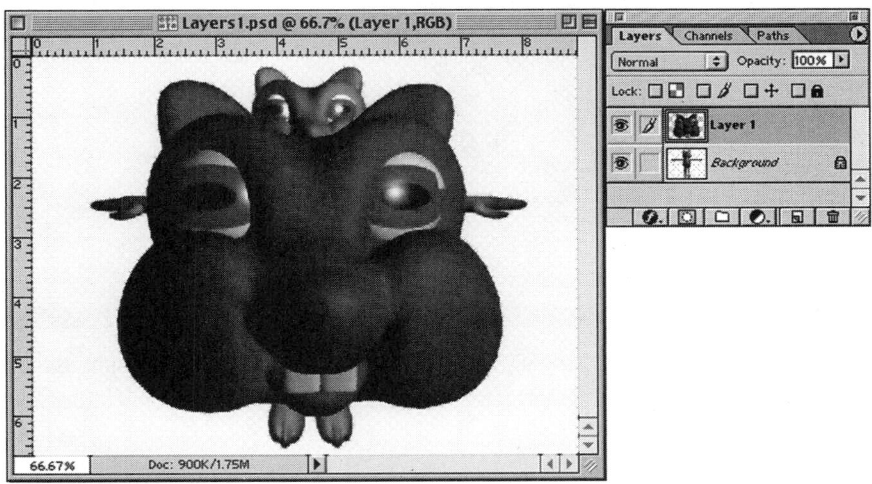

6. To resize the transferred element, choose Edit ➢ Transform ➢ Scale.

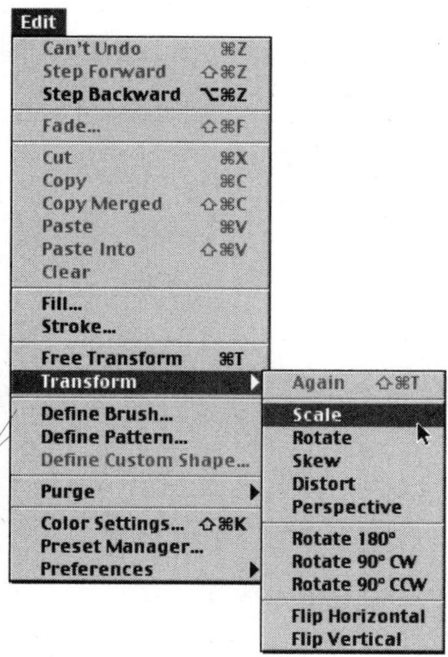

7. A bounding box will surround the element. Place your cursor on one of the corners, hold down the Shift key, and drag inward to resize the layer to fit better.

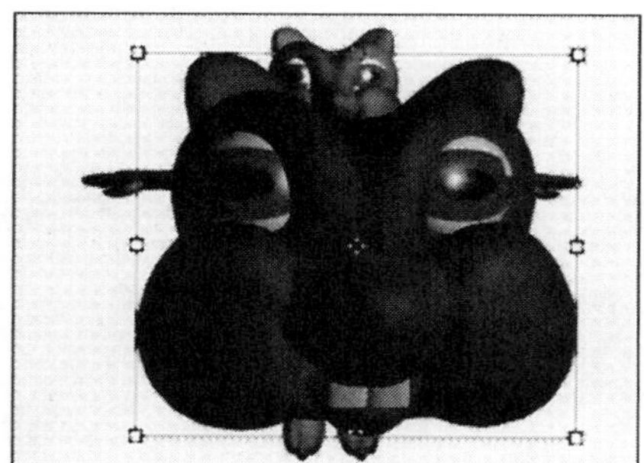

Note

Holding down the Shift key while dragging constrains the proportions of the image so that it retains the correct dimensions. Otherwise, your resized image might be taller or wider than the original.

8. Drag the image anywhere in the workspace, either before you accept the change, by double-clicking inside the bounding box, or after resizing, by selecting the Move tool.

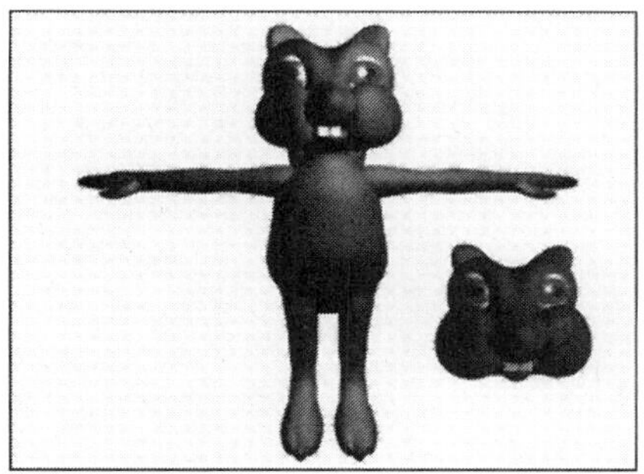

Note

If you simply select the Move tool after resizing the image, a dialog box will come up, asking if you want to apply the transformation. Click the Apply button to accept the change.

9. To duplicate this layer, click the Layers palette menu button (the circular one with the right-pointing arrow in the upper-right corner of the Layers palette) and select Duplicate Layer.

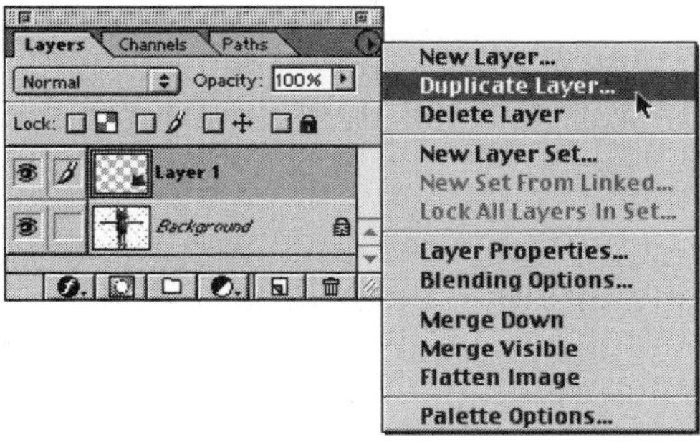

10. Repeat step 9 three times, so that you have the Background and four layers in the Layer palette (Layer 1, Layer 1 copy, Layer 1 copy 2, and Layer 1 copy 3).

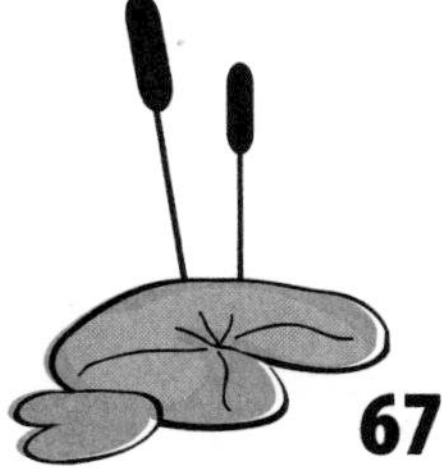

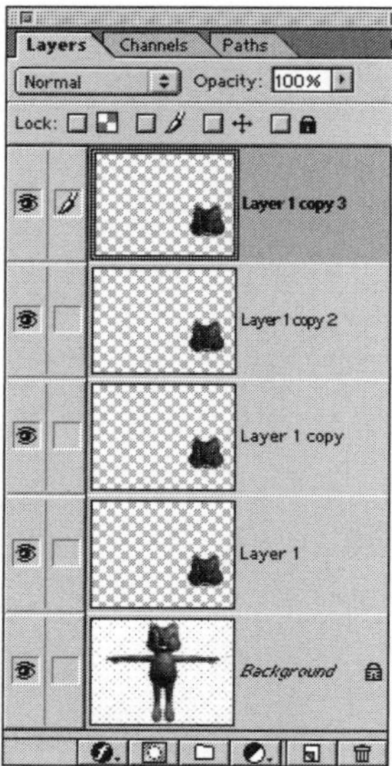

11. Select one of the copied layers and move its image into a corner of the composite file. Repeat this process, so that when you're finished, a duplicated image is in each corner of the file.

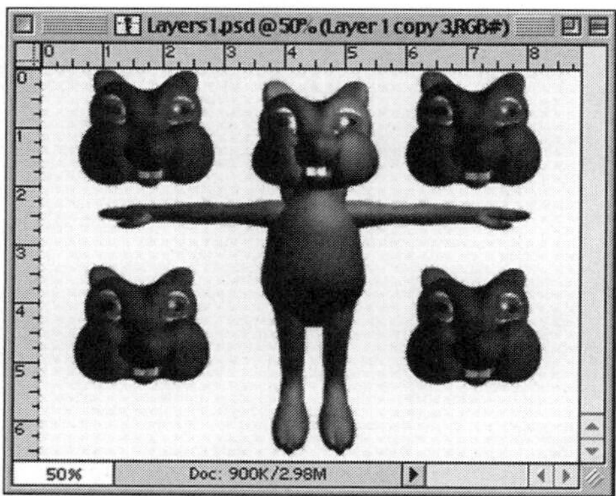

12. Select File ➢ Save. In the Name box, enter **Layers1.psd**. Make sure that Photoshop is selected in the Format box and that Layers is checked in the Save section of the Save dialog box. Keep this file open; you will use it again in the next example.

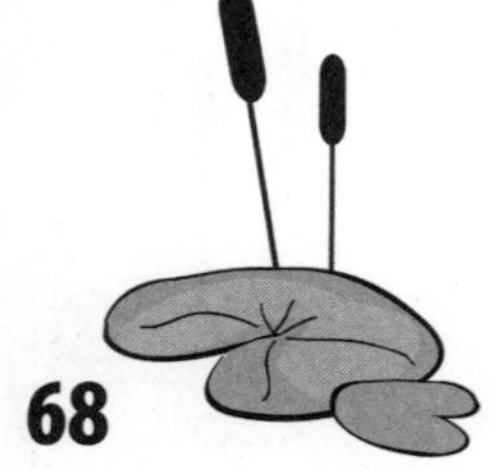

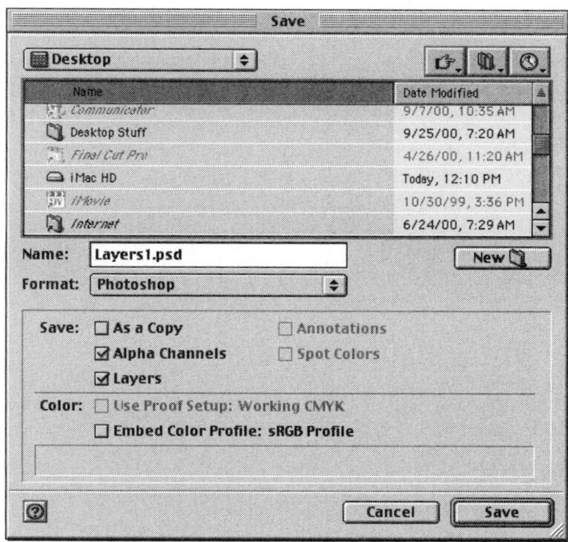

Changing Layer Names

As you can see from the previous exercise, figuring out what is on each layer can become confusing. This is why you might want to name your layers. Let's do that now.

1. Working with the Layers1.psd file you saved in the previous exercise, select Layer 1, which is the bottommost layer (directly above the Background), by clicking it.
2. Click the Layers palette menu button and choose Layer Properties.

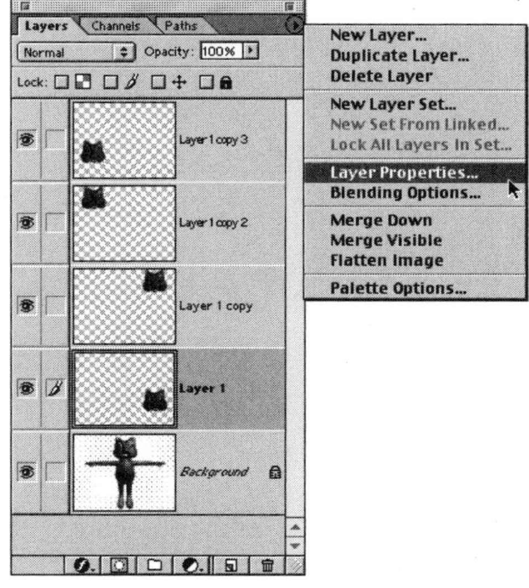

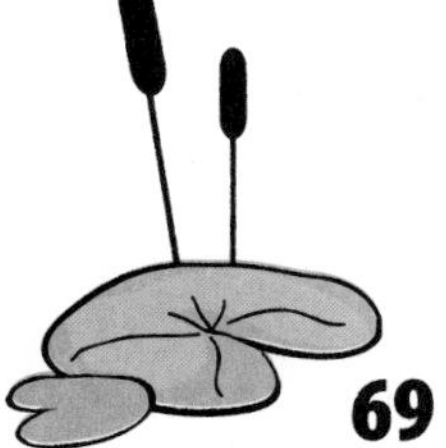

3. In the Layer Properties dialog box, change the layer name to something more descriptive. If you want to assign a color to make it easier to identify this layer in the Layers palette, click the button at the end of the Color box and select a color.

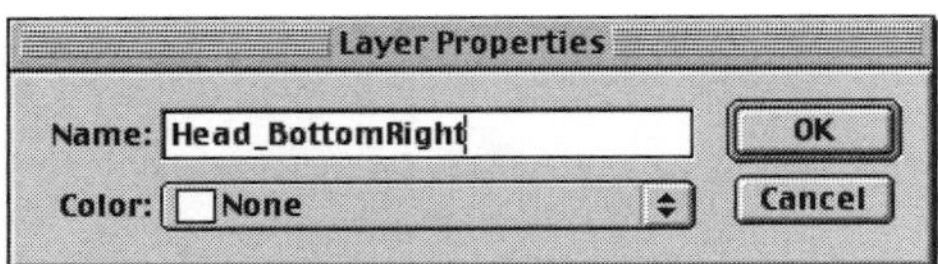

4. Repeat steps 1 through 3 to name the Layer 1 copies.

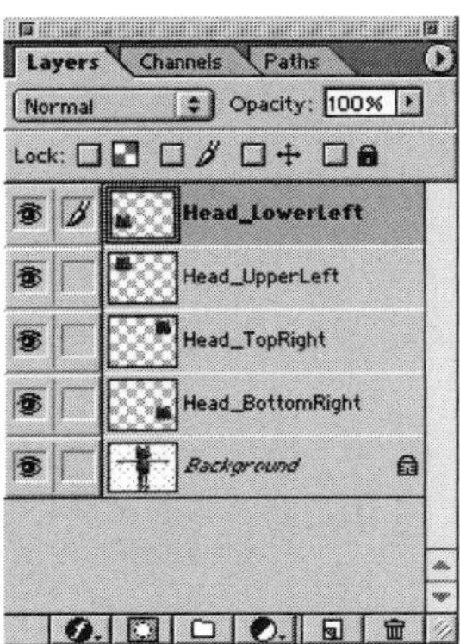

Manipulating Layers

The true power of layers is that you can manipulate them in a number of ways. For example, you can reposition layers, merge them, and apply effects to them.

Changing Layer Positions

The position, or stacking order, of your layers determines which layers are on top of other layers. You can easily change a layer's position by dragging it up or down in the Layers palette.

As an example, let's rearrange the layers in the Layers1.psd file. In this example, suppose that you want the lower head layers and the upper head layers to be positioned together.

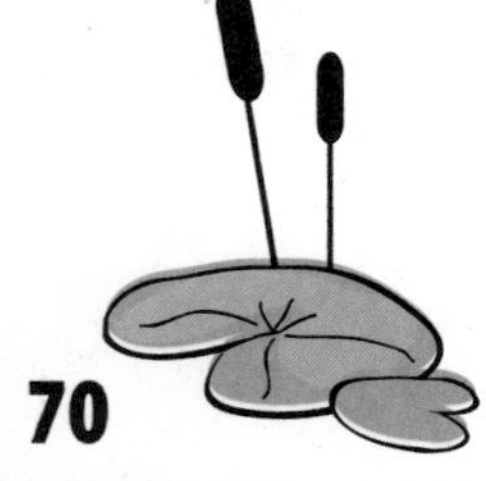

1. To move the Head_LowerLeft layer to directly above the Background, select that layer by clicking it.
2. While holding down the mouse button, drag the selected layer down in the Layers palette to its new position. As you drag, a highlighted line shows where the layer can be moved.
3. When the highlighted line is above the Background, release the mouse button to drop the layer into its new position.

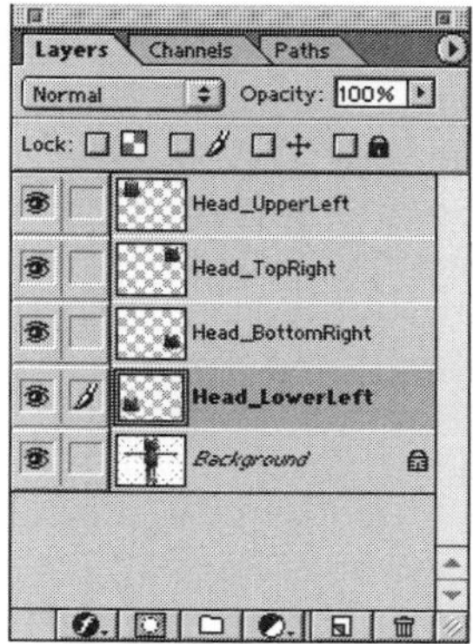

4. Reposition the Head_UpperLeft layer below the Head_TopRight layer.

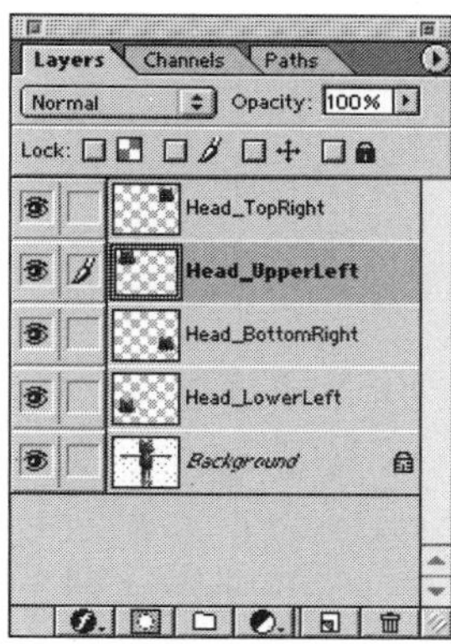

Merging and Adding Effects to Layers

Layers help you to add special effects more efficiently. For example, you can easily add drop shadows to the file you've been working with in the previous

exercises. In this next exercise, you will first merge the layers, then duplicate the new layer before adding the effect.

1. To unclutter the screen, hide the Background. Do this by clicking the eye icon next to the Background on the Layers palette. The eye icon disappears, and the background image is hidden, leaving only the visible layers in the workspace.

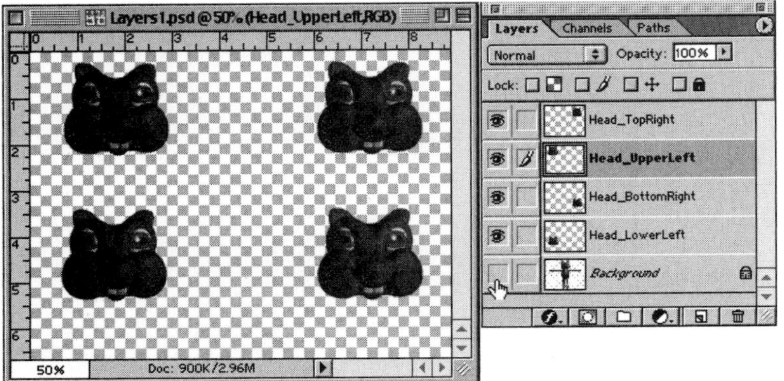

2. With any of the other layers selected, click the Layers palette menu button and choose Merge Visible.

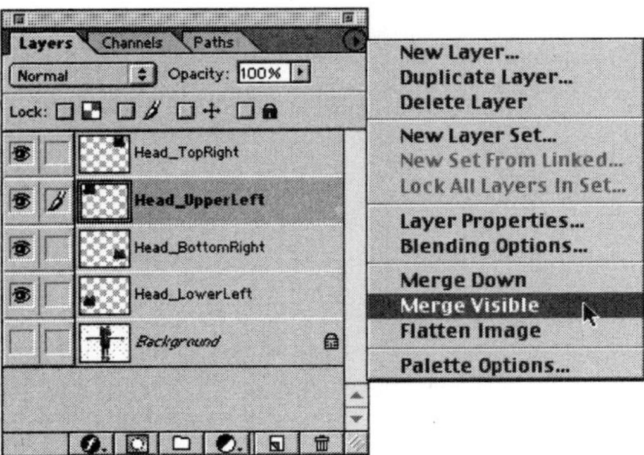

3. Click the merged layer, click the Layers palette menu button, and choose Layer Properties. In the Layers Properties dialog box, name this layer **FloatingHeads**.

4. Duplicate the FloatingHeads layer by dragging it to the Create New Layer icon at the bottom of the Layers palette.

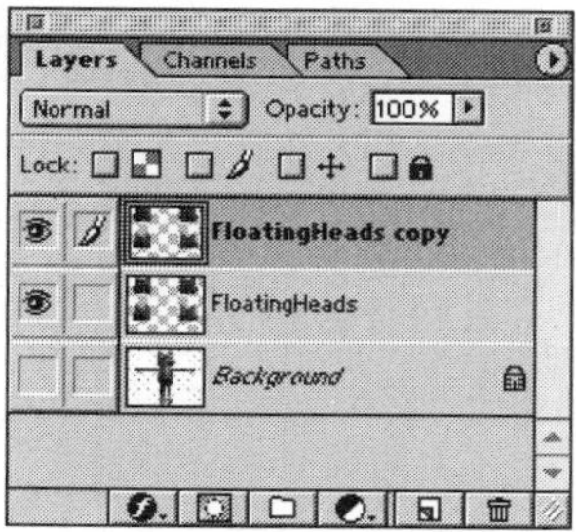

5. Select the first FloatingHeads layer in the Layers palette and choose Edit ➢ Fill. In the Fill dialog box, set Use to Foreground Color and make sure that Preserve Transparency is activated. (The foreground color should be Black for this exercise.)

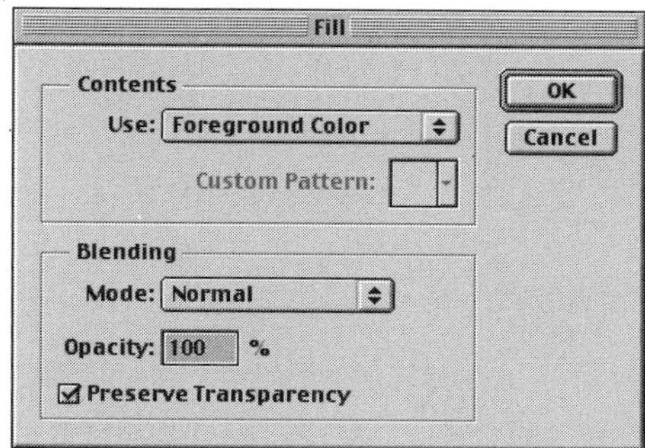

Note

Preserve Transparency makes sure that only nontransparent portions of the layer are filled. If this were not selected, the entire layer would be filled with the color or pattern you choose.

6. Select Filter ➢ Blur ➢ Gaussian Blur and change the Radius setting to 3.0 pixels.

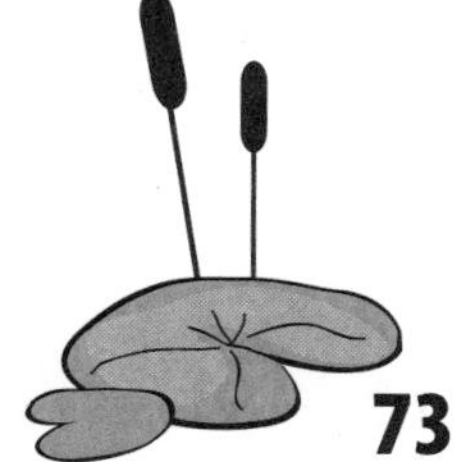

Tip

You can click the – (minus) and + (plus) buttons directly beneath the preview image in the Gaussian Blur dialog box to zoom in or out on the layer image. To move the image around in the preview, place the cursor inside the preview and hold down the mouse button. The cursor will turn into a hand, allowing you to drag the image.

7. Choose the Move tool and drag the FloatingHeads layer into another position that is down and to the right of the FloatingHeads copy layer.

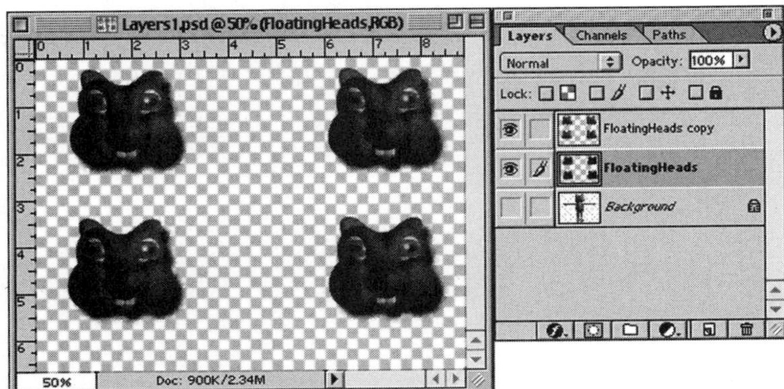

8. Change the FloatingHeads copy layer's opacity by clicking the arrow next to the Opacity box at the top-right side of the Layers palette. Select 40, for an opacity of 40%.

9. Click where the eye icon appeared next to the Background in the Layers palette to make the Background visible again. Now you can see how your new drop shadows look.

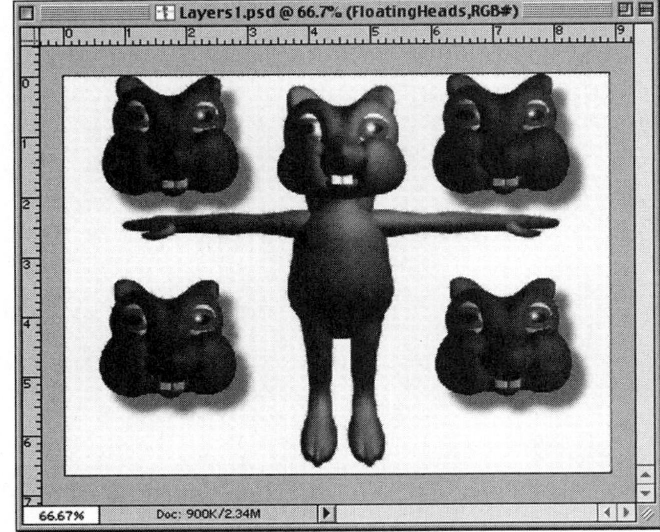

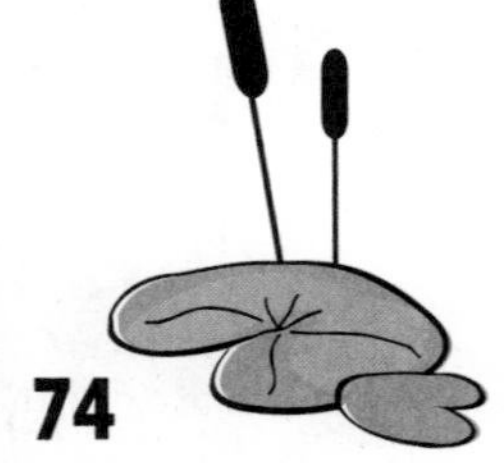

Working with Channels

In Photoshop, each image has **channels** that contain the image's color information. Since red, green, and blue are the main colors that make up a full-color image, working directly within a specific color channel lets you modify an image in a more precise way.

channel
An area that stores information about an image's color. Channels include Red, Green, Blue, and Alpha when in RGB mode. In CMYK mode, the channels are Cyan, Magenta, Yellow, Black, and Alpha. By working with an image's color channel, you can create many different special effects, changing the entire appearance of the image.

Introducing the Channel Controls

The Channels palette provides controls for working with channels. Open a color image and select the Channels tab at the top of the Layers palette.

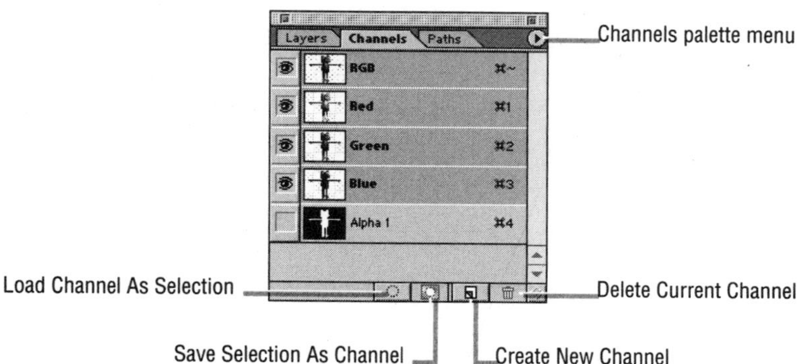

The Channels palette lists Red, Green, and Blue channels, as well as RGB and Alpha channels. The individual Red, Green, and Blue channels let you modify each of those colors separately. The RGB channel activates all of the channels, so you see your full-color image. The Alpha channel controls the masking assigned to an image.

Along the bottom of the Channels palette are four buttons:

- The Load Channel As Selection button allows you to load saved channels or channels that you have worked on previously.
- The Save Selection As Channel button lets you save modifications to a selection as a new channel in the image.
- The Create New Channel button adds a new channel to the list.
- The Delete Current Channel button removes a channel from the list.

The Channels palette menu, displayed by clicking the circular button with a right-pointing arrow in the top-left corner, provides some channel-specific options.

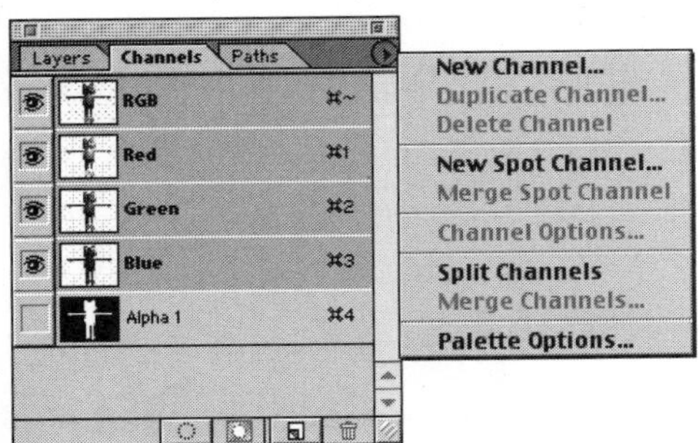

The Channels palette menu options work as follows:

- New Channel creates a new channel in which you can paint masking information.
- Duplicate Channel makes a copy of the selected channel or channels. This is an excellent option when you want to try out different effects on a specific color channel without losing the original channel information
- Delete Channel removes the channel from the list.
- New Spot Channel lets you create a channel that adds a spot color to the image. This is a professional printing technique that requires a separate film layer.
- Channel Options works with **Alpha** and Spot channels, allowing you to assign how masked, selected, or spot colors are represented on the screen.
- Split Channels closes the color file and opens the Red, Green, Blue, and Alpha channels as separate image files. These files are represented as black-and-white images.
- Merge Channels returns the split channels back to one full-color image.
- Palette Options allows you to change the size of the channel thumbnail.

Alpha channel
A stored selection from an image. An Alpha channel is a grayscale representation. Black represents transparent areas; white is opaque.

Creating a Channel Effect

Channels provide flexibility for working with the colors in your images. To demonstrate what you can do by working with channels, you will create a new channel and apply a special effect to it.

1. Open a color image that you would like to experiment with and display the Channels palette (open the Layers palette and click the Channels tab).
2. Select the Blue channel by clicking it.
3. Click the Channels palette menu button (the right-pointing arrow in a circle at the top right) and choose Duplicate Channel.
4. In the Duplicate Channel dialog box, enter **BlueEFX** in the As box.

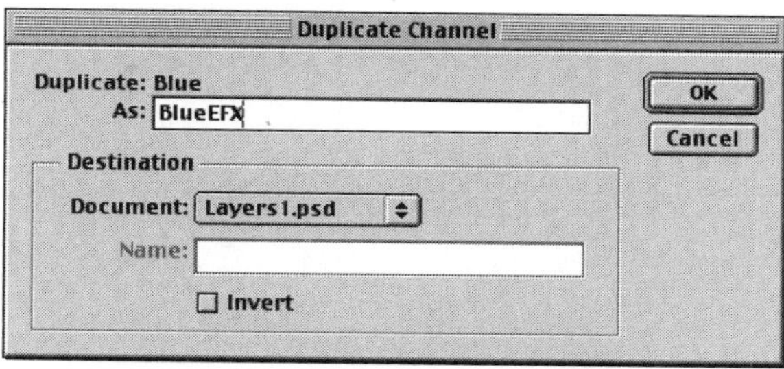

5. With the BlueEFX channel selected, select Filter ➢ Sketch ➢ Note Paper.

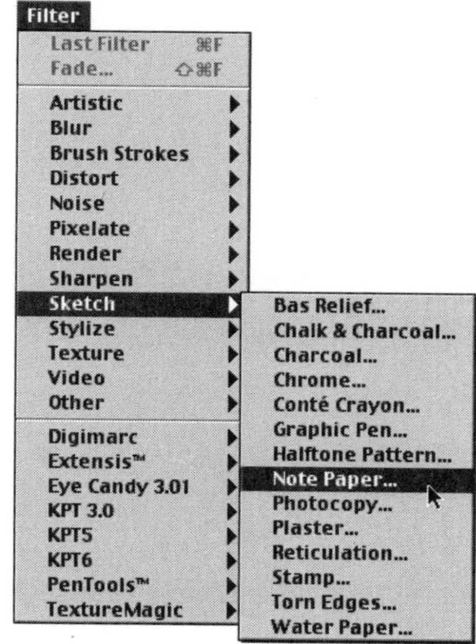

6. In the Note Paper dialog box, set Image Balance to 31, Graininess to 15, and Relief to 14. This will create a paper-like texture in this channel. Click OK to close the dialog box.

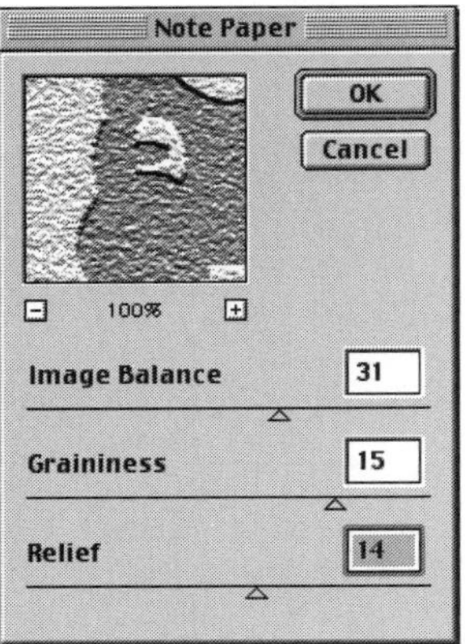

7. Now look at how this new channel interacts with the image.

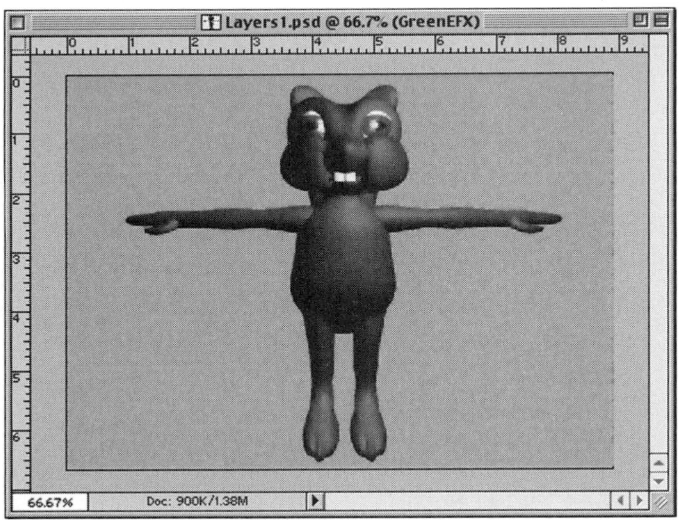

As you become more familiar with Photoshop, you will find that working with the various RGB and Alpha channels can help you create some exciting effects that would be either very time-consuming or almost impossible to do in any other way.

Note

For more information about using Photoshop channels, you can search through the Photoshop documentation or invest in *Mastering Photoshop 6* (published by Sybex).

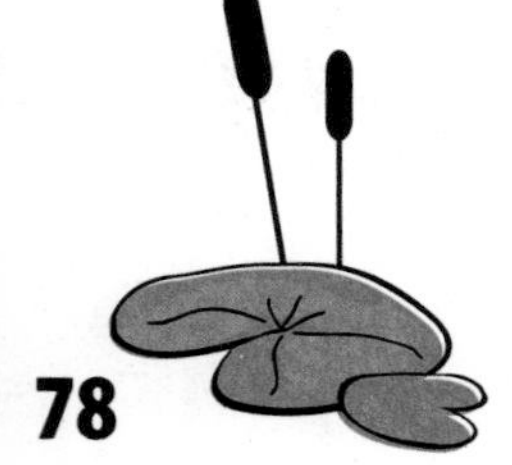

Working with Paths

Paths allow you to create straight lines and curves with precision, but their extraordinary versatility stems from their use to mask off areas of an image or create unusual effects directly within Photoshop. They can also be exported to other programs that read this type of information (called vector-based applications), such as Adobe Illustrator and LiveMotion.

path

An object composed of anchor points and line segments, created using the Pen tool. A path defines the outline of a shape. You can use a path to hide areas of an image or layer, define an area to become a selection, or create a clipping path that will show only the selected area when the image is brought into a page layout program such as InDesign or QuarkXPress.

Introducing the Path Controls

The Paths palette provides controls for working with paths. To access this palette, select the Paths tab at the top of the Layers palette.

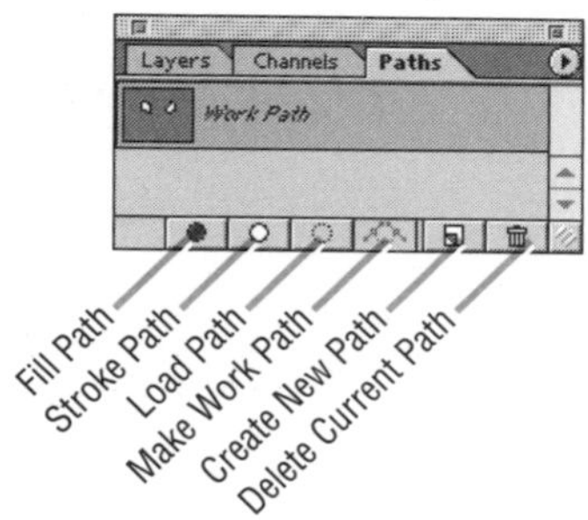

The main area in the Paths palette shows the paths you've created. You can select a path here in order to modify it. The six buttons across the bottom of the Channels palette work as follows:

- The Fill Path button fills the interior of the path with the color of your choice.
- The Stroke Path button lets you assign a color to the path edge, allowing you to create effects like neon signs and more.
- The Load Path button lets you load saved paths.
- The Make Work Path button gives you the ability to create a temporary path.
- The Create New Path button creates a new path.
- The Delete Current Path button lets you delete the path you have selected.

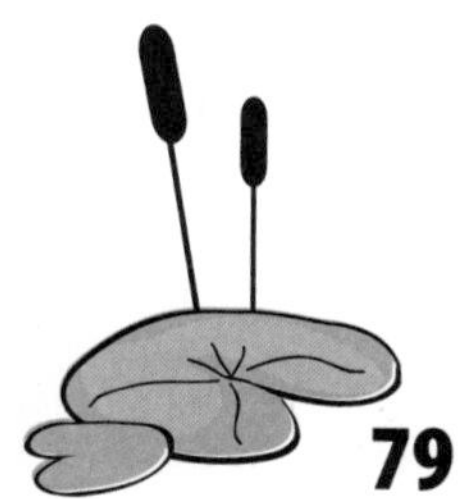

The Paths palette menu, displayed by clicking the circular button with the right-pointing arrow in the top-right corner of the palette, offers more options for working with paths.

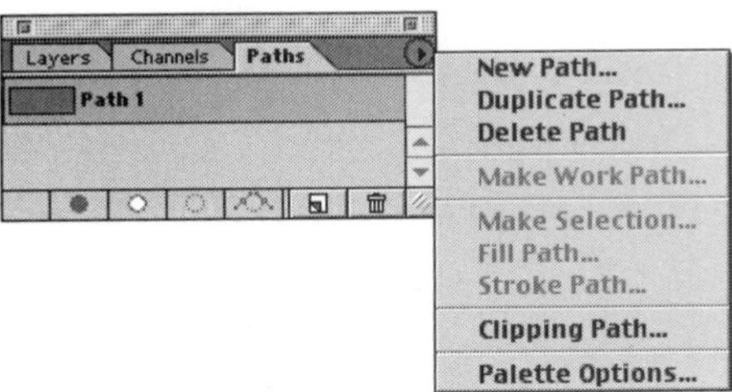

The Paths palette menu options work as follows:

- New Path creates a new path.
- Duplicate Path lets you duplicate the selected path.
- Delete Path allows you to delete the selected path.
- Make Work Path lets you create a temporary path (called a **work path**).
- Make Selection turns the path into a selected area, much like that created with the Lasso tool.
- Fill Path fills the interior of the path with the foreground color of your choice.
- Stroke Path adds color to the path outline.
- Clipping Path isolates the image surrounded by the path from the rest of the image so that the unselected portions do not show when imported into programs such as Illustrator or LiveMotion.
- Palette Options lets you change the size of the path thumbnail.

work path
A temporary path you create using the Pen tool. The work path can be modified and edited.

Creating a Path and Mask

To create a path, you use the Pen tool. The Pen tool works by laying down points when you click your mouse. Each consecutive point is connected to the last one. Let's create a path and then use it to make a mask.

1. Open a file and display the Paths palette (by clicking the Paths tab in the Layers palette).

2. Select the Pen tool from the toolbox.

3. You will use the Pen tool to create a path that follows a shape in your image. Lay down the first point of your path by clicking next to the shape that you want to draw around.

4. Move the mouse to another point along the area you want to outline and lay down a second point. If you need to create a curve in the path, before releasing the mouse button, drag the cursor until the path matches the curve as closely as possible.

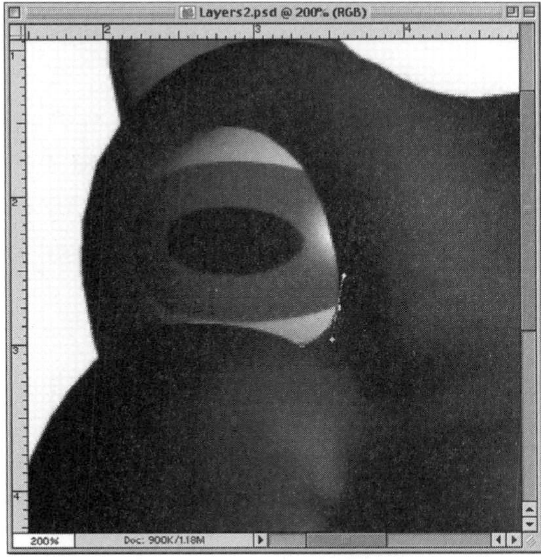

5. Continue to lay down points in this manner until the entire selection is outlined. To close the path, connect the last point and first point by clicking the first point.

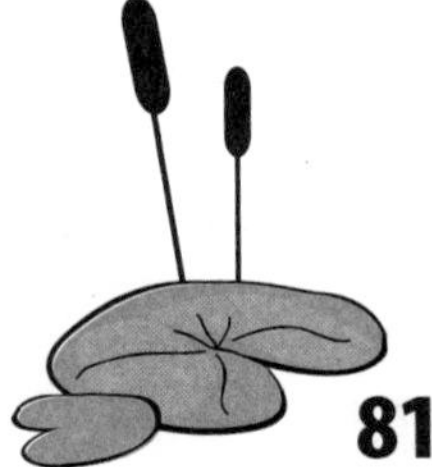

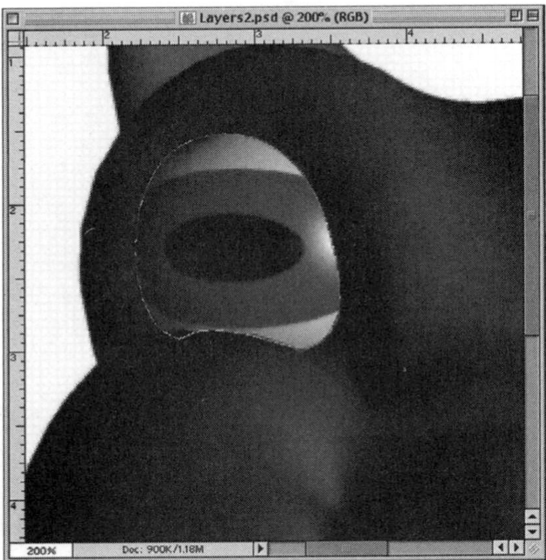

6. To modify some of the points so the path outlines your selection better, select the Convert Point tool in the toolbox.

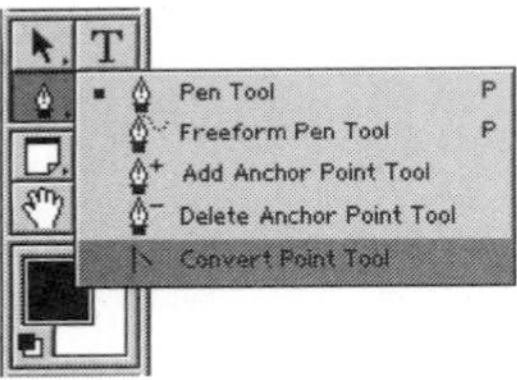

7. Click the path you created. You'll see modifier handles on the points. Click and hold down the mouse button on the point where you want to make modifications. Drag the handles until the curve fits more precisely.

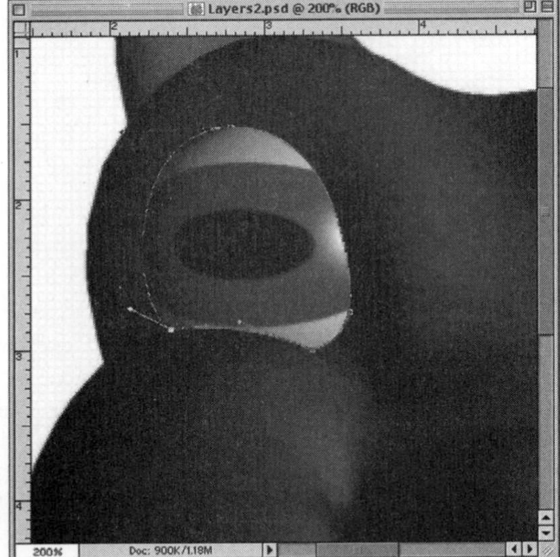

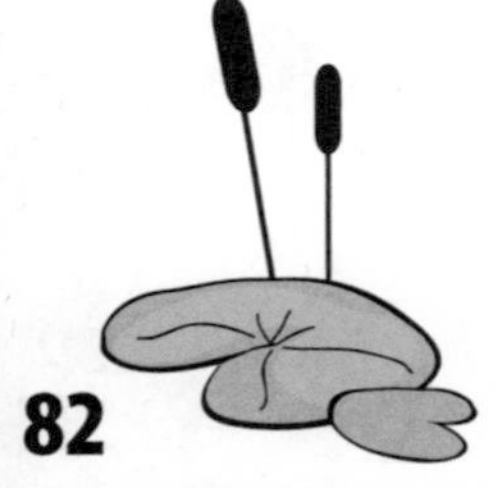

Tip

You can create sharp corners by holding down the Alt (Option) key while dragging a point with the Convert Point tool.

8. If there is another area of the image you want to create a path around, do so before moving onto the next step.
9. Select Make Selection from the Paths palette menu.

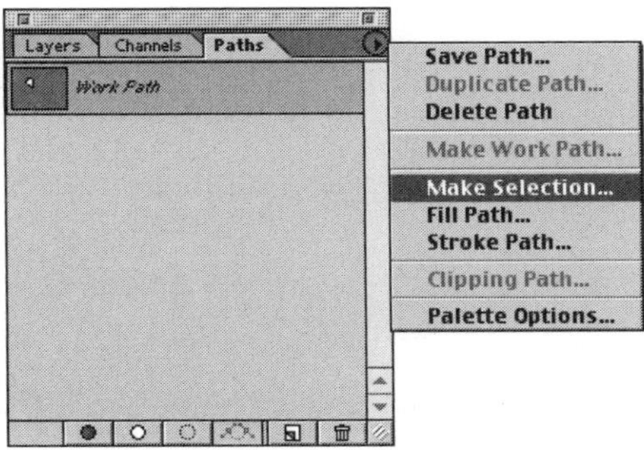

10. In the Make Selection dialog box, change the Feather Radius to 5 pixels. Make sure Anti-aliased is activated. Then click OK.

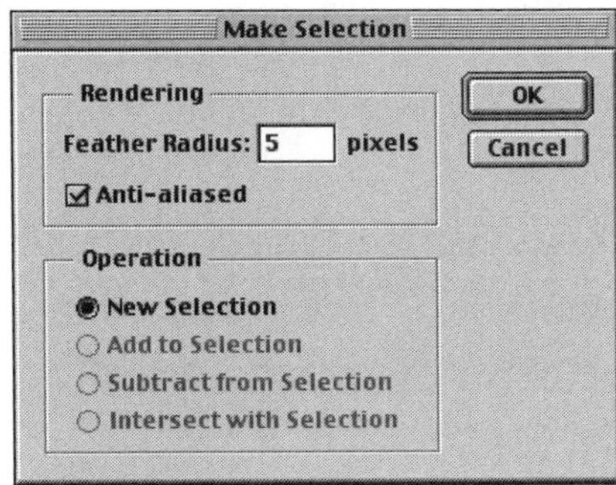

11. The path turns into the marching ants outline. Click the Layers tab at the top of the Channels palette to switch to the Layers palette.
12. Duplicate the Background by dragging it to the Create New Layer icon at the bottom of the palette.

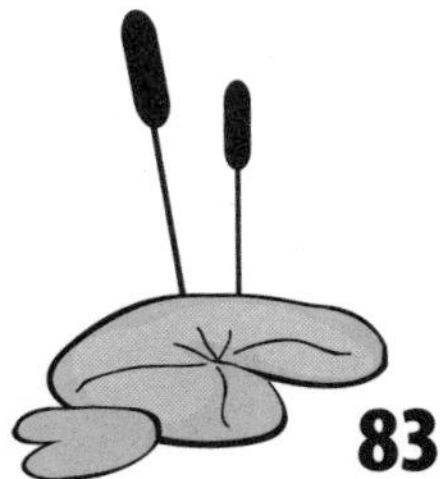

13. With this new layer active, click the Add Mask button at the bottom of the Layers palette. A mask icon with the paths you created is added to the layer.

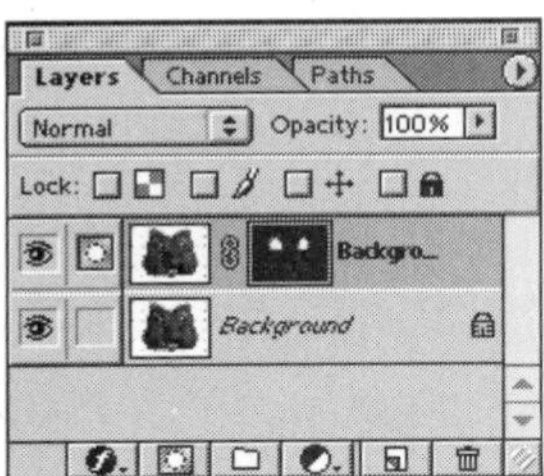

14. Select the original Background. Choose Edit ➢ Fill and fill the background with black. All that will be left is your masked areas, surrounded by black.

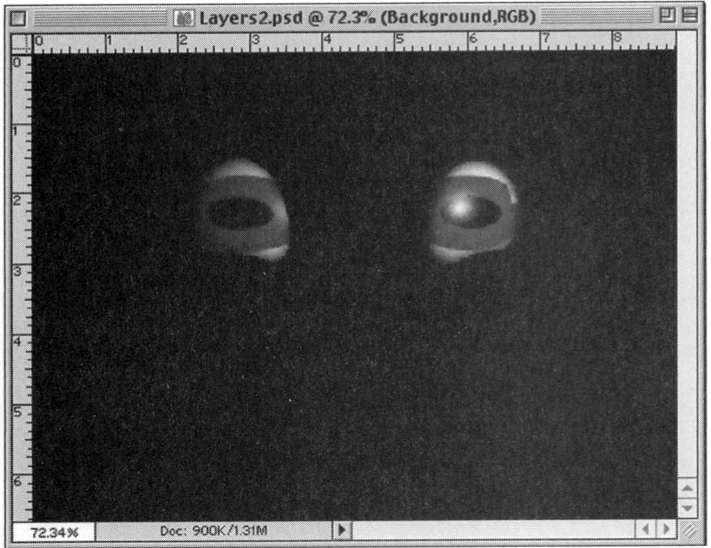

You can change the background, adding different patterns, colors, or images (using the techniques covered earlier in this chapter) to see how your new mask looks.

Moving On

As you have seen, there are many controls available through the Layers, Channels, and Paths palettes. These controls allow you to create fascinating and high-quality images. These features are what Photoshop is famous for, and why it is the de facto professional photo-manipulation program on the market.

Another major feature of Photoshop is its wide array of modification tools. In the next chapter, you'll learn how to use Photoshop's tools for fixing mistakes, creating effects, and using photographic techniques.

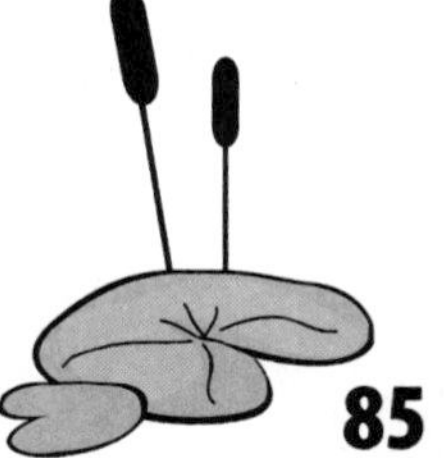

Chapter 4

Using Image-Modification Tools

You've already experimented with some modification tools (back in Chapter 2). Now it's time to work with some of the more advanced ones. The tools that you'll learn about in this chapter deal with erasing areas from an image, forms of cloning, and emulating a photographer's darkroom techniques. Many of these tools are best used on layers, which were the subject of Chapter 3.

Here, you'll learn how to use some of the more sophisticated image-editing tools:

- The Eraser tools, for removing parts of your images
- The History Brush and Art History Brush tools, for painting layers over layers
- The Blur, Sharpen, and Smudge tools, for changing an image's focus
- The Dodge and Burn tools, for lightening and darkening image areas

Erasing with the Eraser Tools

As you would expect, the Eraser tools allow you to erase portions of your image. Photoshop provides three separate tools for erasing: Eraser, Background Eraser, and Magic Eraser. As their names imply, these tools have specific functions to help you manipulate your images. To select a specific eraser, move your cursor over the Eraser tool in the toolbar and press and hold down the mouse button to make the pop-up menu appear.

Straightforward Erasing with the Eraser Tool

The Eraser tool simply erases anything it comes in contact with, which allows you to create some interesting layered effects. You will first try it with its default settings, and then see the effects of changing some tool options.

1. Open an image to practice on and select the Eraser tool in the toolbar by clicking it.

Tip

Before working on any of your images, make sure to duplicate them in the Layers palette. This way, you won't harm your original picture. See Chapter 3 for information about duplicating layers.

2. Move the cursor over the portion of the image you want to erase and, while holding down the mouse button, drag the Eraser tool over the area you want to remove.

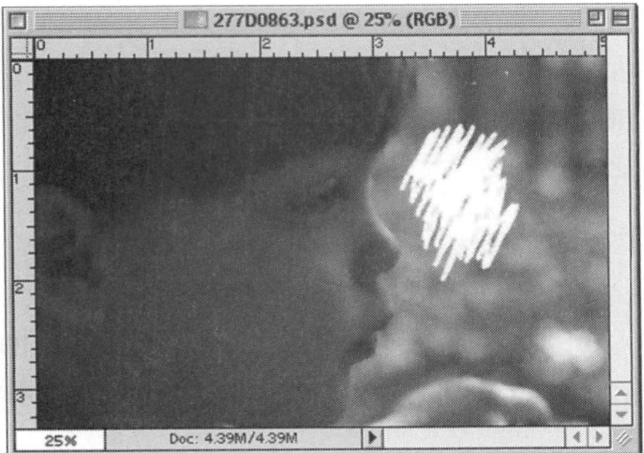

3. Select Edit ➢ Undo Eraser to return the image to its original state.
4. In the options bar, change the brush size to Soft Round, 100 pixels and select the Wet Edges check box.

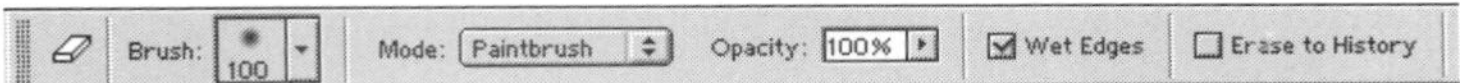

5. Erase the same area of your image. This time, as you continue holding down the mouse button, the erased area expands as if something wet were spreading across the image.

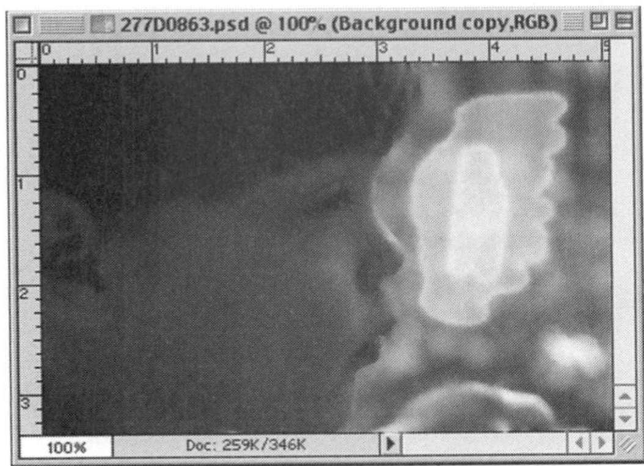

Note

The Wet Edges feature doesn't erase a selected area completely, because it is simulating erasing with water. To fully erase an area, go over it a few times. Make sure to release the mouse button and then press it down again before continuing to erase.

As you've seen, the Brush setting works in a similar way to how it does with the tools you've experimented with in previous chapters. The Wet Edges option gives a "wet brush" effect, where the edges of the erased area fade back to 100 percent opacity. The other settings on the Eraser tool's options bar work as follows:

- The Mode setting determines the way that the Eraser tool interacts with the image, giving you more control over the look of the erased area. Access the different modes by clicking the pop-up menu button.

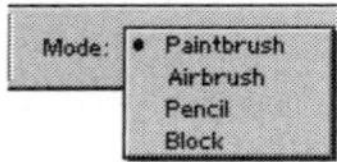

- The Opacity setting lets you determine the strength of the eraser effect: 0% has no effect on your image, and 100% completely erases the selected area. You can either type in a percentage or use the pop-up control.

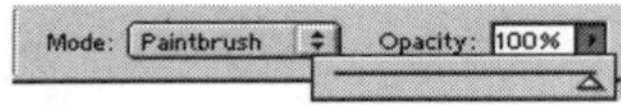

- The Erase to History setting determines how the Eraser tool is affected by the History parameters you have assigned (see the "Painting with the History and Art History Brushes" section later in this chapter).

Getting More Control with the Background Eraser

You played with the Background Eraser tool a bit in Chapter 1, where you saw that it can be used to erase the background elements in an image, creating a transparency in the affected area. In the toolbar, the Background Eraser is represented by a pair of scissors over the eraser.

The Background Eraser's options bar includes several settings that give you more control over the area that is to be erased.

The Brush setting works the same as it does with the main Eraser tool. The other options work as follows:

- The Limits setting specifies how the eraser will interact with the area. You have three choices:

  Discontiguous erases a sampled color no matter where it appears in the image.

  Contiguous erases only the area where the eraser is, removing the pixels surrounding that particular spot.

  Find Edges preserves the sharpness of the nonselected areas near the area you want to erase.
- The Tolerance setting controls the color range for erasing. A low tolerance (down to 0%) erases a small range of colors; a higher tolerance (up to 100%) erases a wider area of colors.
- The Protect Foreground Color option protects areas of the picture that match the foreground color.
- The Sampling setting controls how colors are erased. There are three choices:

  Continuous erases colors continuously as you drag the eraser across the image.

  Once erases only the color you first click, which is handy for erasing single colored areas.

  Background Swatch erases only the color specified in the background swatch in the toolbox.

Tip

The best use of the Background Eraser tool is to quickly create a "safe area" around a subject so you can erase the rest of the unwanted parts of your image more easily.

Let's try using the Background Eraser tool with some color controls.

1. Open an image that has a subject that can be separated from the background.

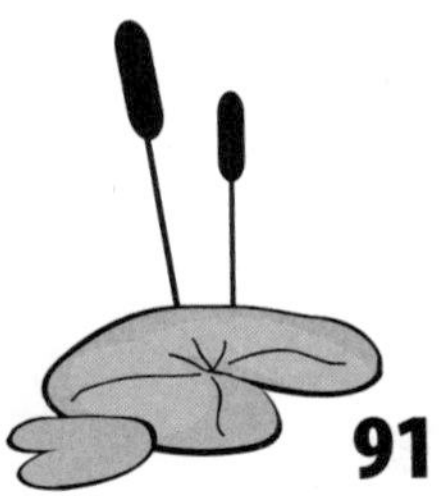

2. Select the Eyedropper tool in the toolbox.

3. Select a color in the subject.

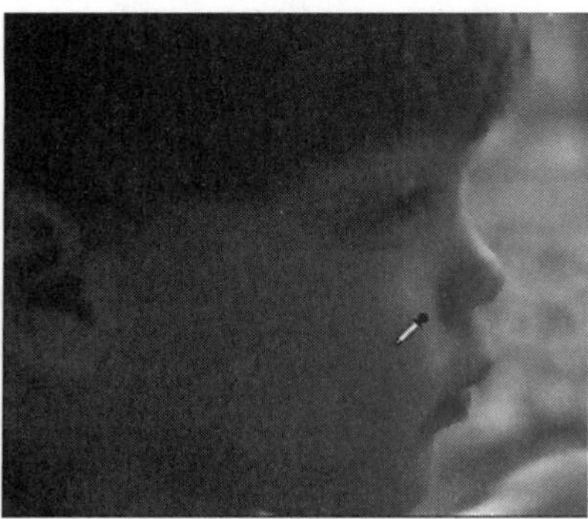

4. Select the Background Eraser tool in the toolbox.
5. In the Background Eraser tool's option bar, set the following options:

   Brush: Hard Round, 13 pixels

   Limits: Contiguous

   Tolerance: 50%

   Protect Foreground Color: Selected

   Sampling: Continuous
6. Begin erasing the area next to the color you just selected in your subject.

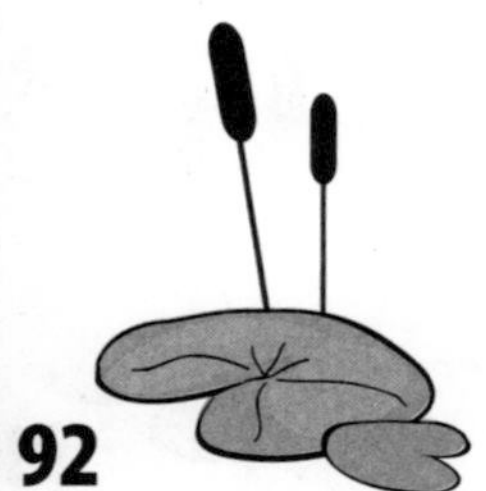

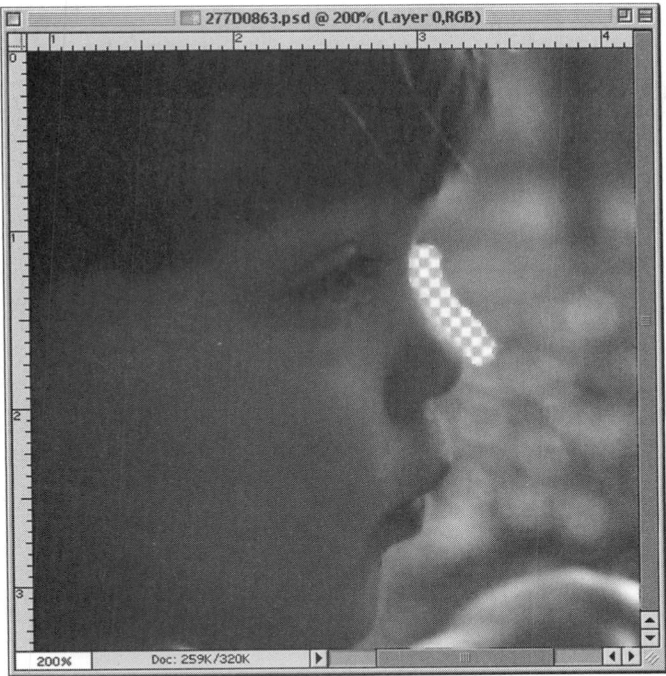

7. When you move into a new area of the picture where the subject color has changed, resample the color with the Eyedropper tool.
8. Select the Background Eraser and erase some more of the background.
9. Repeat steps 7 and 8 until you've outlined your subject.

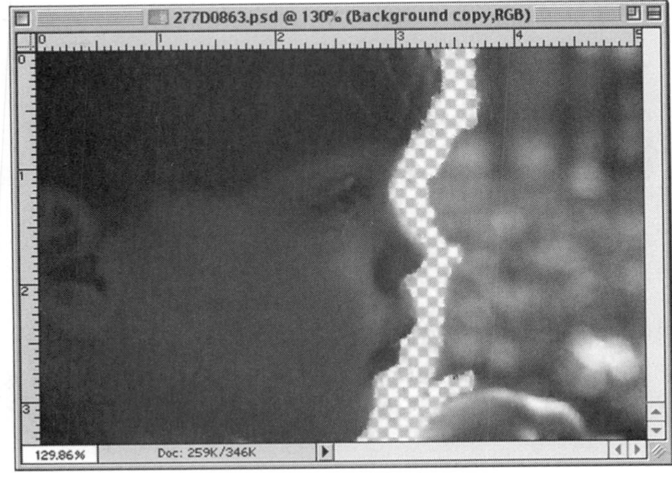

Color Erasing with the Magic Eraser Tool

The Magic Eraser tool is another tool you were introduced to in Chapter 1. As you saw in the example in that chapter, the Magic Eraser tool erases the specific color you select. The Magic Eraser tool's options bar lets you control how colors will be erased.

These options work as follows:

- The Tolerance setting determines how many variations of a color the tool will affect. The lower the number, the fewer color variations it will recognize; the higher the number, the more variations it will affect.
- The Anti-aliased option smoothes the edges of the erased area.
- The Contiguous option erases colors only in the area you choose. If this option is not selected, all instances of the selected color throughout the picture are erased.
- The Use All Layers option allows you to choose colors to be erased from any layer that might be in your document.
- The Opacity setting controls how strong the erasure effect is. Its range is 0% (no affect) to 100% (the chosen color will be completely erased).

Painting with the History and Art History Brushes

The History Brush and Art History Brush are two fascinating tools that can help you create some fantastic effects. To work with these tools, you will need to have the History palette open, because they use a previous version of your image.

Painting Layers with the History Brush

In a nutshell, the History Brush tool allows you to paint areas of one layer onto another. It can be used to create sophisticated montages or to build other effects that would otherwise take a lot more time to create.

montage
An image made up of a number of separate images.

As an example, you will add some light effects to an image using the History Brush tool.

1. Open an image that could use some light effects.
2. Select Window ➢ Show History to open the History palette.

Note

Photoshop's History palette keeps track of all of the changes you've made to an image during the current working session, as a series of states. You can revert to a previous state simply by clicking it in the History palette. You can also save snapshots of an image at any stage in its development and quickly retrieve the snapshot version from the History palette. You'll learn more about the History palette in Chapter 6.

snapshot
A saved version of an image. Using the History palette, you can save the current image to a snapshot to preserve that state of the image.

3. Click the circular button with the right-pointing arrow in the upper-right corner of the History palette and select New Snapshot from the palette's options menu.

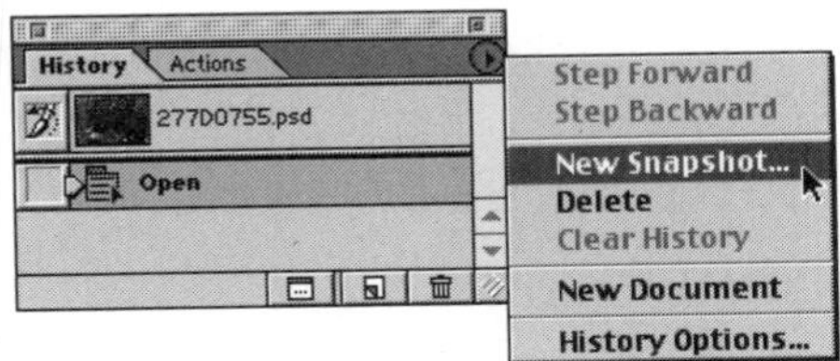

4. The New Snapshot dialog box will open. You can give the snapshot a name and tell Photoshop where the snapshot information will come from. In this case, leave the defaults and click OK.

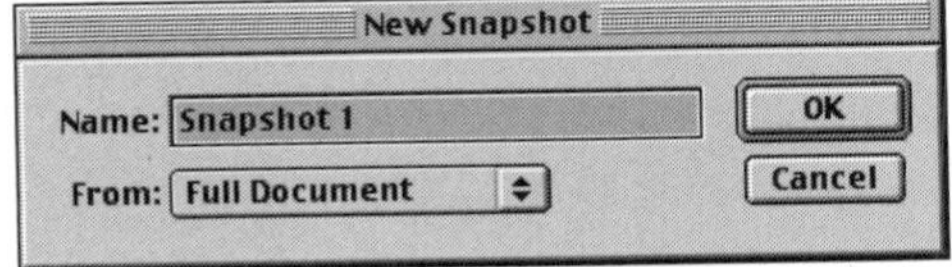

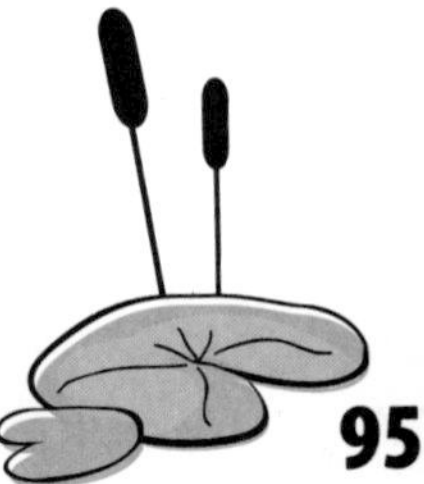

5. A new element named Snapshot 1 has been added to the History palette. Click this element to activate it.

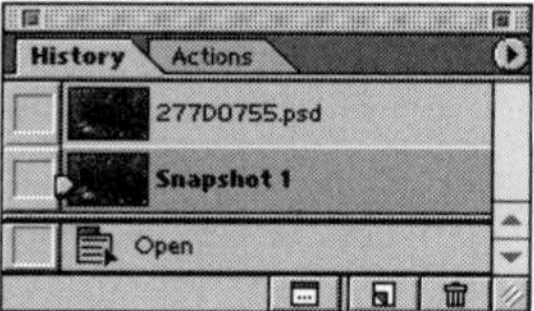

6. Open the Layers palette if it isn't already displayed (select Window ➢ Show Layers) and click the Create New Layer button. Click the eye icon for the Background to make it invisible. (This way, you will be able to see the History Brush effect.)

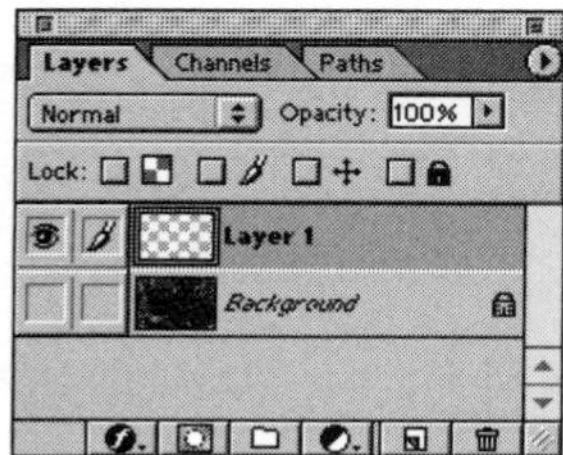

7. With this new layer selected, click the check box next to Snapshot 1 in the History palette. A paintbrush icon will appear.

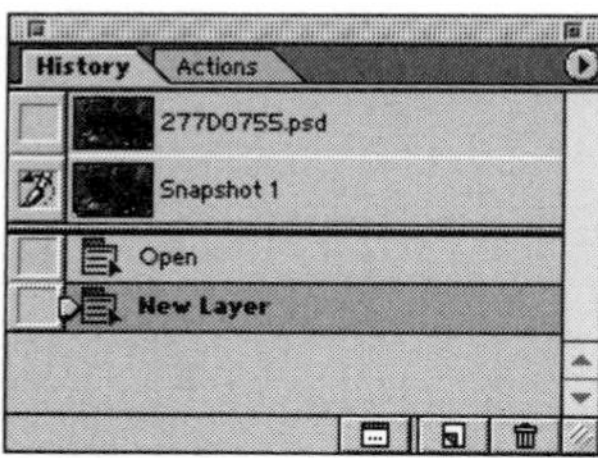

8. Select the History Brush in the toolbox.

9. In this example, you want to create streaks of light across the image. Set the following options in the History Brush's options bar:

   Brush: Soft Round, 65 pixels

   Mode: Dissolve

   Opacity: 100%

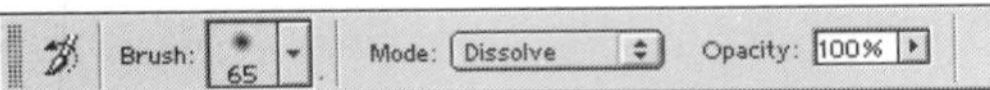

10. With the History Brush, paint a few streaks across the layer. As you do, you'll see the image you used as your snapshot appear.

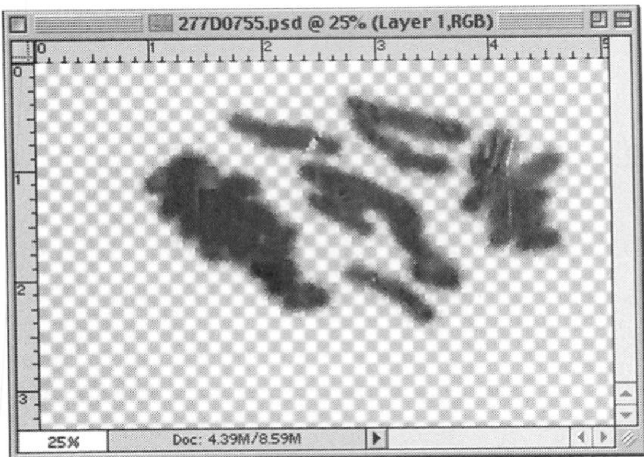

11. Change the Mode setting to Screen and paint over the streaks you already created. Notice how the image becomes much lighter.

12. Make the Background visible (click to display its eye icon in the Layers palette) to see how your streaks of light look.

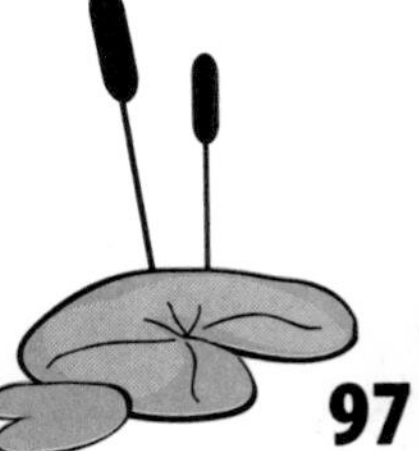

Tip

By using the History Brush with Mode set to Screen again, you can continue to lighten the areas for a stronger effect.

As you saw in this example, the Brush setting for the History Brush determines the size of the brush you will "paint" with. The Mode selections are the same as those in the Layers palette, but here they affect the brush strokes only. (You can also combine layer Mode effects with the History Brush.) As with the other tools, the Opacity setting determines how clear or opaque the brush strokes will be.

Making Masterpieces with the Art History Brush

With the Art History Brush tool, you can turn your image into a Picasso or van Gogh, or even an original masterpiece that looks like a painting. The keys to creating art effects with this tool are located in its options bar. Along with the same Brush, Mode, and Opacity settings as the History Brush, the Art History Brush offers these options:

- The Style setting determines how the "paint" is laid onto the layer. Access the different styles by clicking the pop-up menu button.

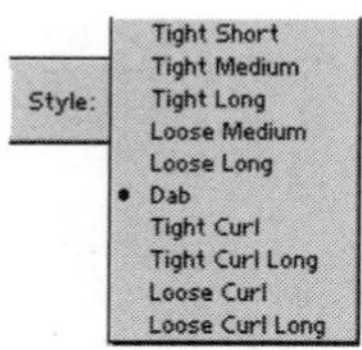

- The Fidelity setting determines how true to the original the colors are. The lower the fidelity, the more variance there is from the original.
- The Area setting specifies how large an area is covered by the paint strokes.
- The Spacing setting determines how far apart the paint strokes are when they are laid onto the layer.

To create a painterly masterpiece, continue working with the practice document you've been using for the previous exercises or open another image, and then do the following:

1. Open the History palette's options menu, select New Snapshot, and click OK in the New Snapshot dialog box to accept the defaults.
2. In the Layers palette, select the snapshot you just created. Then click the Create New Layer button to add a new layer. (Keep the Background visible.)
3. With this new layer selected, click the check box next to Snapshot 2 in the History palette.
4. Select the Art History Brush from the toolbox.

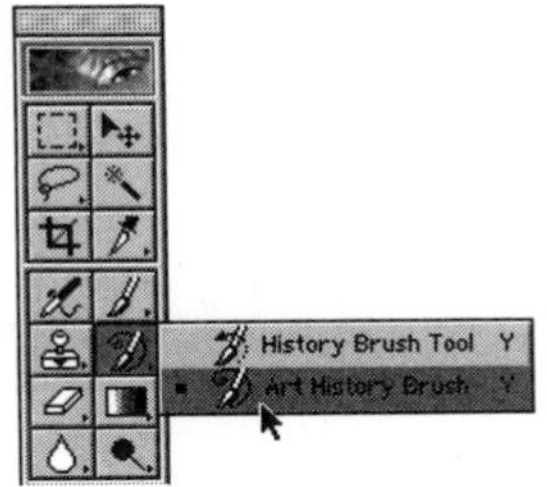

5. In the Art History Brush's options bar, set the following options:

   Brush: Chalk, 23 pixels

   Mode: Normal

   Opacity: 100%

   Style: Dab

   Fidelity: 61%

   Area: 5 px

   Spacing: 48%

6. With the Art History Brush, paint onto Layer 1.

7. Select File ➢ Save and save this file as a layered Photoshop (.psd) file. We'll use it later in the book when discussing lighting effects.

Using Photographer's Tools

Now let's look at the tools included in Photoshop that emulate techniques photographers use to modify photos: the Blur, Sharpen, Smudge, Dodge, and Burn tools.

Softening Areas with the Blur Tool

Sometimes, a photograph needs a little help to make it really stand out. In many cases, you can improve a picture by separating the subject from the background. This is where the Blur tool can come in handy. (The Blur tool is the one that looks like a big raindrop in the toolbox.)

Let's see how the Blur tool works.

1. Open a photograph that has a subject that needs to stand out from the background.
2. Select the Blur tool in the toolbox.

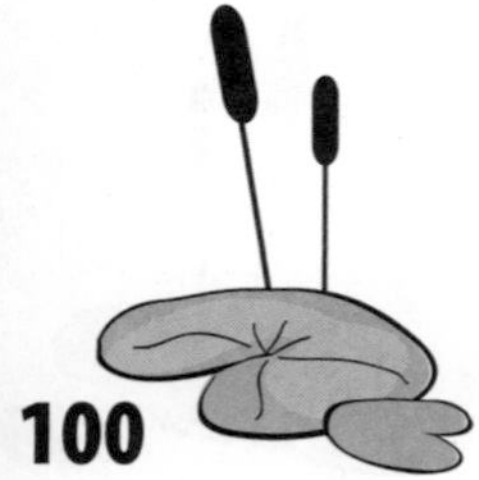

3. In the Blur tool's option bar, select a large brush and change the Pressure setting to 95%. Leave the other settings at their defaults.

4. Click and drag the Blur tool over the image background. You can do this as many times as you like (make sure to release the mouse button and then depress it again before going over an area you've already worked on).

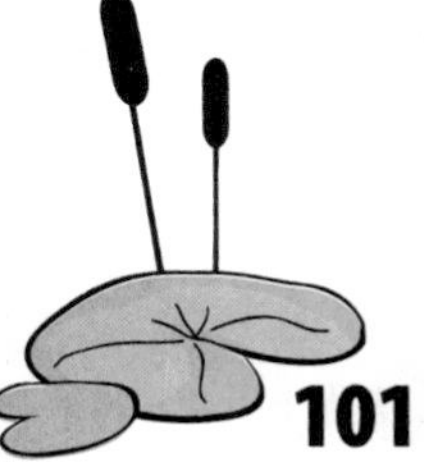

To protect your foreground or your subject, use the Lasso tool and outline the subject, then choose Select ➢ Inverse to reverse the outlined and selected area.

Gaining Clarity with the Sharpen Tool

If there are areas in your photograph that you would like to make clearer, you can try using the Sharpen tool. You can continue working with the photo you used the Blur tool on to see how the Sharpen tool works.

1. Click and hold down the mouse button on the Blur tool icon, and then select the Sharpen tool from the pop-up list.

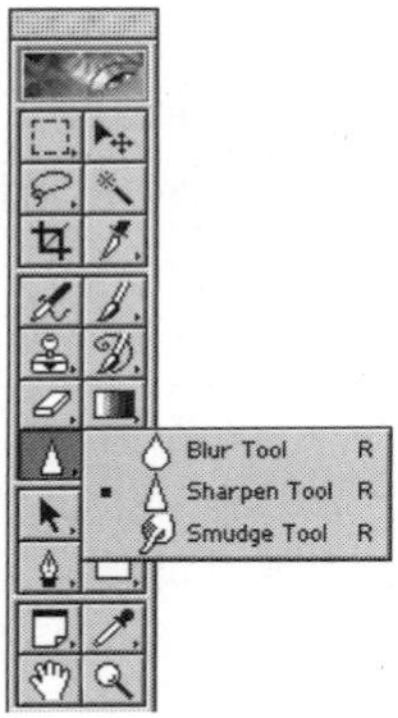

2. In the Sharpen tool's option bar, set the brush size to Soft Round, 100 pixels and the Pressure setting to 100%. Leave the other settings at their defaults.

3. Click and drag the Sharpen tool over the area of the image that you want to sharpen.

Warning

You can oversharpen an image very quickly, making the sharpened area look strange to the viewer. Make sure you go over an area only once with the Sharpen tool.

Smearing Areas with the Smudge Tool

You can use the Smudge tool to do quick repairs on a damaged photograph, to make edges blend better, or to get rid of unwanted blemishes or dark rings under the eyes. The tool works by literally smearing the pixel information. Because it functions this way, you should be careful to work with small strokes as you use this tool.

Tip

With careful use of the Smudge tool, you can make your girlfriend or wife look ten years younger. So if you do this type of work on a photograph, expect grateful hugs and kisses afterward.

The Smudge tool is in the same toolbox spot as the Blur and Sharpen tools. To select it, click and hold down the mouse button on the Blur tool icon, and then select the Smudge tool from the pop-up list.

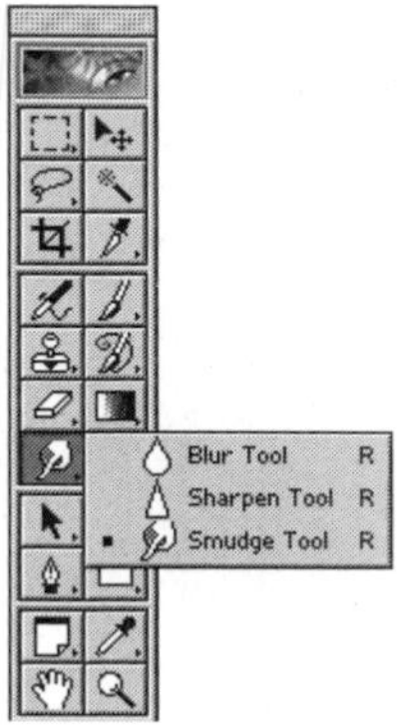

As an example, notice the circles under this poor author's eyes. Using the Smudge tool with a brush size of Soft Round, 21 pixels and a Pressure setting of 25%, I can make those bags quickly disappear.

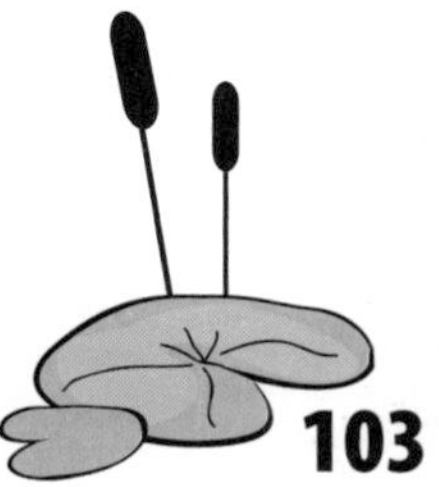

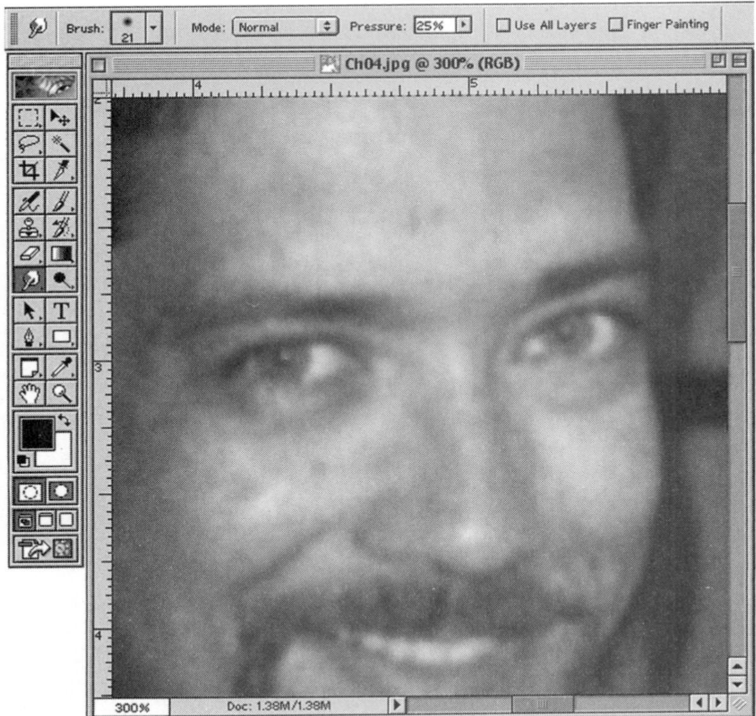

You blend from your starting point to your ending point. So to make this work, I start from beneath the lower eyelid and move upward slightly, until the bags are gone.

The Smudge tool's Finger Painting option lets you add color while smudging. When you select this option, the Smudge tool smudges using the selected foreground color at the beginning of each dragged stroke.

Lightening Shadows with the Dodge Tool

Some of your photos may have unwanted shadows. You will want to lessen their effect on the overall image by lightening them, called **dodging** in photographic jargon. This is what the Dodge tool can do. You can, through the tool's Range setting, lighten the shadows, **midtones**, and highlights of the image to give it a whole new look.

dodge
In photographic terms, to lighten an area of a picture. Photoshop's Dodge tool performs this operation.

midtones
The colors that fall in the middle of the overall range of colors in your image.

Tip

Make sure to keep the Exposure control set fairly low. Much like the Opacity control, Exposure determines how drastically a modification affects the image. By keeping it low, you can incrementally make changes until you have the image just the way you want it.

Try using the Dodge tool on a photo with dark areas, such as the example shown here.

1. Choose the Dodge tool (which looks like a straight pin with an oversized ball on top) from the toolbox.

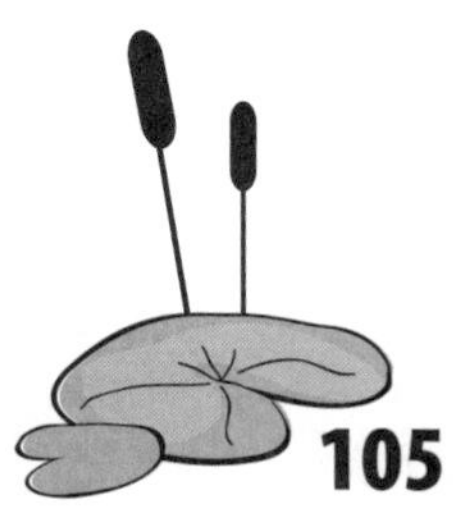

2. In the Dodge tool's options bar, set the following options:

   Brush: Soft Round (any size you like)

   Range: Midtones

   Exposure: 11%

3. Click and drag with the Dodge tool to lighten areas of the photo. Use small strokes as you work with the Dodge tool, focusing on specific areas first, and then the surrounding areas afterward. This will allow for a nicer blending effect.
4. Switch between Midtones and Highlights until you have lightened the features, such as the eyes in this example, as you want them.

Note

In this example, if I had used the Shadow selection for the Range, I would have lightened the eyelashes too much, because this tool works on the darkest pixels first.

Darkening Areas with the Burn Tool

Burning, in the photographic sense, means to darken an area. That's just what the Burn tool does—it darkens areas that might be overexposed. To see how this affects your photograph, do the following:

burn
In photographic terms, to darken an area of an image. Photoshop's Burn tool performs this operation.

1. Select the Burn tool from the Dodge tool toolbox position's pop-up list. (It's the one that looks like a hand.)

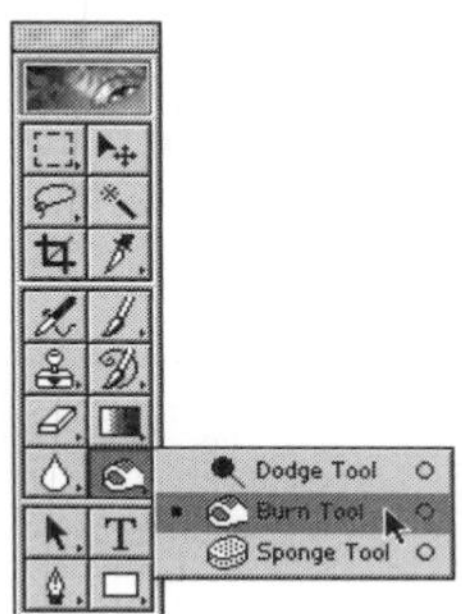

2. In the Burn tool's options bar, set the following options:

   Brush: Soft Round (any size you like)

   Range: Highlights

   Exposure: 10%

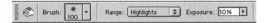

3. Click and drag the Burn tool over the brightest area of your picture. For example, in the photo used in the previous exercise, spots on the shirt are too bright. Dragging the Burn tool over them tones down the bright areas.

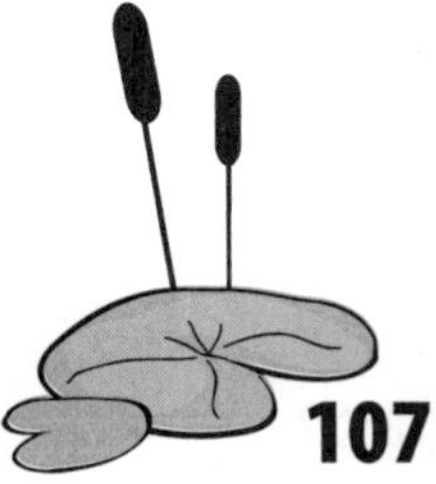

4. Switch between Highlights and Midtones until you're satisfied with the look of your image.

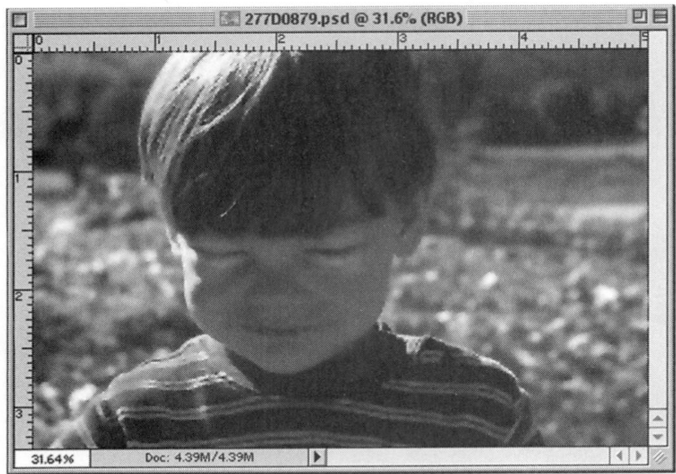

Moving On

The trick to Photoshop and many of its tools is to work in small areas and make incremental changes to the image. To correctly manipulate a photograph takes patience, but the rewards can be enormous. Using the tools discussed in this and previous chapters is only the beginning of your experience with Photoshop. The tools you've learned about will be your workhorses. But to make these workhorses really shine, you need to combine them with the other features of this powerful program.

In the next chapter, you'll learn how to add text and then create text effects that will blow your mind—not to mention what they'll do to your friends' and family's minds. Then, combined with what you've already learned about the program, you'll be well on your way to Photoshop panacea.

Part 2

Image Manipulation

Getting to know Photoshop's image-manipulation tools is essential for design success. Many of these tools can be applied to text, allowing you to create interesting text effects. Photoshop's History and Actions palettes also offer many features for manipulating your images. And when you need to fine-tune the coloring or tones in your images, you can use Photoshop's image-adjustment controls.

Image Manipulation

A Photoshop 6 Gallery

Main image

Normal

Multiply

Screen

Overlay

Hard Light

Soft Light

Color Dodge

Color Burn

Darken

Lighten

Difference

Exclusion

Hue

Saturation

Color

Luminosity

You can create subtle and not-so-subtle effects by changing the mode settings for your tool, as well as for different layers.

Selecting areas of a picture and using the Color Balance controls can produce interesting effects.

To create special text effects, you can use layers and the underlying image. Photoshop offers many tools for manipulating text, including a new text-warping feature.

You can create interesting backgrounds in Photoshop using the Lasso and Airbrush tools. In this case, the stripes were created using the Lasso tool. The shadows on the curtain were created using layers and the Airbrush tool. A canvas texture was added after the image was completed.

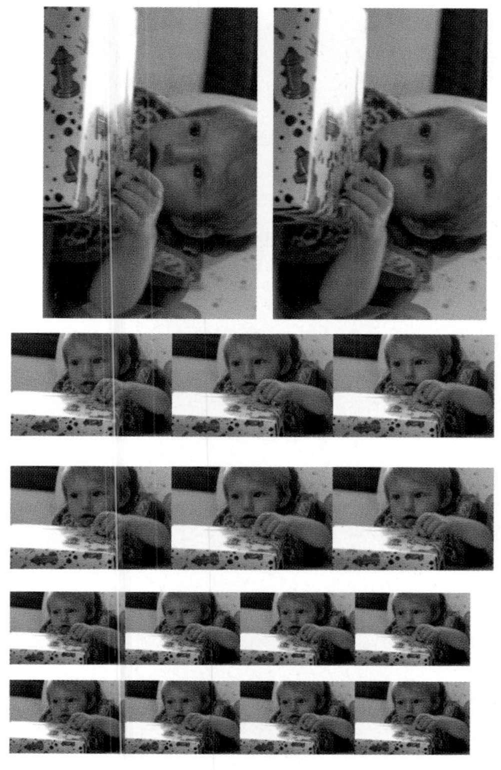

Photoshop's Picture Package feature lets you quickly produce multiple copies of the same image at various sizes.

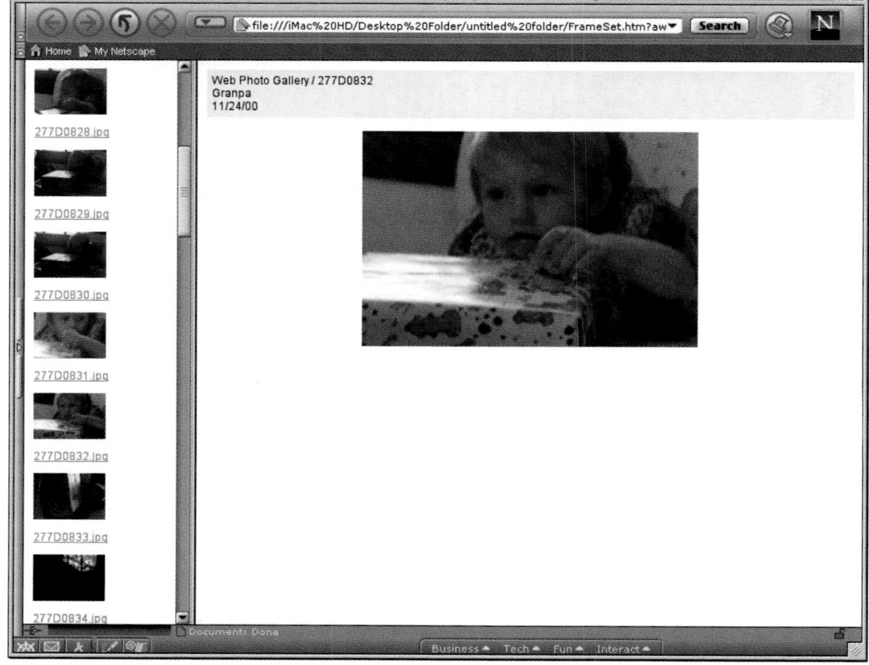

Photoshop's Web Photo Gallery feature automatically creates photo pages for the Web, complete with thumbnails and links.

AMERICA'S LARGEST COUNTRY RADIO NETWORK

25% Of All Country Stations Already Rely On JSN To Provide Them With HIGH QUALITY, UNIQUE Programming Which Helps Them Solidify Their Position In Their Local Market!

CD Country

New Country

A Competitive Format Choice For Markets With A Mainstream Country Station

Mainstream, Contemporary Country

The Nation's Most Popular Radio Format

U.S. Country

PRODUCED BY JIM OWENS & ASSOCIATES, INC.

4-Hour Weekend Countdown Show Hosted By Lorianne Crook & Charlie Chase

Featuring The Top 40 Country Hits, Exclusive Interviews, and Music City News

JONES SATELLITE NETWORKS®

The Nation's Largest Provider Of 24-Hour Music Formats...
Including Rock Alternative, Adult Hit Radio, Soft Hits, Good Time Oldies,
FM Lite, The Word In Music, Z Spanish.
A Division Of Jones Intercable, Inc., Which Provides Great American Country, A New Country Music Video Channel.

©1996 Jim Owens Radio Used by permission

©1998 Jim Owens Companies Used by permission

I created these designs for my clients. The image on the previous page shows how the curtain was incorporated into an ad that appeared in a broadcast industry publication. The Crook & Chase Country Countdown ad also appeared in an industry publication. The Summer Of '66 image was created for a CD-ROM of the musical.

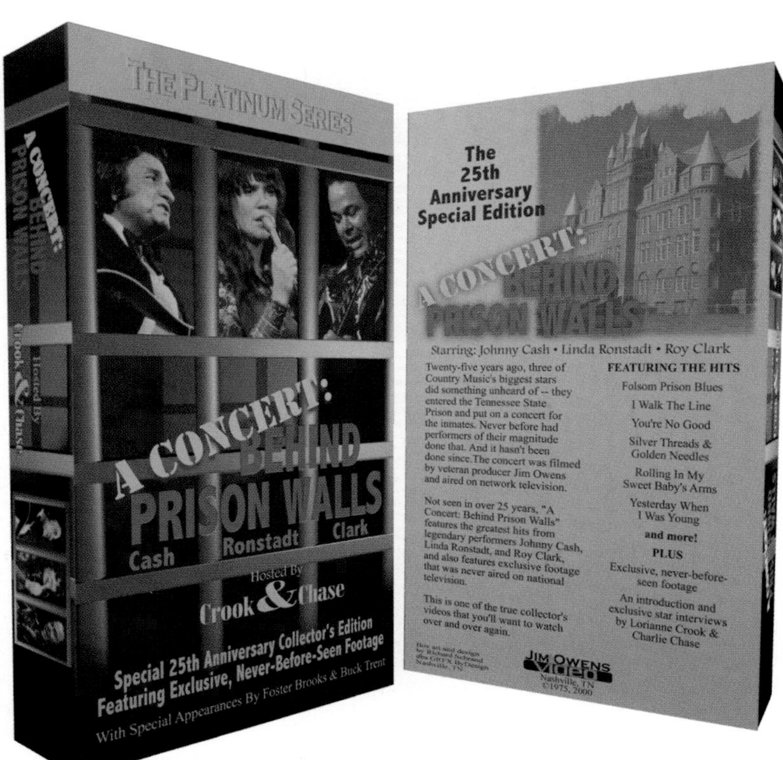

These video case designs were created using various Photoshop tools and techniques, including the Lasso tool and layers.

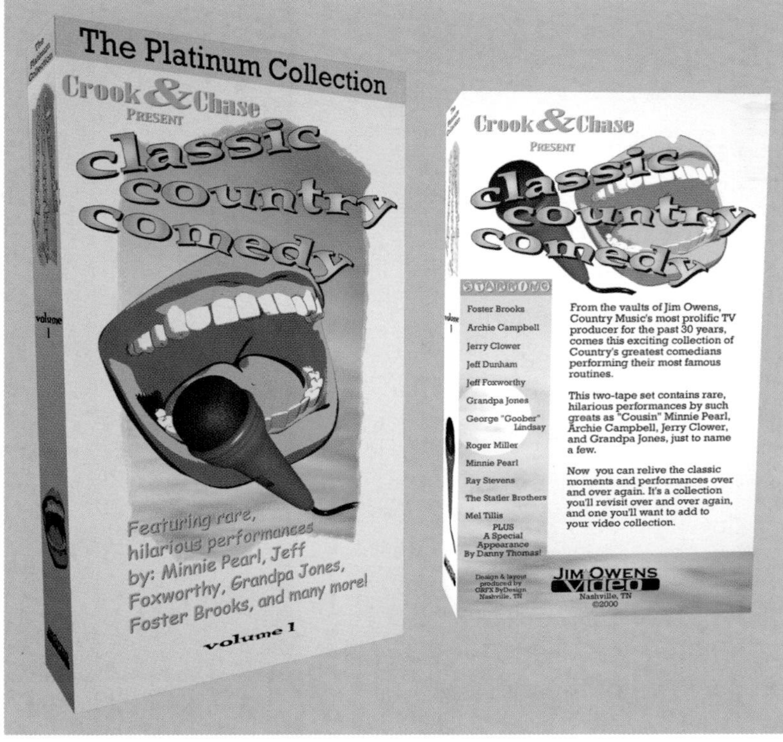

Designs and layouts by the author

Chapter 5

Working with Text

Text is an important part of any type of work you do in Photoshop, whether for personal use or professionally. You may just need to add credit and copyright information to your images. On the other hand, you might want to create sophisticated text effects with drop shadows, depth, and possibly images within each letter. Photoshop provides many options for setting your text's appearance, ranging from simple alignment to warping and layer effects.

In this chapter, you'll learn how to create and modify text with Photoshop's tools and features:

- The Type tool, for adding text
- The Layer ➢ Layer Style command, for adding layer effects
- Drop shadow effects
- The Warp Text feature, for shaping text
- The Edit ➢ Paste Into command, for creating layer masks

Adding Text with the Type Tool

To use the Type tool, you simply select it in the toolbox, click in the workspace, and begin typing. Of course, Photoshop provides plenty of ways to control how your text appears. Let's go ahead and create some text on a blank workspace and try out a few of the options.

1. Create a new document by pressing Ctrl+N (Cmd+N). Make the new file 5 × 3 inches and 72 pixels dpi. Open the Layers palette (select Window ➢ Show Layers) if it isn't already displayed.
2. Select the Type tool from the toolbox (it's the one with the *T*).

3. Click anywhere in the workspace. Notice how a new layer is automatically added. This layer is represented by a T icon in the Layers palette.

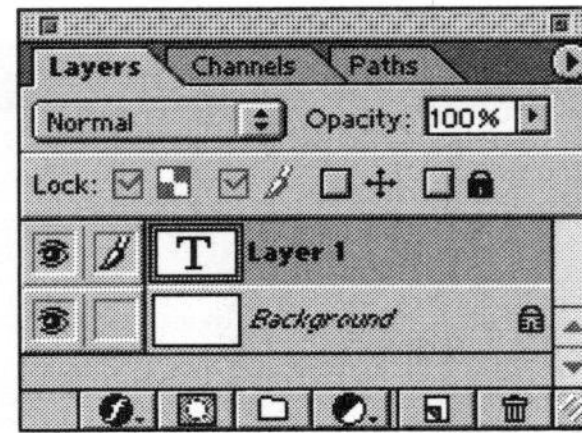

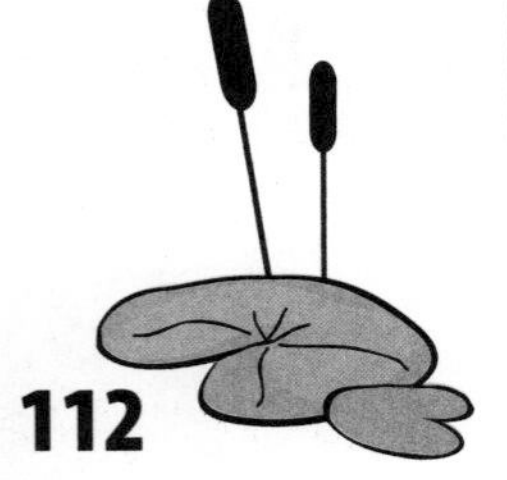

4. Type in a word or phrase. For this example, enter **HELLO**.
5. Before you can make any changes to the text, you need to select it. With the Type tool still selected, click and drag across the text to highlight it.

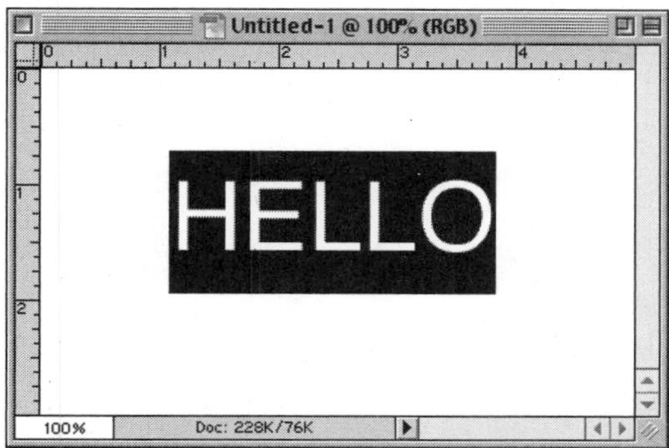

6. In the Type tool's options bar, click the drop-down arrow next to the font name (Helvetica) and select a different font family. For this example, you can use Times New Roman, a font that is readily available on most systems.

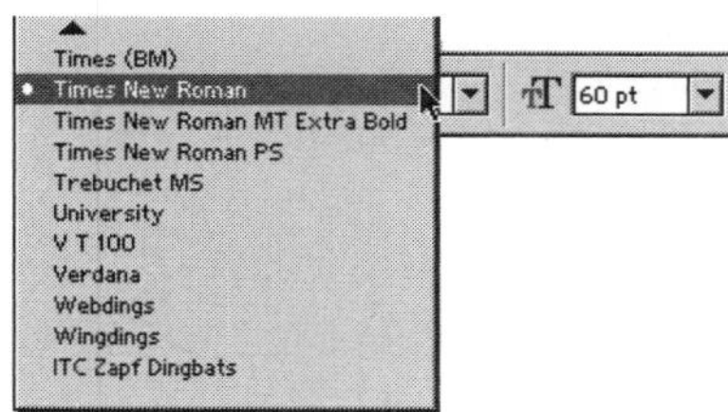

7. Click the font style drop-down arrow in the options bar and choose Bold.

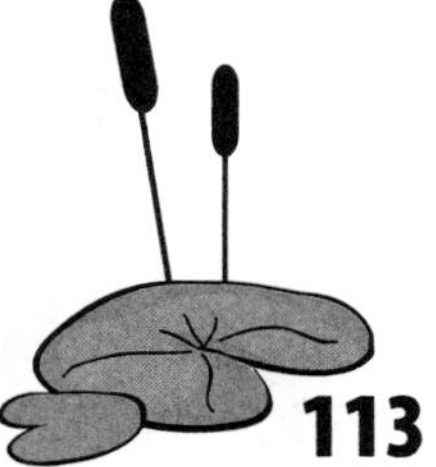

8. In the options bar, click the size drop-down arrow and change the size to 48 pt (points).

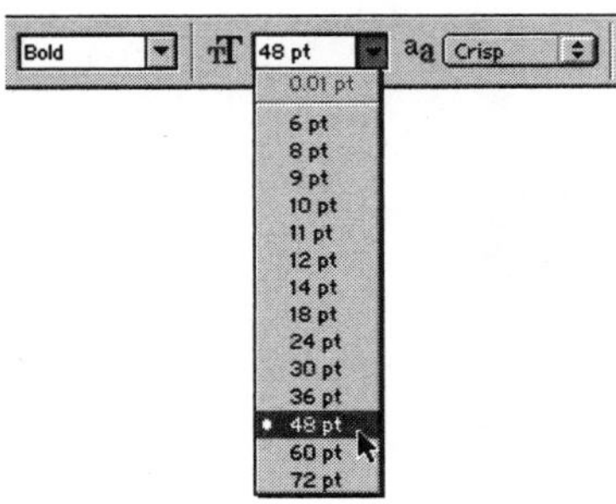

9. Click the color swatch button (the third from the right end of the options bar) and change the text color to red.

You should now have 48-point, bold, red, Times New Roman type in your new document.

Setting Type Options

Now let's take a look at the settings available on the Type tool's options bar.

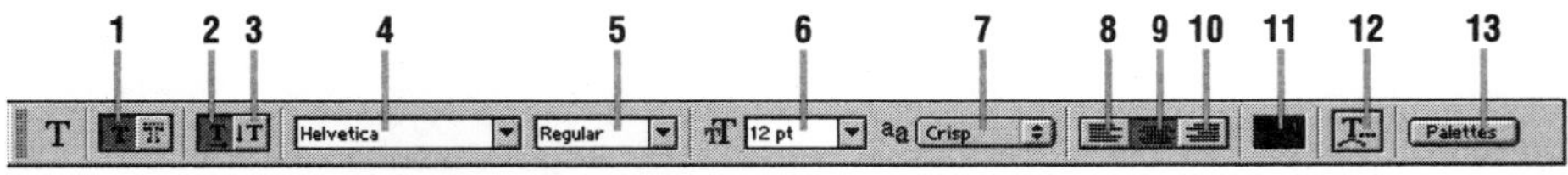

1. Create Mask
2. Horizontal Orientation
3. Vertical Orientation
4. Font Family
5. Font Style
6. Font Size
7. Anti-aliasing Method
8. Left Align
9. Center Align
10. Right Align
11. Text Color
12. Warp Text
13. Show Character and Paragraph Palettes

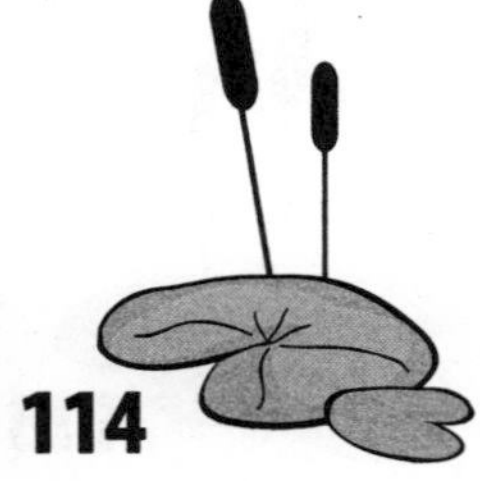

These controls work as follows:

- The Create Mask option creates type that can be turned into a mask.
- The Orientation options control how the text is oriented. With Horizontal Orientation, the text runs from left to right. With Vertical Orientation, the type runs from the top of the screen to the bottom.
- The Font Family option lets you choose a text style. The number of font families is determined by how many fonts you have loaded on your computer.
- The Font Style option lets you choose from Bold, Italic, Outlined, and Bold Italic font styles.
- The Font Size option allows you to choose the size of your text, measured in points.
- The Anti-aliasing Method option determines how smooth or jagged your text will appear. You have the following choices:

  None does not assign any anti-aliasing to the text.

  Crisp makes type appear sharper.

  Strong gives text the appearance of being thicker.

  Smooth makes the text look smoother.
- The Alignment options control how the text is aligned. You can choose to have text aligned along the left side, centered, or aligned along the right side.
- The Text Color option allows you to choose the color for your text.
- The Warp Text option allows you to warp the text along different paths. You'll experiment with the Warp Text feature later in this chapter.
- The Show Character and Paragraph Palettes option opens these palettes, which contain settings that reflect the selections you've made in the options bar.

rasterize
To convert vector information into pixel-based information. When you rasterize type, you can apply filters and other effects that do not work on vector-based type. However, after you rasterize type, you cannot edit the individual characters.

Repositioning and Rasterizing Text

After you've finished typing, you can position the text anywhere on the document and to make other basic changes. **Rasterizing** text changes it from single,

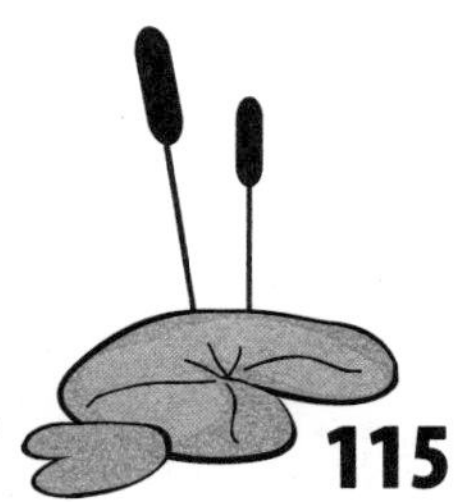

individual editable characters to an image, in which all of the characters are a unit. When you rasterize the text, it tells Photoshop you're finished working with it and you want it to remain in this form.

1. Select the Move tool and click the text. While holding down the mouse button, drag the text to the upper-left side of the document window.

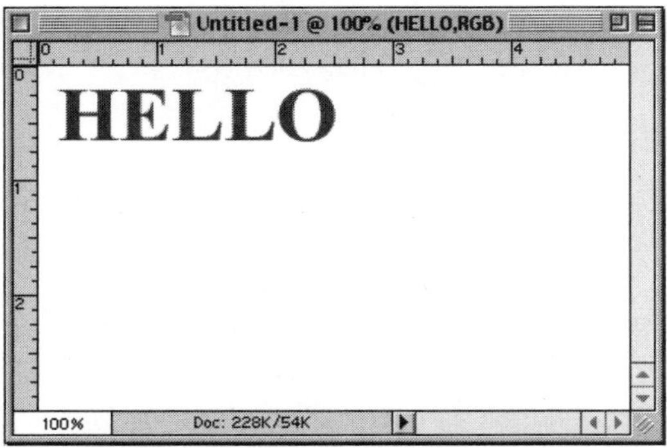

2. Choose Layer ➢ Rasterize ➢ Type.

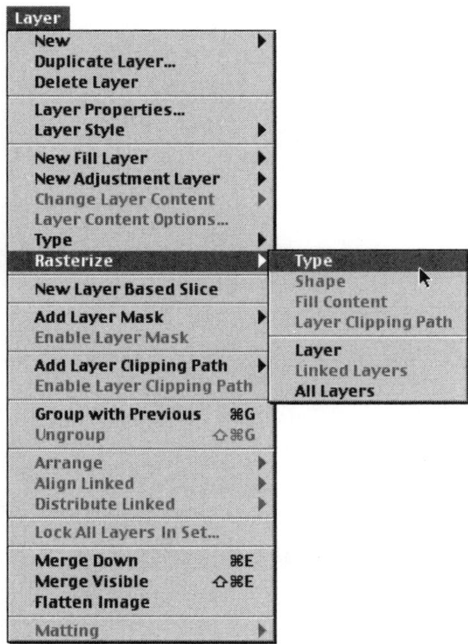

Note

Once you rasterize the text, you can no longer add effects such as Warp Text or Blending Options.

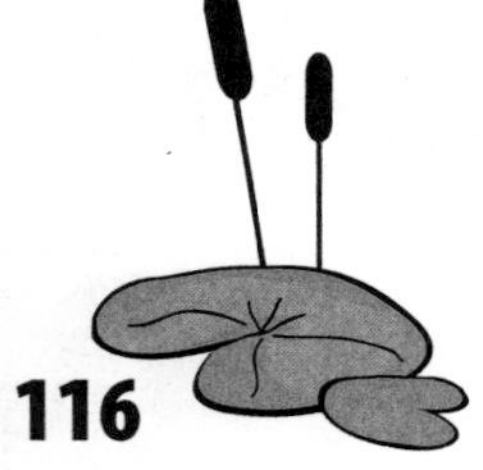

3. Choose the Rectangular Marquee tool. With this tool, you can select rectangular portions of an image.

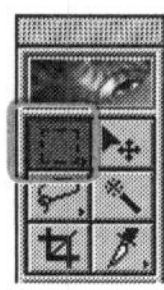

4. To select all of the letters except the first one, click to the left of the *E* and drag right to after the *O*.

HELLO

5. Switch back to the Move tool and drag the selected letters down below the *H* in the document window.

Note

If you hold down the Ctrl (Cmd) key while you are dragging an item with the Move tool, the movement is constrained to a straight line up, down, or angled. You can also use the arrow keys on your keyboard to move the text 1 pixel at a time in the direction the arrow is pointing. Hold down the Shift key while doing this to move the selection 10 pixels at a time.

6. After positioning the letters, press Ctrl+D (Cmd+D) to deselect the text.

H
ELLO

Tip

If you need to, press Ctrl+plus (Cmd+plus) to zoom in on your text. You can zoom the document up to 1600%.

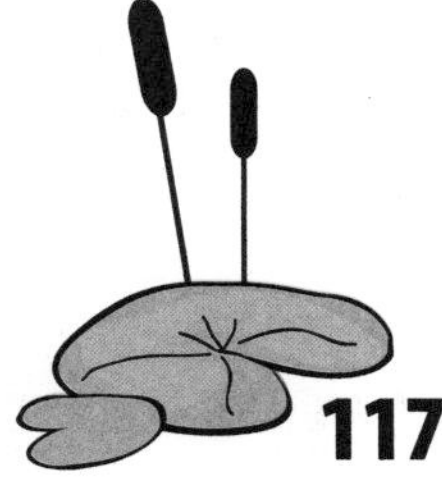

7. Repeat the procedure in steps 3 through 6 to position each letter diagonally down the document window.

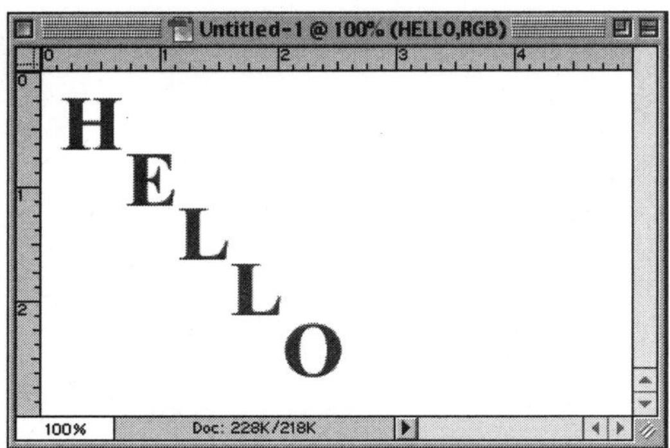

Creating Text Effects

Before rasterizing your text, you can create all sorts of special effects with it. Here, we'll look at some of the layer styles that you can apply and Photoshop's new text-warping feature.

Using Layer Styles to Create Text Effects

Photoshop gives you the ability to create very complex effects at the click of a button through its layer styles. In this section, you'll experiment with two different layer styles.

1. Press Ctrl+A (Cmd+A), then Delete to remove the text you created in the previous sections.
2. Select the Type tool and type a new line of text (perhaps the name of your company or your own name).
3. In the options bar, change the font family to the thickest one you have in your system. For this example, I used a font called Impact. Set the size to 48 points and the style to Bold (if it's available for that font family). Change the color (to blue or any color you prefer).

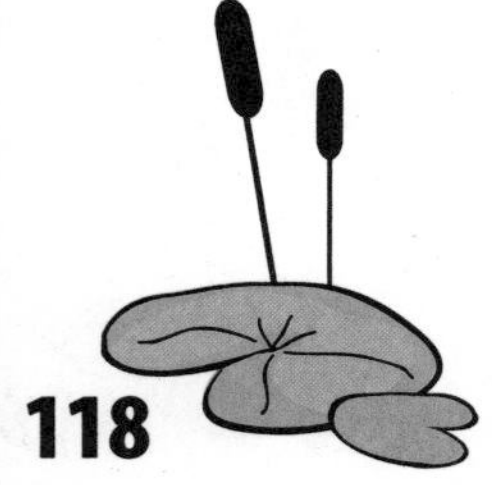

4. Choose Layer ➢ Layer Style ➢ Blending Options.

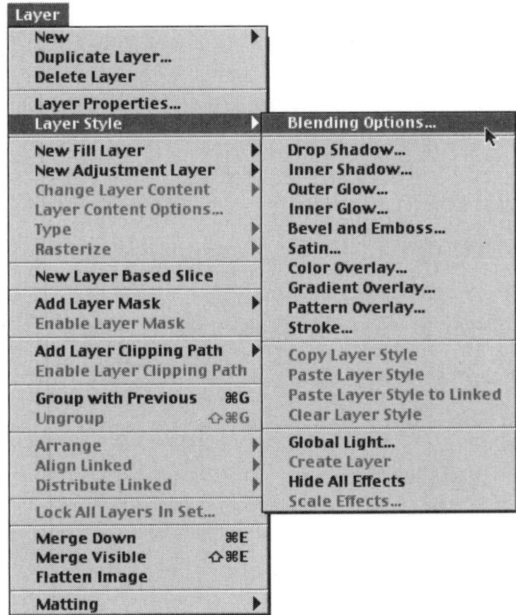

5. In the Styles list on the left side of the Layer Style dialog box, click the check box next to Bevel and Emboss to see the options for this effect. If the Preview check box on the far right side of the dialog box isn't checked, click to select it.

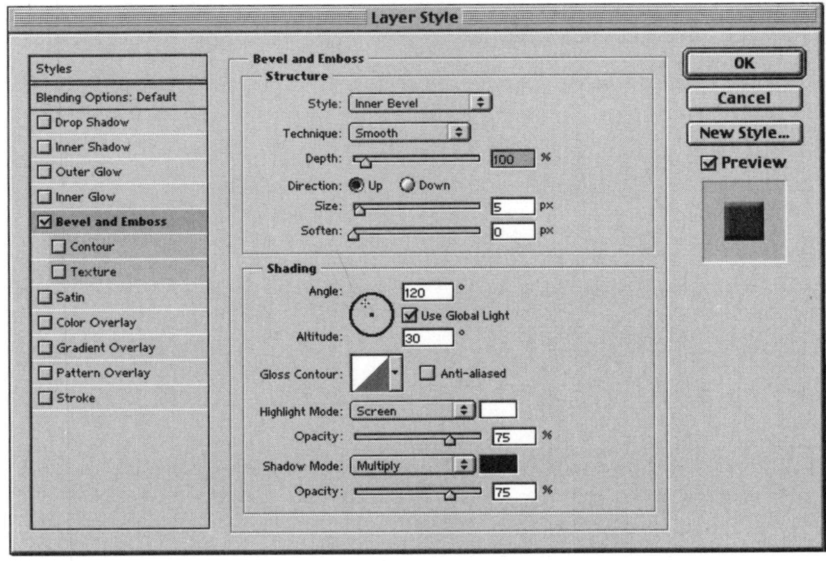

Tip

If you have a large enough screen, when the Preview option is selected, you can move the Layer Style dialog box to another location on your Desktop and be able to see the effects on your image file before accepting your changes.

6. In the Structure section of the dialog box, change three settings: Direction to Down (by clicking the Down button), Size to 10, and Soften to 1. These settings increase the depth of the effect and give the shadow that we will add a softer edge. (We'll look at some of the other interesting Bevel and Emboss settings after this exercise.)

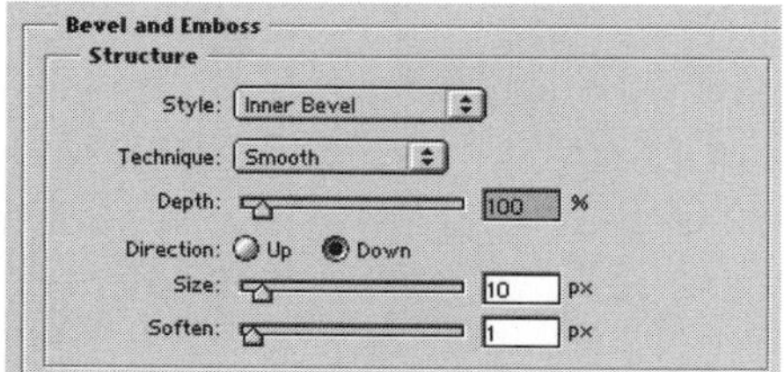

7. In the Styles list, click the Drop Shadow check box. Change Opacity to 65%, Distance to 4 pixels, Spread to 24%, and Size to 5 pixels. This will create a nice drop shadow.

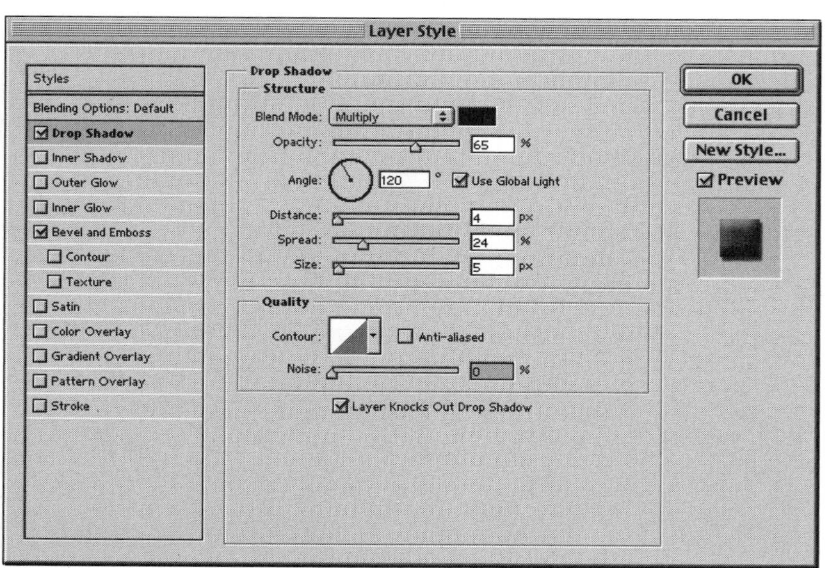

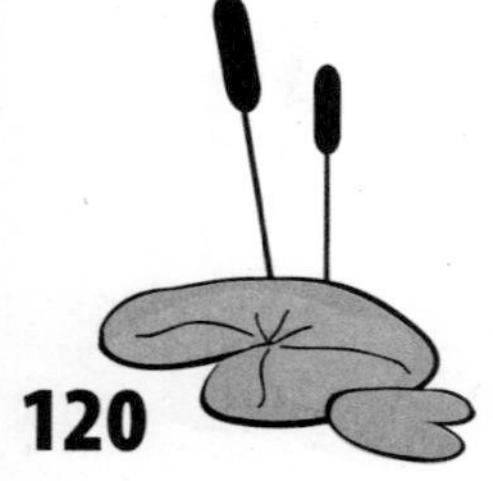

8. Click OK to close the Layer Style dialog box and see what you've just created.

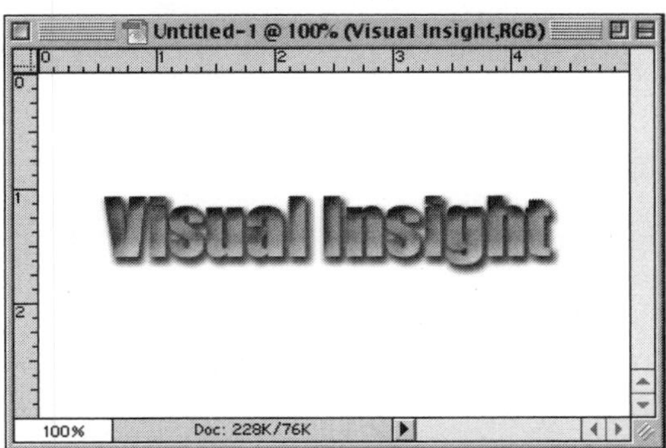

Note

The Drop Shadow layer style is a great feature for creating basic drop shadows. There are other ways of creating drop shadows that give you more control, as you will learn later in this chapter (in the "Creating a Warped Drop Shadow" section) and in upcoming chapters.

For this example, you didn't change any of the settings in the Shading section for the Bevel and Emboss options in the Layer Style dialog box. However, you should take a look at them now, because they can provide some fascinating effects. You can change the direction the light is coming from by moving the little cross-hair inside the Angle circle and change the Altitude setting to a different number of degrees.

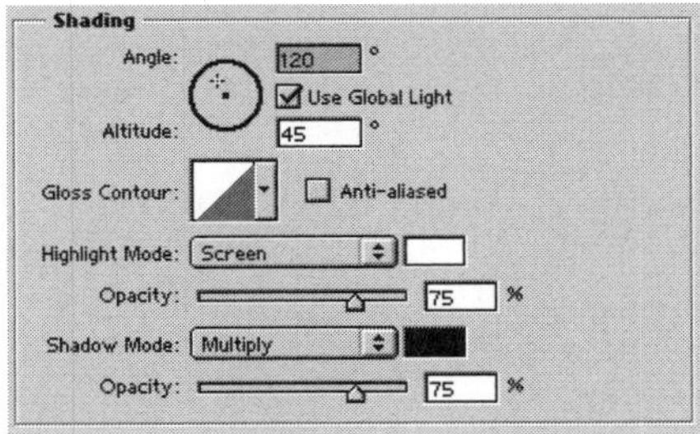

One other control to mention is the Gloss Contour setting. Clicking this option's drop-down arrow displays different contour styles that you can choose to affect how an external or internal bevel will look—from standard to fancy.

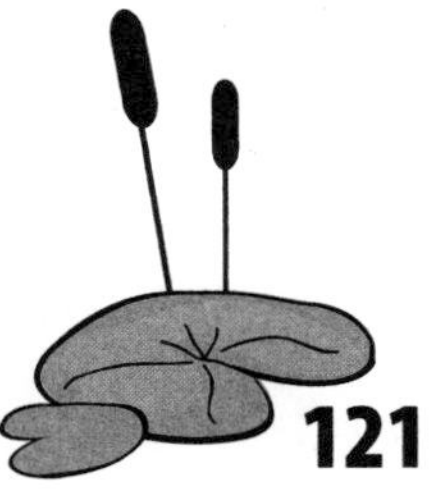

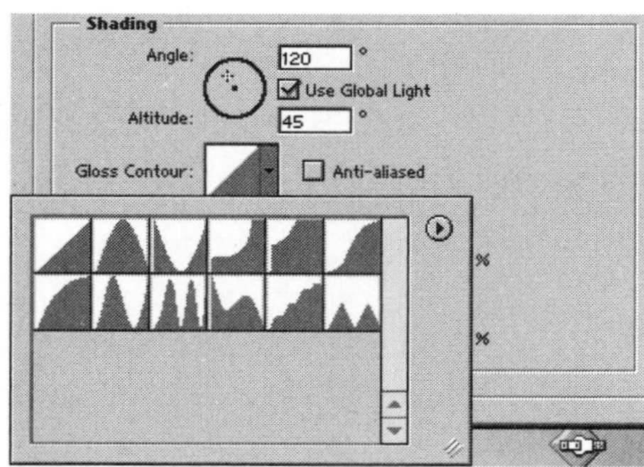

Warping Text

Until Photoshop 6, if you wanted to create text that followed along a wavy path or that looked balloon-like, you needed to either buy software that added that ability to Photoshop or use another program like Adobe Illustrator. Photoshop now offers a series of special warp effects to help you create compelling text styles.

system fonts
Fonts that come already installed on your computer when you buy it.

To use the Warp Text option, your text must be in a font family that includes an outline. Usually, standard **system fonts** have outlines. If you have downloaded fonts from the Internet, an outline might not be associated with that style. If there isn't one, Photoshop will display a message saying to choose a different font.

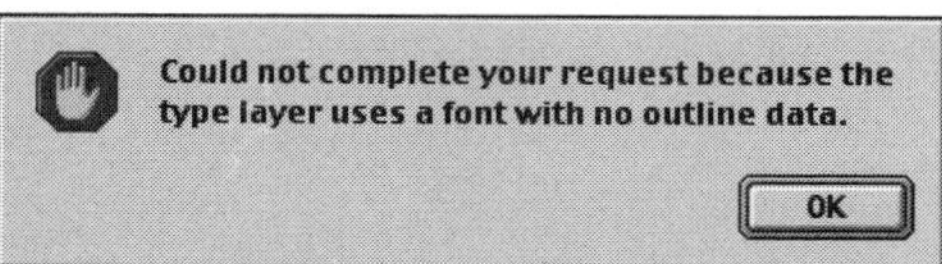

Let's experiment with one of the warped text styles.

1. Select File ➢ New to create a new file. Make the file 5 × 3 inches.
2. Select the Type tool and change the font to either Arial or Helvetica. (These fonts have outlines as part of the family.)
3. Type a word, such as **WARPED**. If you need to, use the Move tool to center the text on the workspace.

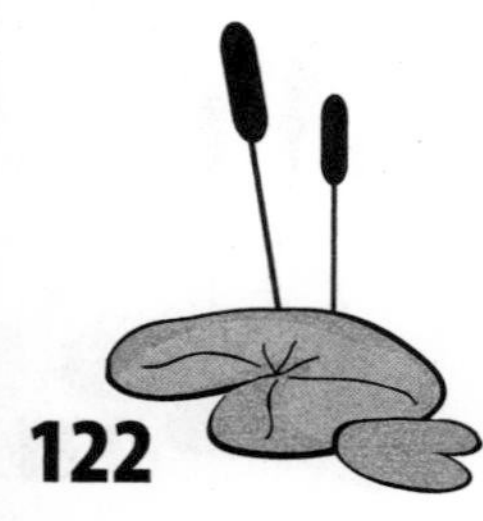

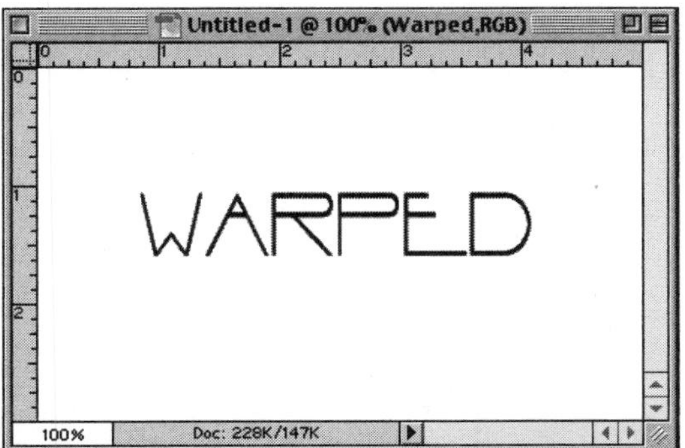

4. If you moved the text, select the Type tool again. In the options bar, click the Warp Text button (the one just to the left of the Palette button) to bring up the Warp Text dialog box.

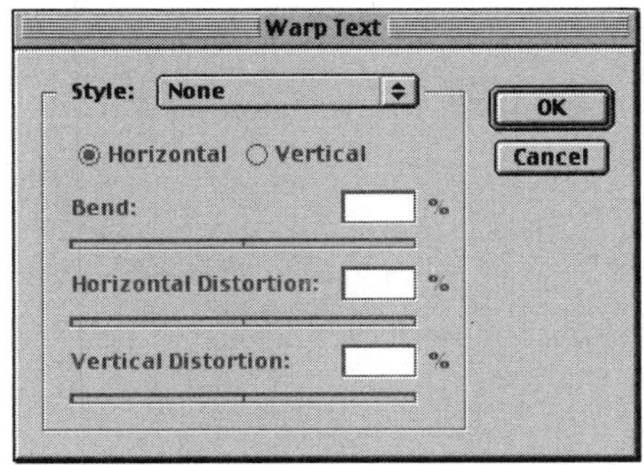

5. Click the Style drop-down arrow. The pop-up menu offers 15 preset text warp effects.

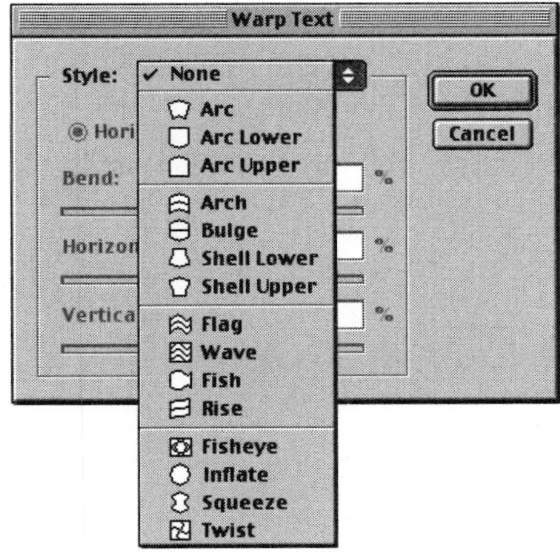

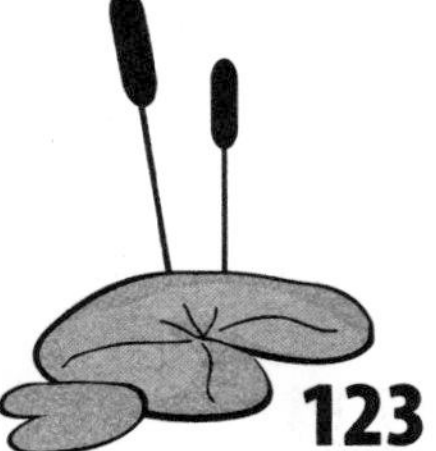

6. Choose Bulge. After you select an effect, the Bend, Horizontal Distortion, and Vertical Distortion controls become available.

7. With Horizontal selected, set Bend to +70%, Horizontal Distortion to −5%, and Vertical Distortion to 7%.

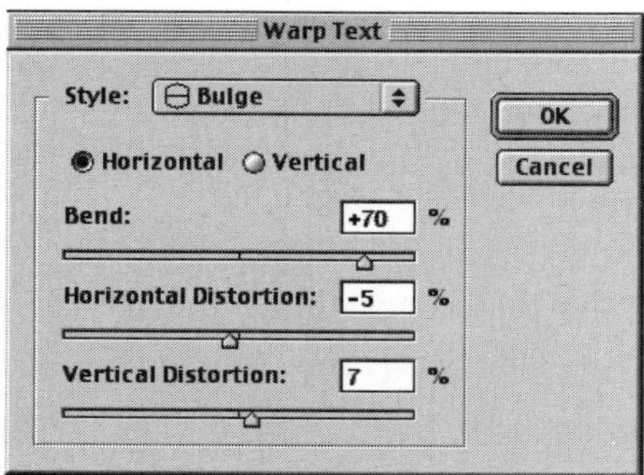

8. Click OK to close the Warp Text dialog box. As you can see, the text is shaped as you indicated. Leave this file open, because you'll continue working with it in the next section.

Creating a Warped Drop Shadow

While simply warping your text is great, you can also use the Warp Text feature to create some nifty drop shadow effects that are very different from the standard ones you see all the time. Here's how to create a specialized drop shadow:

1. Press Ctrl+Z (Cmd+Z) to undo the Bulge effect and return the text to its original form. If you typed the word in all capital letters, as in the previous examples, change it to have only the first letter capitalized.

2. Create a duplicate text layer by clicking and dragging the layer in the Layers palette to the Create New Layer button (the one immediately to the left of the trashcan icon at the bottom of the palette).

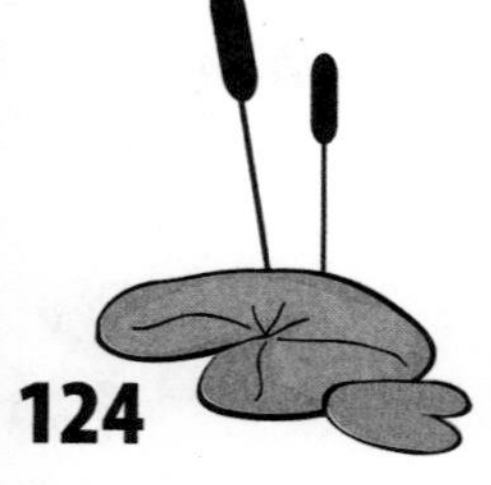

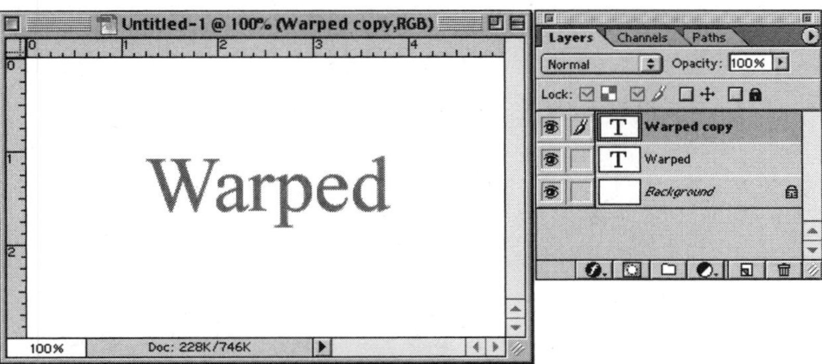

3. Activate the original text layer by clicking it in the Layer palette.
4. Select the Type tool and click the Warp Text button in the options bar.
5. In the Warp Text dialog box, click the Style drop-down button and select Rise. Leave the default settings and click OK.

6. In the Layers palette, change the Opacity setting for the Warped copy layer to 50%. Your warped text is now beginning to look like a drop shadow.

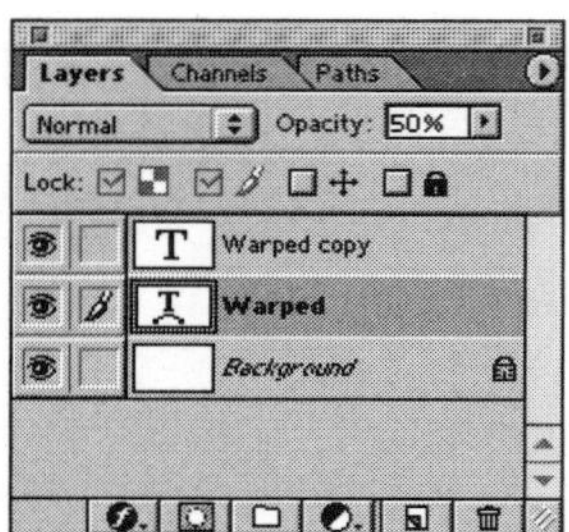

7. Choose Layer ➢ Rasterize ➢ Type to rasterize the Warped copy layer's text.
8. Choose Filter ➢ Blur ➢ Gaussian Blur and set the Radius to 3.

9. To change the color, click the color swatch in the toolbar and select black. Select Edit ➢ Fill. Make sure that Foreground Color is chosen in the Use field and the Preserve Transparency option is selected. Then click OK.

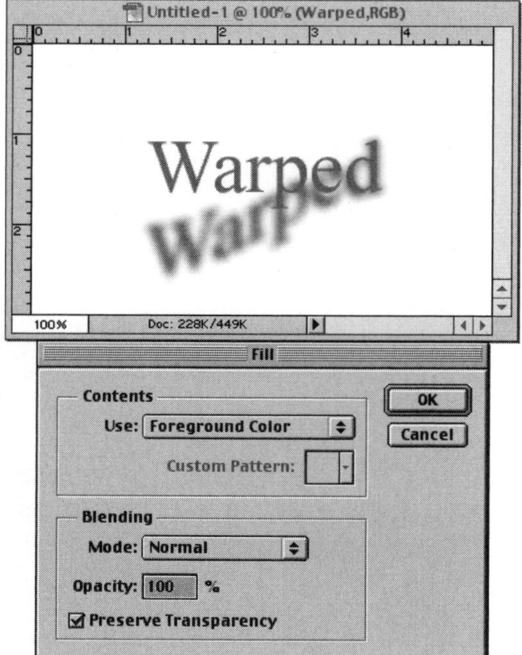

Note

After you rasterize type, you can no longer change its color through the Type tool's options bar.

10. To further modify the drop shadow layer, select Edit ➢ Transform ➢ Distort.

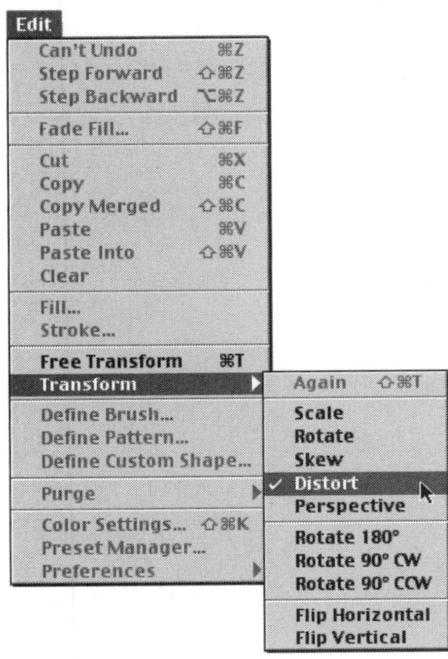

11. A bounding box appears around the text. Click and drag the upper-left and lower-left handles (the little boxes) on the bounding box to reshape the text. For this example, drag the upper-left control box to the upper-left corner of the workspace and the lower-left control box to just to the left of the bottom of the *W*.

12. When the text appears as you want it to, double-click anywhere inside the bounding box to accept your changes.

You now have a creative drop shadow. By using various effects in this manner, you can create extremely realistic drop shadows that look as if they are reacting to their environment.

Adding Text to Images

So far, you've discovered how easy it is to create some cool text effects. But you've worked with text alone on an otherwise blank canvas. Now you'll learn how to add text to images.

Making Text Fit a Photograph

Let's go ahead and add some text to a photograph. We'll begin by capturing a color for the text from the photo itself.

1. Open a photograph in Photoshop.
2. Use the Eyedropper tool to select a color from your image. Make sure that it's a color that will stand out against your background. For this example, I selected the color of the nose on the character's face (on the cake lady's dress).

3. Select the Type tool. Choose a font family you like from the pop-up menu and make sure that your font is sized to fit comfortably in the image. Then type some appropriate word or phrase.

Note

Since your image might be larger or smaller than the one used in the example shown here, you will need to set the point size that is appropriate for your image.

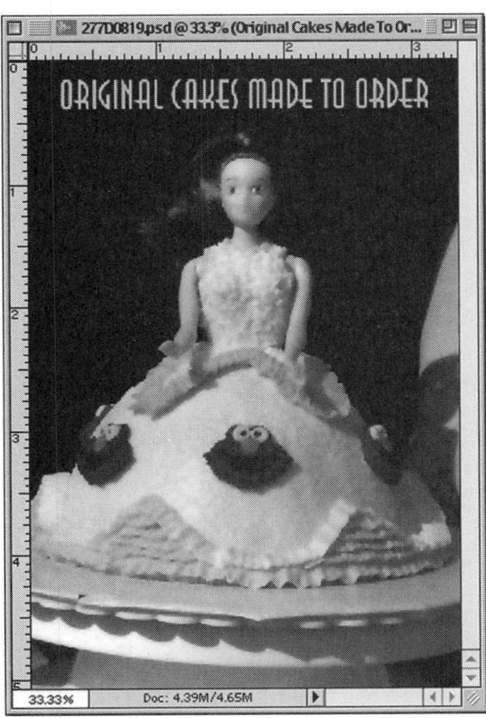

4. Choose Edit ➢ Transform ➢ Rotate. Place your cursor over one of the corners of the bounding box and rotate the text.

5. Switch to the Move tool and position the text so that if fits the area of the photograph. Click Apply when you're prompted to save the changes.

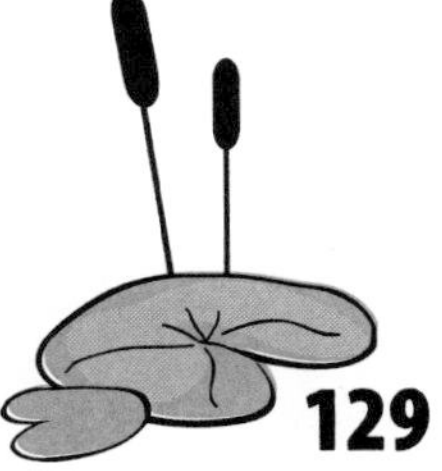

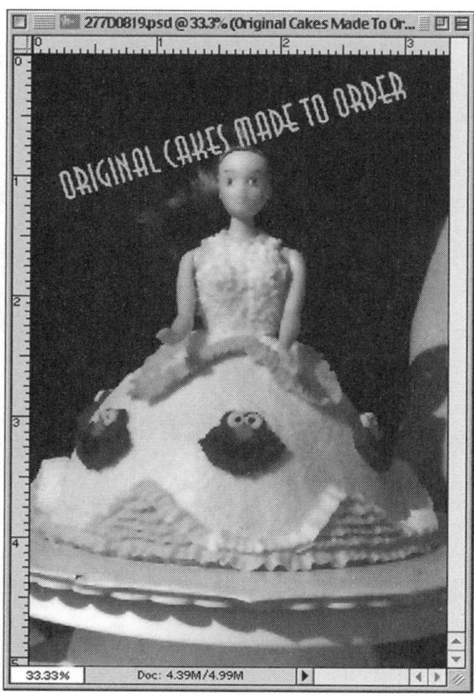

6. Click the Warp Text button in the options bar. In the Warp Text dialog box, click the Style drop-down button and select Arc. Change the Horizontal Distortion to +58%. This will make the text look like it is coming toward the viewer.

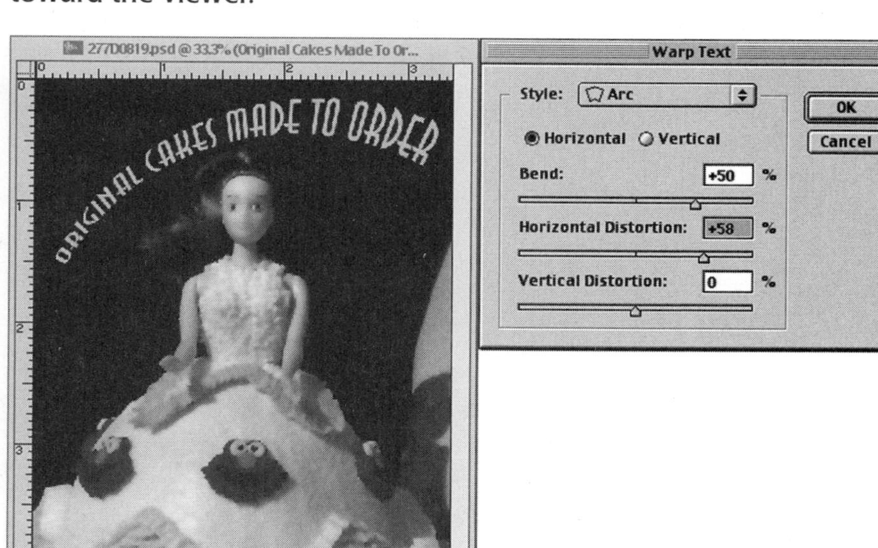

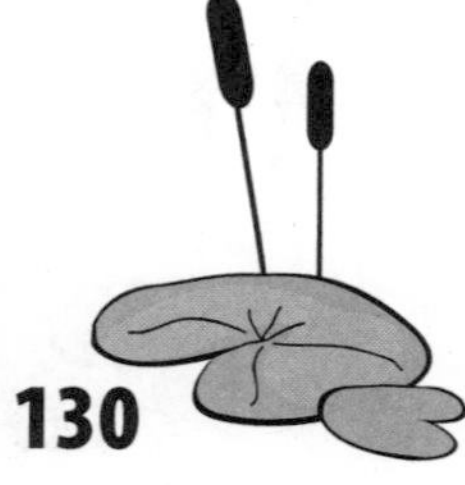

Note

Some warped text effects cause your text to expand outside the edges of the image. Use Edit ➢ Transform ➢ Scale to make the text fit correctly.

Adding an Image to Your Text

Another great effect is giving the impression that the text is actually popping out from the image itself. To create this effect, you use the Paste Into command, a filter, blending options, and a blending mode.

1. Open an image that has an interesting background or area that you can use within your text. For this example, I chose a photo with a leafy foreground.

2. Select the Type tool and choose a very thick font and large point size. I used the Impact font, set at 48 points. Type an appropriate phrase.

Tip

There are dozens of sites that offer free fonts or fonts at extremely low prices. One good starting point in your search for additional fonts is at `www.fontdiner.com`. You can search the Web to locate other sites.

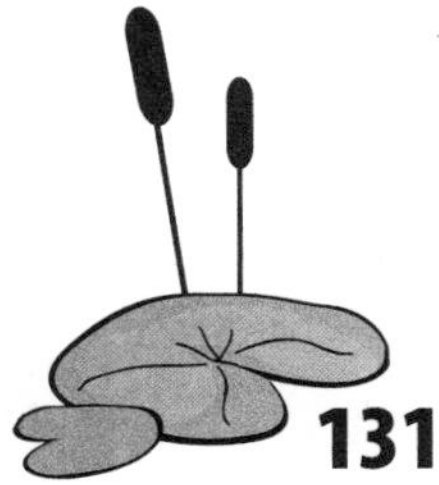

3. Select the Move tool and position your text where you want it.
4. In the Layers palette, select the Background. Then select the Rectangular Marquee tool to surround the text.

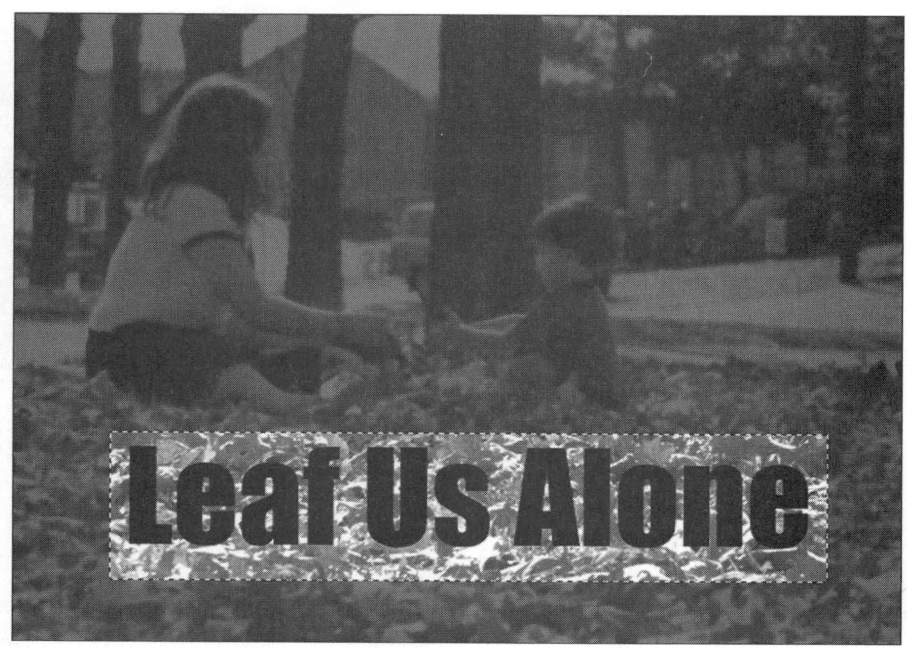

Note

I modified the image in this example somewhat to make the selected area stand out.

5. Press Ctrl+C (Cmd+C) to copy the selected portion of the background image. After you have copied it, press Ctrl+D (Cmd+D) to deselect the area you surrounded with the Rectangular Marquee tool.
6. Select the text layer in the Layers palette.
7. In the Layers palette, Ctrl-click (Cmd-click) the text layer. This will automatically select the text in the image.
8. Select Edit ➢ Paste Into. Your text will seem to disappear. Don't worry; you have just pasted the image you copied into the text, and it's blending perfectly with the image.

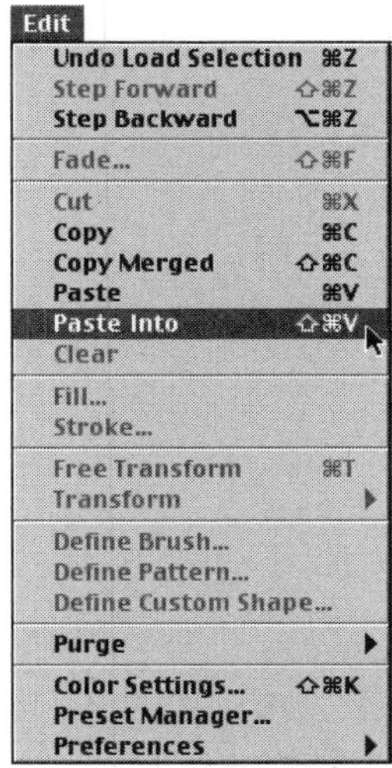

Note

The Edit ➢ Paste Into command pastes the contents of the Clipboard (whatever you cut or copied there) inside another selection and places it on a new layer. The selected area the copy is pasted into is converted into a layer mask.

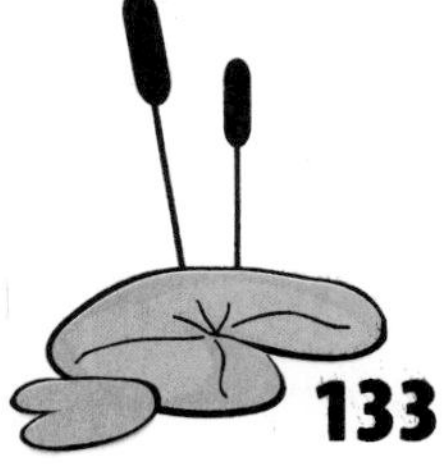

9. Select the original text layer (not the one you pasted the image into) and choose Layer ➢ Rasterize ➢ Type to rasterize this text.

10. Choose Filter ➢ Blur ➢ Gaussian Blur. Set the Radius to anywhere between 5 and 10—whatever looks best to you.

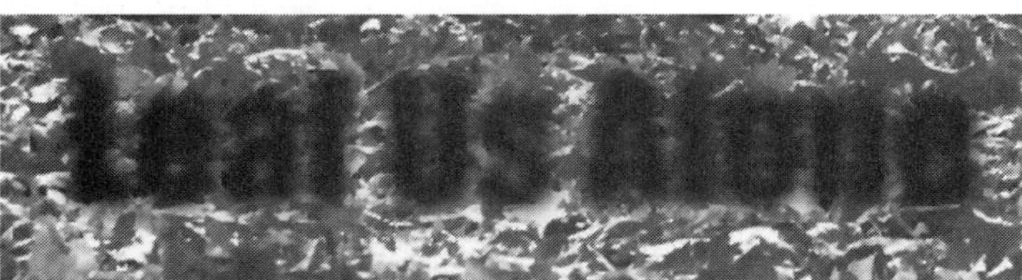

11. Select the text layer you added the effect to (the one called Layer 1 in the Layers palette). Right-click (Control-click) on the Layer mask thumbnail (the black thumbnail on this layer) to pop up the layer mask options. Choose Apply Layer Mask.

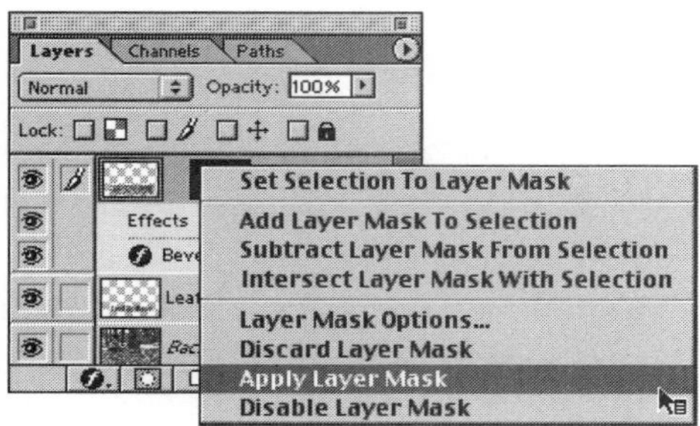

12. Select Layer ➢ Layer Style ➢ Bevel and Emboss. Change Depth to 241, Size to 13, Soften to 0, and Altitude to 28. This gives this text layer a beveled appearance that stands out from the background image.

We'll look at another way to tweak this effect in the next section.

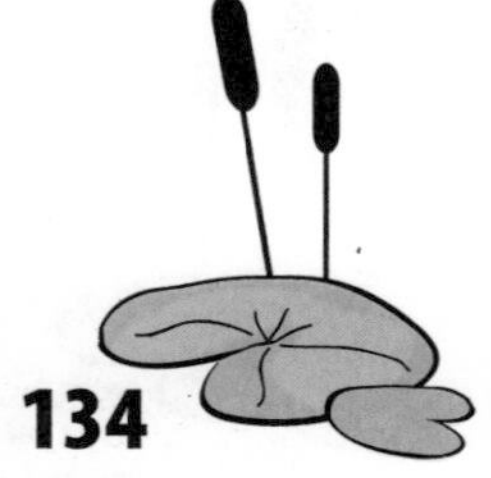

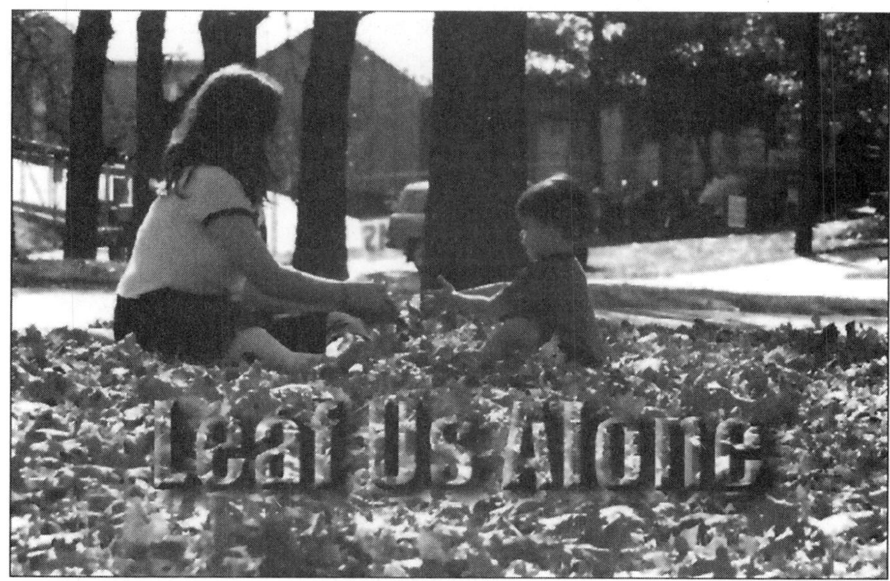

Making Image Text Stand Out

You might want to try something a bit different with the image text effect described in the previous section, to help make the text stand out more from the picture.

1. Move the blurred text layer down and to the right slightly, and then duplicate that layer.

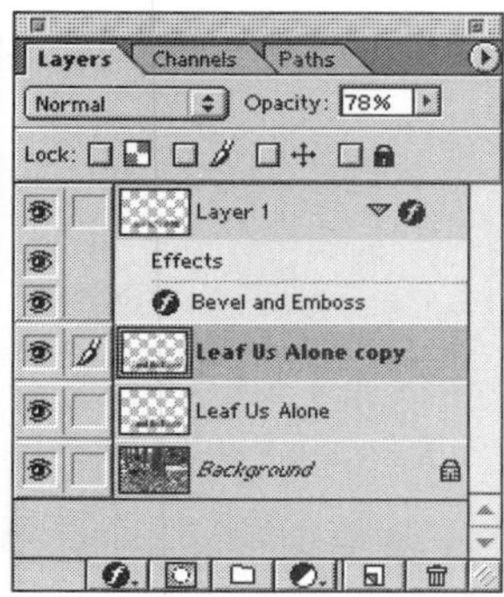

2. Move this new (copied) layer up and to the left.

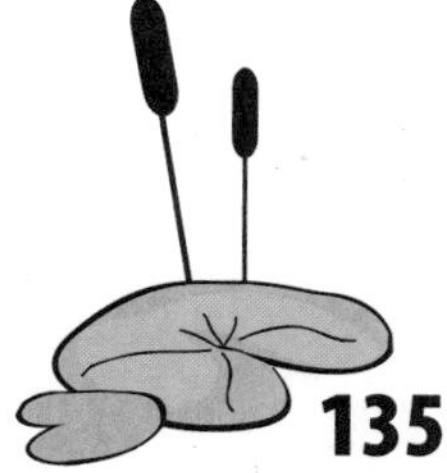

3. Activate the layer that has the Bevel and Emboss effect assigned to it (the top layer in the Layers palette).

4. Select Image ➢ Adjust ➢ Levels.

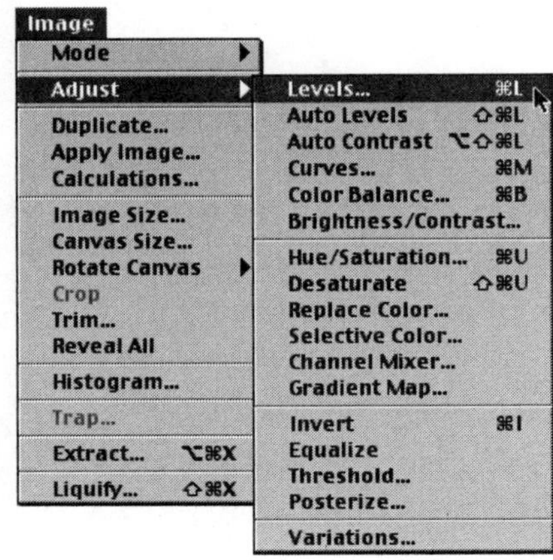

histogram
A graphical representation of the color values in an image. The leftmost area is black, rightmost is white, and the area in between represents the midtones (the other colors or shades of gray that make up the image).

5. In the Levels dialog box, move the rightmost triangle under the **histogram** to the left. This has the effect of lightening the image on that layer. Then move the middle triangle (which controls midtones) slightly to the left. Move the leftmost triangle (which controls blacks) to the right.

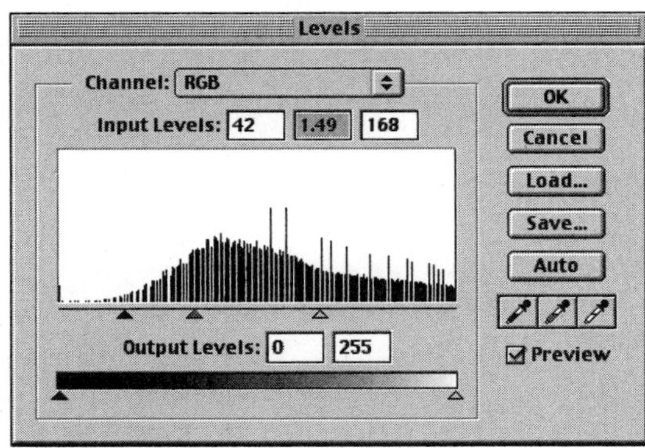

Tip

The controls in the Levels dialog box allow you to change the brightness and darkness of an image. If your photograph is too dark, you can make most of your fixes right here.

6. Click OK to close the Levels dialog box.

Now your text not only stands out from the rest of the image, but it also is separated from the image thanks to the drop shadows.

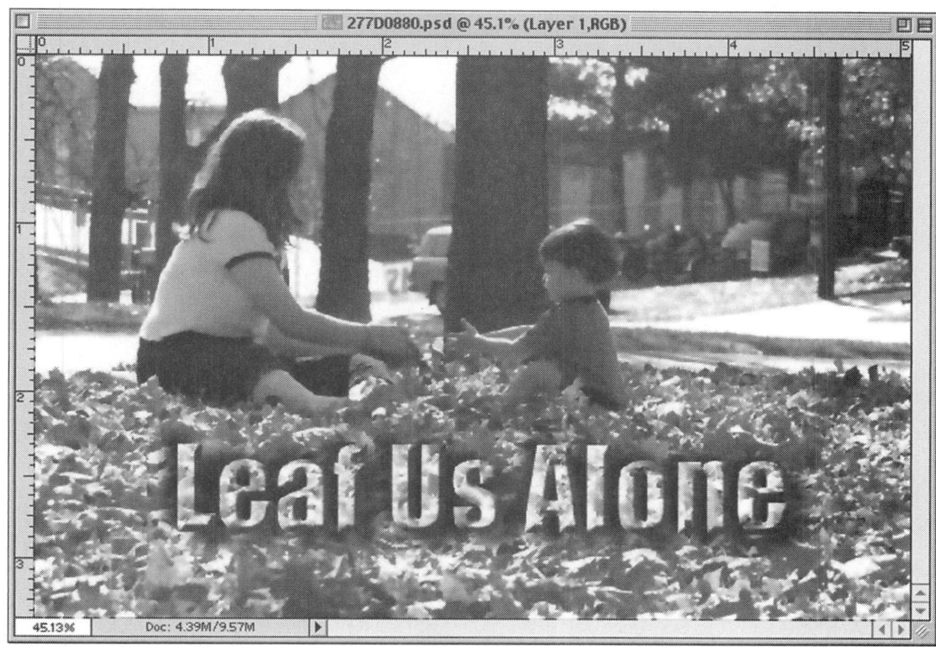

Moving On

In this chapter, you became acquainted with the Type tool and some of the really cool things you can do with type in Photoshop. You'll want to experiment with the other layer styles and see how they affect your text. Also, we only looked at two of the Warp Text styles (Bulge and Rise). You'll have a lot of fun seeing what the other 13 styles do.

In the next chapter, you'll learn about two handy Photoshop features: the History palette and the Actions palette. As you learned in Chapter 4, the History palette keeps a record of all of your actions during a session. The Actions palette allows you to record and play back a series of image-editing steps.

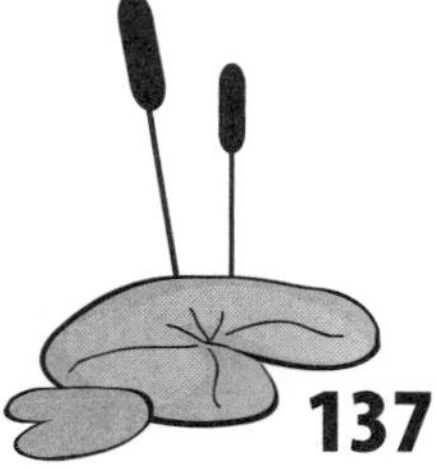

Chapter 6

Working with History States and Actions

Photoshop allows you to undo one previous task by using either the Ctrl+Z (Cmd+Z) key combination or the Edit ➢ Undo command. However, sometimes Undo will not be enough to get your image back to the desired point. That's where the History palette can save the day.

Grouped with the History palette is the Actions palette (unless you've rearranged the palette groupings). You may have noticed during the previous chapters that you duplicated certain operations over and over again. With the Actions palette, you can automate groups of operations.

This chapter covers Photoshop's tools for discarding changes and automating tasks, as well as some handy techniques for creating effects:

- The History palette
- The Actions palette
- Duotone mode
- Layers with effects

Working with the History Palette

As you build your Photoshop files, the History palette keeps a record of everything you do during that particular session. This is a great tool if you need to go back and see what steps you took to create a particular image. It's also a handy tool for fixing problems that might have occurred at some point in the creation process. But the usefulness of the History palette doesn't end there—you can use it to create special layered effects as well as experiment with different ways to work on an image.

Exploring the History Palette

state
Adobe's terminology for the particular way an image appears at any given time. As you change the look of the image, you are changing the image's state.

To open the History palette, select Window ➢ Show History. The History palette lists each action, called a **state**, in the order in which they were taken to create the current image.

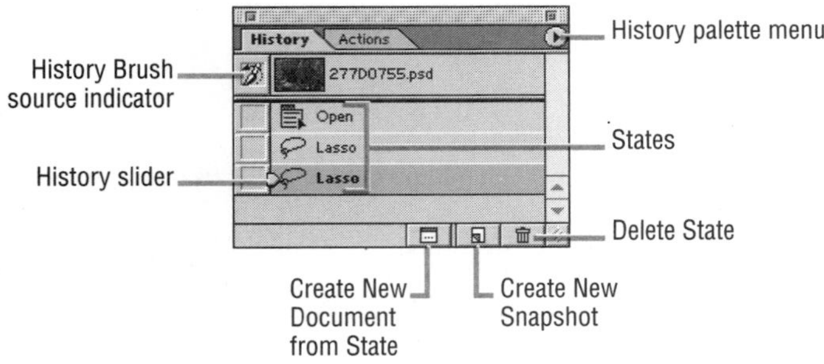

The state shows the tool or command used to produce the image at the stage in its creation. The History Brush icon that appears to the left of a state indicates which state will be painted by the History Brush tool (as described in Chapter 4). The slider arrow next to a state shows the selected state. You can move from state to state by clicking and dragging this slider.

Note

History states only exist during your current work session with a document file. When you close and then reopen the document, the states from the previous sessions are cleared.

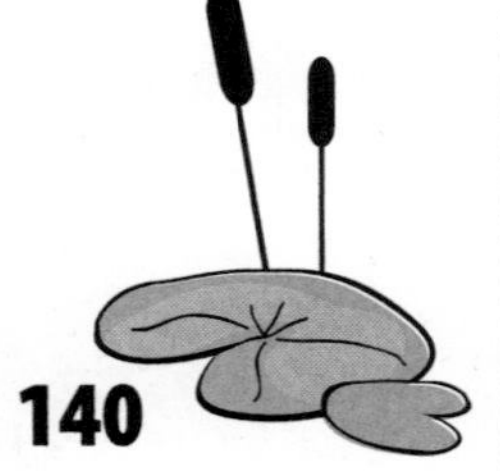

There are three buttons at the bottom of the History palette:

- The Create New Document from State button gives you the ability to create an entirely new document that contains all of the changes you have made.
- The Create New Snapshot button allows you to create a snapshot of a state. As you learned in Chapter 4, after you make a snapshot version of an image, you can retrieve and reuse it for the entire work session.
- The Delete State button deletes a selected state.

Choosing History Options

Like the other palettes, the History palette has its own options menu, which appears when you click the circular button with the right-pointing arrow in the upper-right corner of the palette.

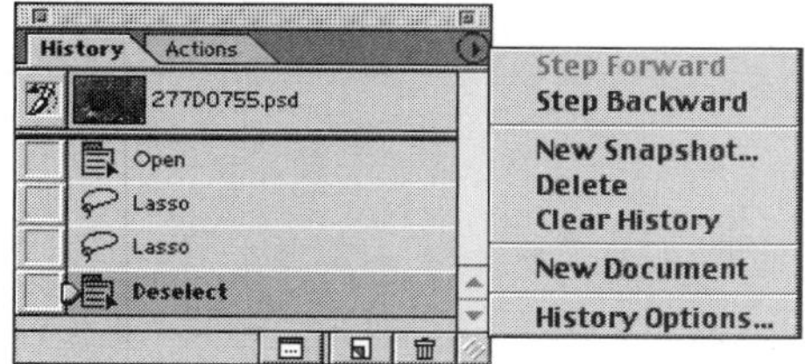

The first six items in this menu do just what you would expect them to do. Choosing History Options displays the History Options dialog box.

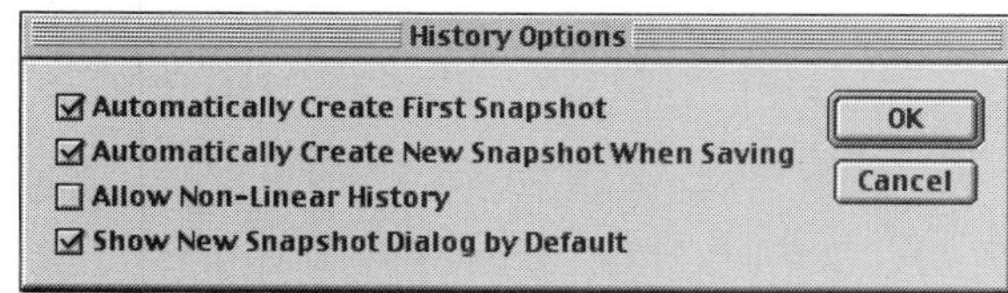

Here, you can set whether or not to automatically create a snapshot of the state of the image when you first open the image file and when you save it. The Allow Non-Linear History option changes the History palette from an ordered control to a more flexible tool. By default, this option is not selected, and deleting a History state earlier in your work will delete all of the changes (states) following that state. When you select Allow Non-Linear History, you can delete any state, without affecting the changes made after it.

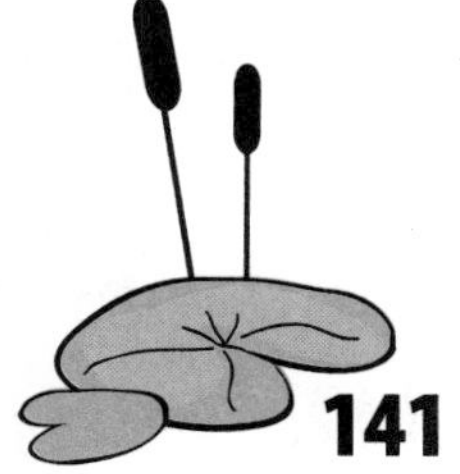

Creating a New Image from a State

As an example of how you can use the History palette, let's see how it lets you experiment with different effects.

1. Open an image you want to work with. If the History palette isn't already displayed, select Window ➢ Show History.
2. Select Filter ➢ Artistic ➢ Colored Pencil. This filter creates the appearance of the image having been drawn with a colored pencil.

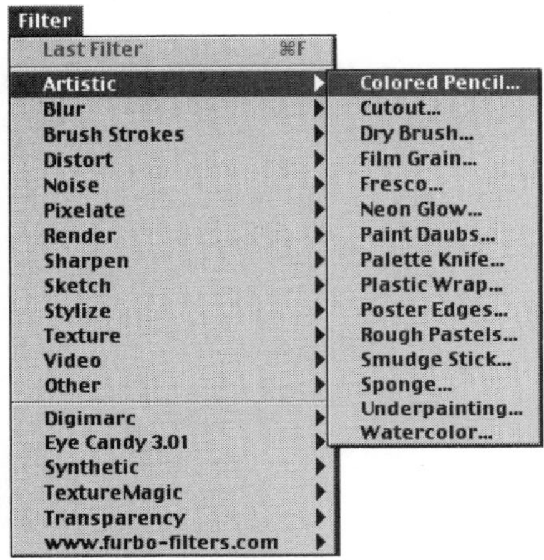

3. Choose Filter ➢ Brush Strokes ➢ Crosshatch.
4. Choose Filter ➢ Sketch ➢ Graphic Pen. You now have an image with three filters applied, and each state appears in the History palette.

5. Select the Crosshatch state in the History palette.

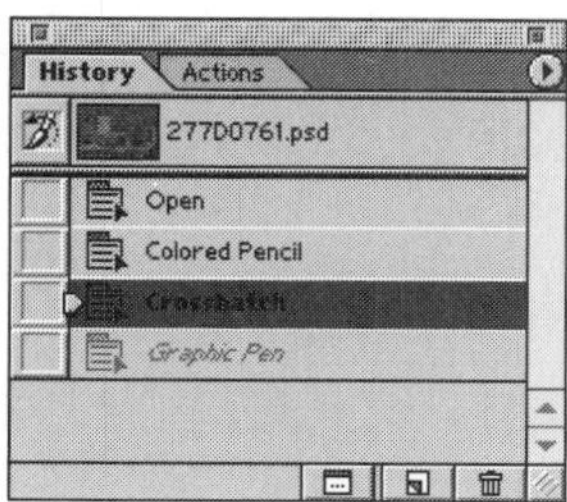

6. Click the Create New Document from State button. You now have a new image that includes the Colored Pencil and Crosshatch effects, but does not include the Graphic Pen filter.

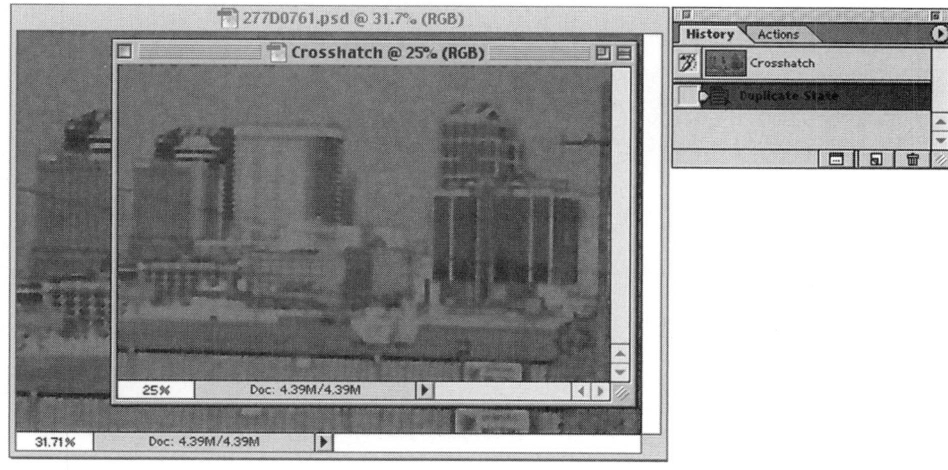

As you can see, you can not only review how different effects work with each other, but you can also replace the effects at any time to create an entirely new picture using the History palette.

action
Another term for command. An action is anything that makes a change to the file you are working on.

Working with the Actions Palette

The Actions palette is grouped with the History palette. With this palette, you can create and save sets of commands and tool operations, called **actions**. You can then play back an action to reuse it and recreate the effects in any image.

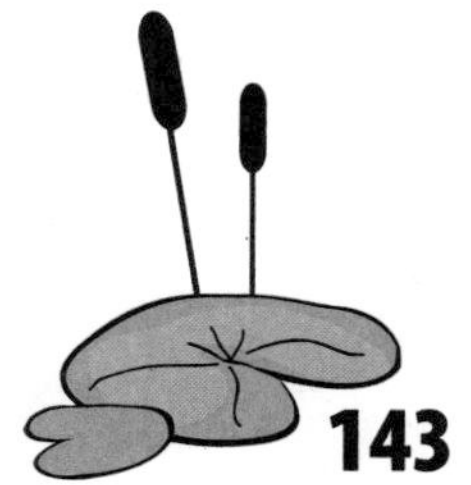

Exploring the Actions Palette

To open the Actions palette, either click the Actions tab from the History palette or select Window ➢ Show Actions. The Actions palette shows any actions you've created, listed by the name you've given them.

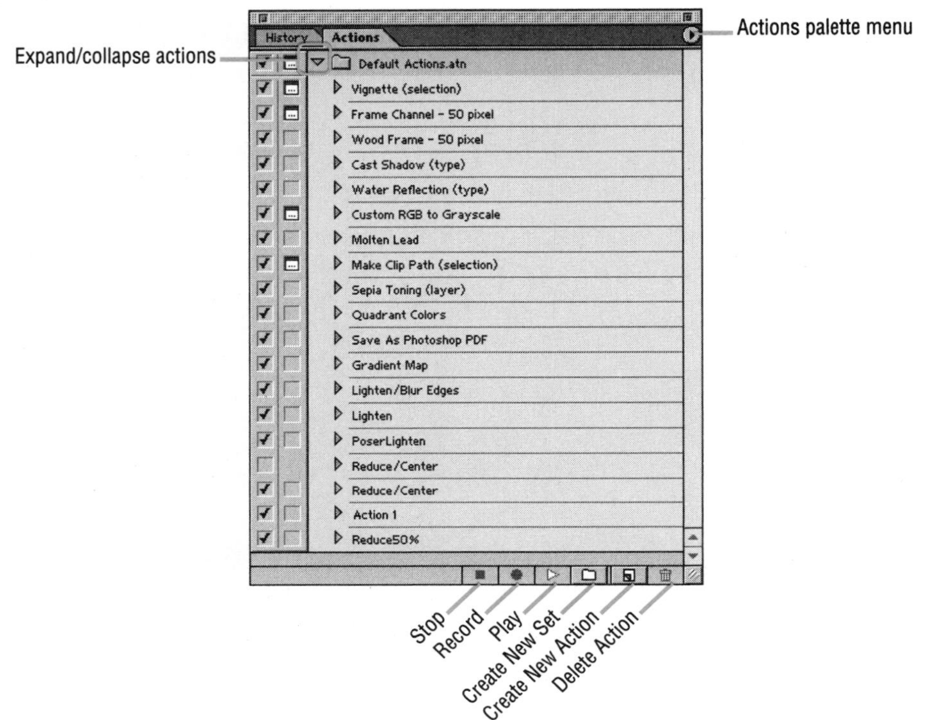

By clicking the triangle that appears to the left of the action name, you can expand the listing to show all of the operations that make up the action. Click it again to collapse the display and show just the action name.

The buttons across the bottom of the Actions palette work as follows:

- The Stop button stops the recording when you are creating an action (telling Photoshop your action is complete) or stops the playback of an action.
- The Record button tells Photoshop to record each step you make to store an action. Everything you do will be recorded until you click the Stop button.

- The Play button recreates the specific action on the image you are working on.
- The Create New Set button creates a folder in the Actions palette where actions can be stored.
- The Create New Action button tells Photoshop to create a new action.
- The Delete Action button deletes a selected action or operation within an action.

Creating an Action

When you click the Create New Action button (or select New Action from the Actions palette's options menu), Photoshop displays the New Action dialog box.

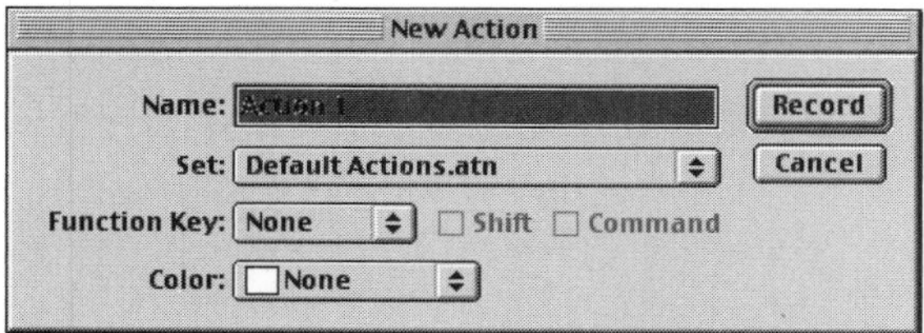

Here, you enter a name for your action, which you'll want to make as descriptive as possible, so that you'll know what happens when you play back your action.

The Set box shows the default actions folder, Default Actions.atn. This is the only choice available in the pop-up menu if you did not click the Create New Set button in the Actions palette. (You do not need to create a new set to record a new action.) The Function Key option allows you to assign a function key (F1, F2, and so on) to your action. This provides a handy way to perform an action from the keyboard. Finally, you can select a color for your action from the Color pop-up menu. Color coding your actions can be helpful to visually group specific actions that are related to each other or to help you identify specific actions quickly.

vignette
A photograph without a defined edge or border. The image fades off gradually at the edges into the background.

As an example, you'll record an action that creates a **vignette**.

1. Open a new file. If the Actions palette isn't displayed, click the Actions tab in the History palette or select Window ➢ Show Actions.

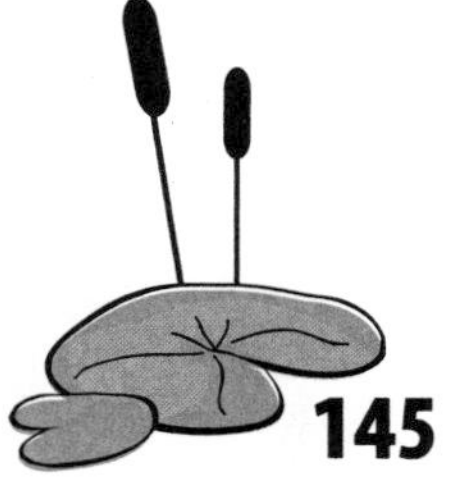

2. Select the Elliptical Marquee tool from the toolbox. This tool works like the Rectangular Marquee (which you used in Chapter 5), but selects an elliptical area rather than a rectangular one.

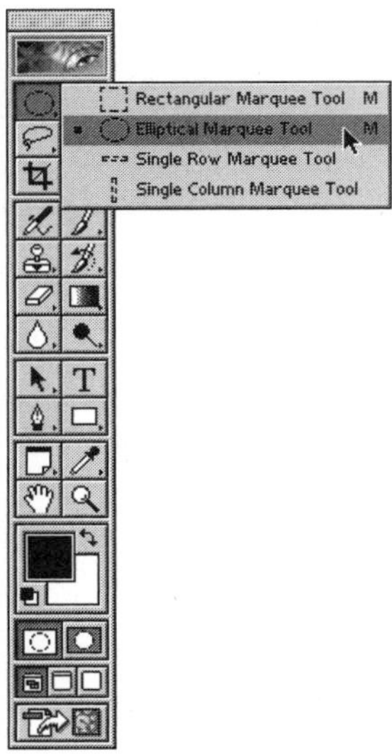

3. Click and drag around the portion of your picture that you want to be the focus of your vignette to select that area.

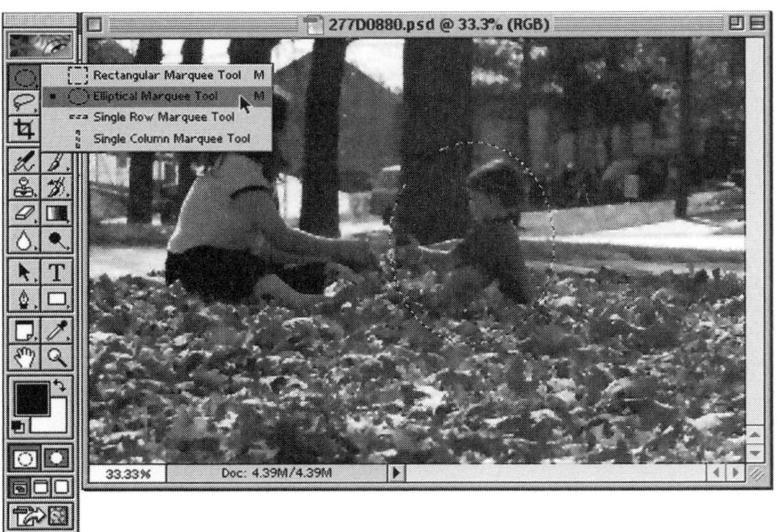

4. In the Actions palette, click the Create New Action button.

5. In the New Action dialog box, enter a name for your new action (**My_Vignette** for this example) and click the Record button. In the Actions palette, you'll see that the Record button is "depressed" and your new action is highlighted.

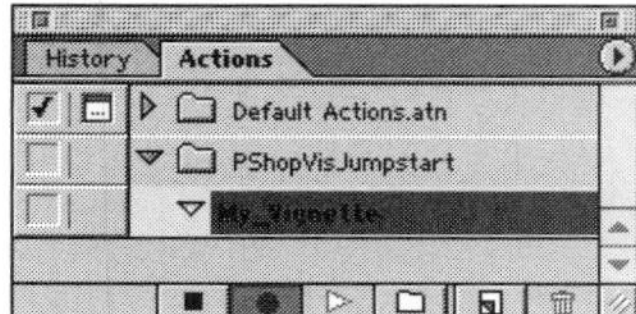

Note

Time is not a factor in Record mode. Recording merely saves each action you assign when you assign it. You can take your time when building your action.

6. Choose Select ➢ Inverse to invert the selected area. Inverse appears in the Actions palette.

7. Choose Select ➢ Feather to open the Feather Selection dialog box. Feathering will create a "blurred" or softened edge around the selected area. Enter **25** for the Feather Radius value and click OK.

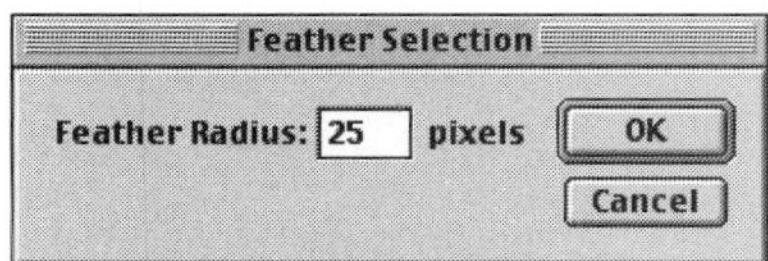

8. Feather now appears in the Actions palette, with an expander triangle next to it. Click that triangle, and you will see that the feather size you assigned is grouped with the Feather operation.

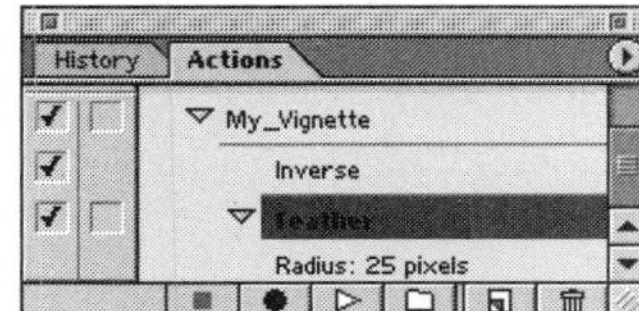

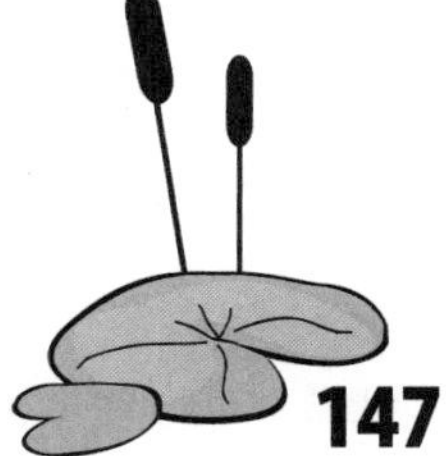

9. Press the Delete key to remove the selected area of the photograph. Press Ctrl+plus (Cmd+plus) to zoom in. Notice the soft edge around the remaining image.

10. Deselect the area by selecting Select ➢ Deselect.

11. Click the Stop button in the Actions palette. Your action has now been recorded.

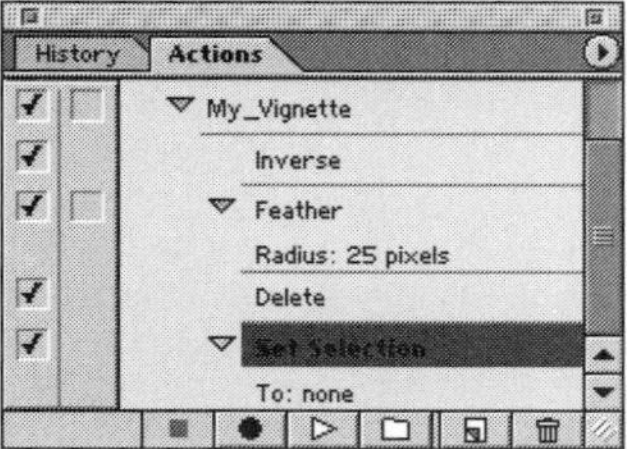

Using Your Recorded Action

Now that you've created an action, let's try using it.

1. Select File ➢ Revert to return your image to its original state. Notice that the action you just created is still available in the Actions palette.

2. Select a portion of your image to use for the vignette (it can be the same area of the image you used to create the action, a different area in that image, or a portion of a different image), using any of the Marquee tools—it makes no difference which one you use.

3. Click the My_Vignette action in the Actions palette, and then click the Play button. You will see Photoshop moving through the steps of the action, with each step highlighted until the action is completed.

4. Select File ➢ Revert to restore your original image. Select the standard (or freeform) Lasso tool and draw a peanut-shaped border around a section of your image. As you can see, the Lasso tool allows you to cre-

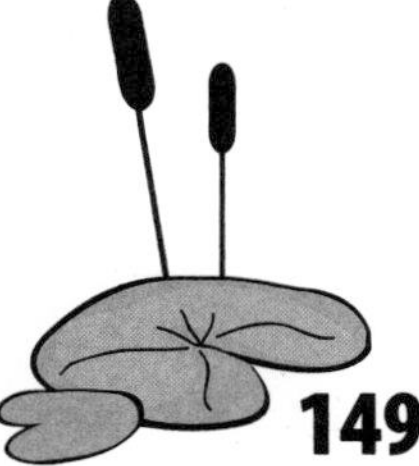

ate selections that use original shapes (see Chapter 2 for more information about the Lasso tools).

5. Click the Play button on the Actions palette to create the new vignette.

sepia-tone
A photograph that has a dark reddish-brown color (sepia) as the main color of the image.

Duotone
A mode that uses two specified colors in your image for specialized effects. The other modes are Monotone (one color), Tritone (three colors), and Quadtone (four colors).

Creating a Duotone Image

Normally, when you think of a vignette, you envision an old picture of your grandparents or famous people from the past. These pictures usually are **sepia-toned** images that evoke a feeling of age and history. You can mimic that effect by using Photoshop's **Duotone** mode.

Let's turn a vignette into a full-fledged, sepia-toned vignette.

1. Select File ➢ Revert to return your image to its original state. Use the Elliptical Marquee tool to select a portion of your image.
2. Select Image ➢ Mode ➢ Grayscale.

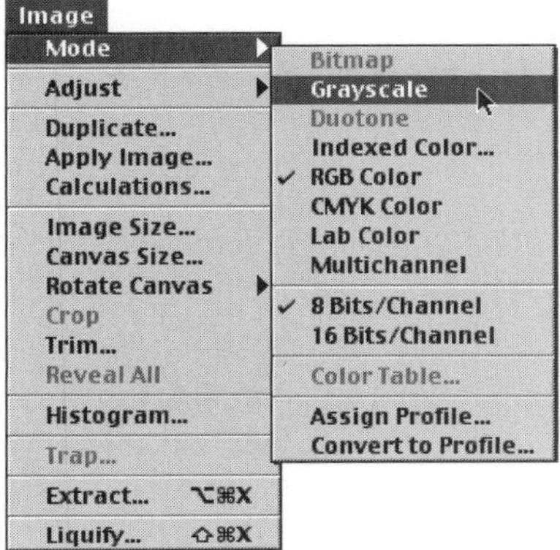

3. Select Image ➢ Mode ➢ Duotone. This brings up the Duotone Options dialog box. Here, you can choose Monotone (the default), Duotone, Tritone, or Quadtone to create interesting photographic looks.

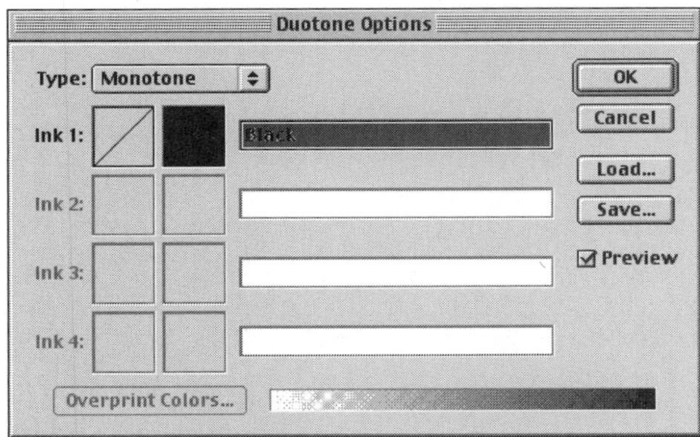

4. From the Type pop-up menu, select Duotone. Then click the Ink 1 color box (the second to the right from the color layer title). This opens your system color palette. Assign a reddish-brown color and give it a name in the text field.

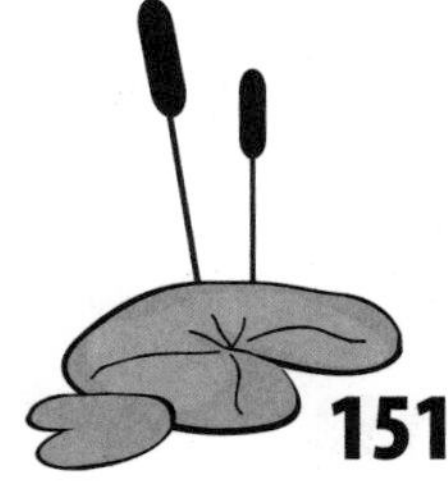

5. Click the Ink 2 color box and select a cream-like color.

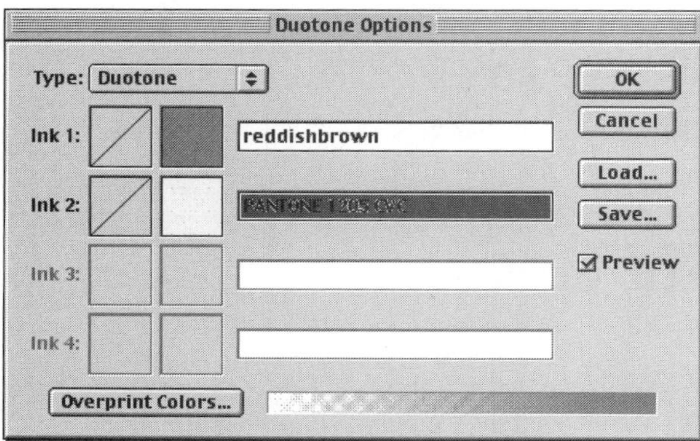

6. Click OK to close the dialog box and view the Duotone effects.

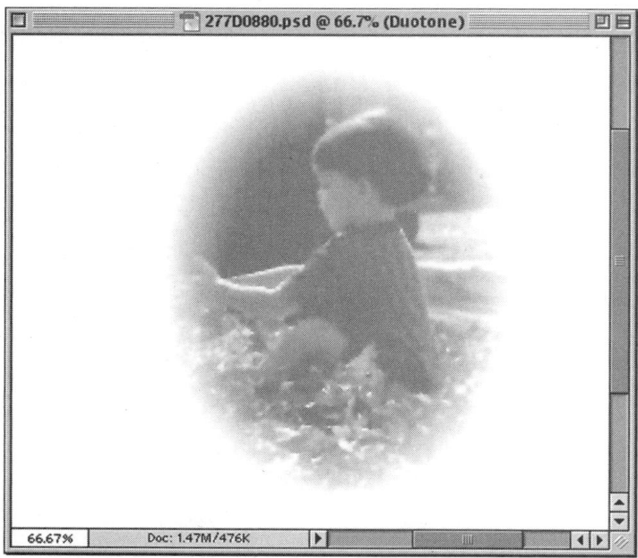

If your sepia duotone looks a little washed out or too dark, don't worry. You'll learn how to fix that in Chapter 7.

Assigning Effects to Layers

After you've set up some effects that you like, you can assign them to different layers. This allows you to create montages and other looks for your images. To

demonstrate how layered effects can help you with your projects, you'll put your vignette on a layer.

1. Open both the Actions and Layers palettes.
2. Select File ➢ Revert to return the image that you have been using throughout this chapter to its original form.
3. Open a second image.

4. Select the Move tool, click the second image, and drag it over the first image.

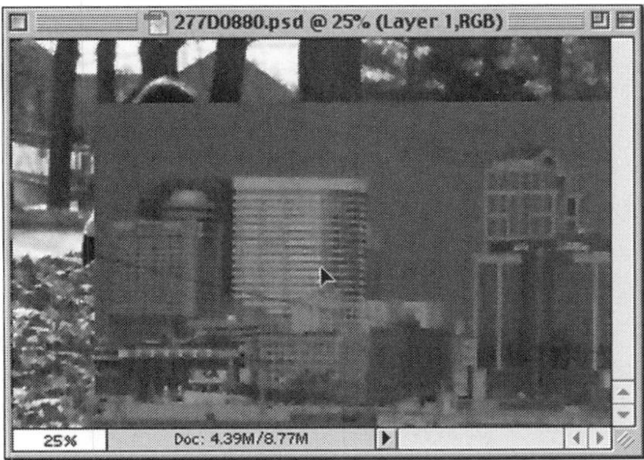

5. Close the window that held the second image. This will help you avoid confusion and reduce the amount of memory Photoshop uses.

6. Use one of the Marquee tools or the Lasso tools to surround an area on Layer 1.

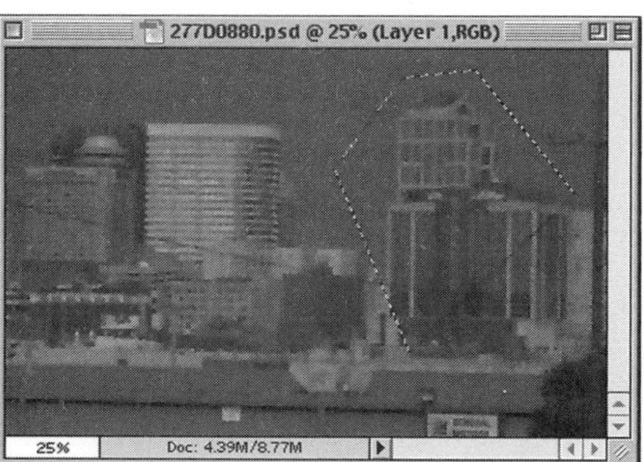

7. Click the My_Vignette action in the Actions palette, and then click the Play button to create a vignette on Layer 1.

8. Use the Move tool to position the image on Layer 1 where you want it to appear.

9. Duplicate Layer 1 by dragging it to the Create New Layer icon at the bottom of the Layers palette.

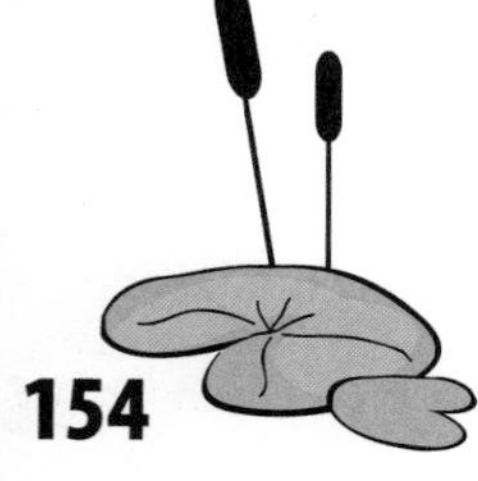

10. Select the original layer and choose Edit ➢ Fill. Make sure Preserve Transparency is checked and fill the layer image with black.

11. Use the Move tool to move this new drop shadow layer down and to the right.

Tip

You can also use the arrow keys on your keyboard to move items. This allows you to move a selection pixel by pixel.

12. Click the eye icon for the Background in the Layers palette to hide it.
13. Open the Layers palette's options menu and choose Merge Visible.
14. Select the first image (the Background).

15. Select an area of that image using the Marquee or Lasso tool and play back your My_Vignette action to create another vignette.

16. Move Layer 1 into a new position.

Now that you have more an idea of the power of layers, you can experiment with mixing different modes in the Layers palette to see how your layers can look.

Moving On

As you learned in this chapter, the History and Actions palettes can help you quickly and easily manipulate your photographs and images. You also learned a few more new tricks: using the Duotone mode and assigning effects to layers.

In the next chapter, we'll look at solutions to a universal problem, which is that no image is perfect. It may have small blemishes, or it might appear too light (to name two potential problem areas). Photoshop provides some tools that allow you to make various adjustments in your images, ranging from adding a bit of contrast to changing the color spectrum dramatically.

Chapter 7

Adjusting Images

Whether you are using scanned-in photographs or images from a purchased collection, you will often need to adjust the images in one way or another. Your adjustments might be as simple as lightening or darkening the image, or as dramatic as changing the entire color spectrum.

Photoshop provides a variety of image-adjustment controls, accessed through the Image ➢ Adjust menu, plus image-sizing options, which you'll learn about in this chapter:

- Variations controls
- Levels controls
- Brightness/Contrast controls
- Hue/Saturation controls
- Image Size settings

Adjusting Image Colors and Tones

Photoshop's Variations controls are the most basic method of modifying the overall look of your image, so they are a good place to start. Through the Variations dialog box, you can adjust an image's coloring, shadows, midtones, highlights, and saturation.

Correcting an Entire Image

When your image needs some lightening or darkening, you can use the Variations controls to fix it.

1. Open an image that might be improved by changing its tones.
2. Select Image ➢ Adjust ➢ Variations.

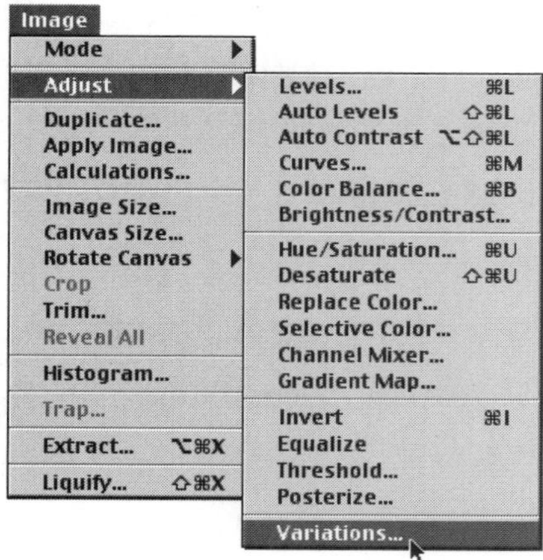

3. As you can see, the Variations dialog box shows a graphical representation of your image in its original form and one that shows whatever changes you make based on the colors and lightness/darkness controls. The colors represented in the main area of the Variations dialog box represent opposites in the color spectrum.

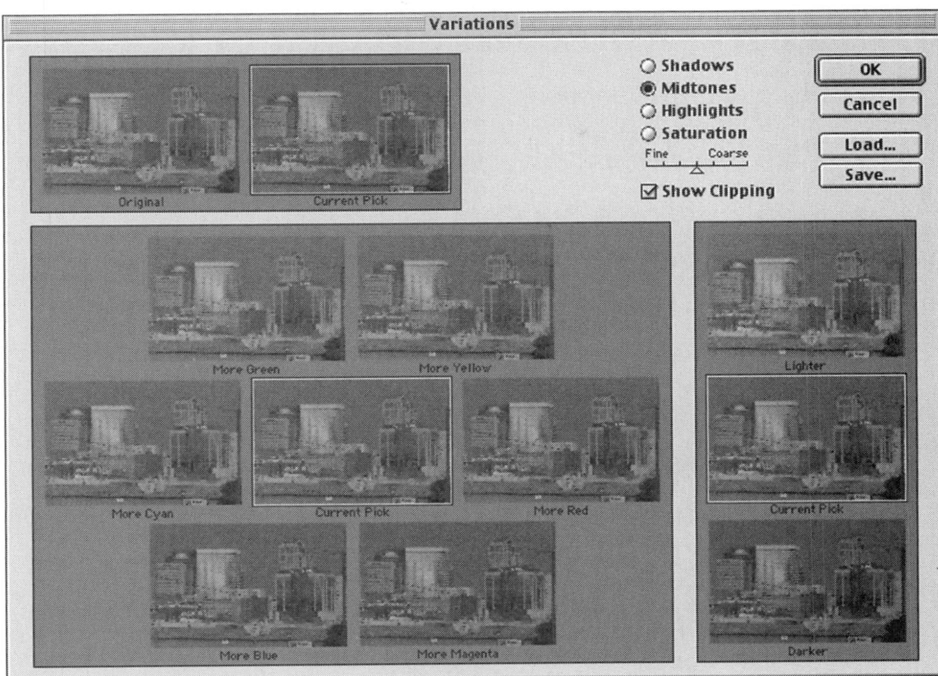

4. If your image is too light or dark, click the Lighter or Darker image representation. Then check the difference in the Current Pick representation.

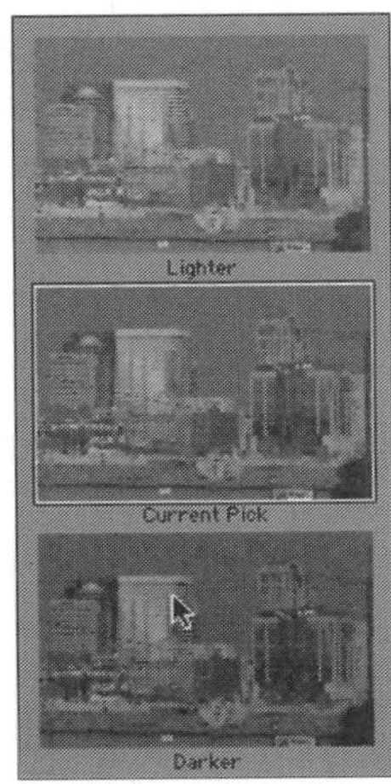

Continuing to click a control adds more of that choice to the image. Unless there is something drastically wrong with an image, you won't want to click more than two or three times (on the outside) on a particular variation.

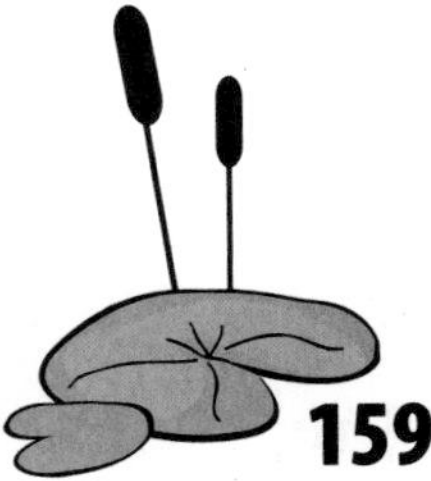

Adjusting a Specific Portion of the Image

You can also assign variations to a particular portion of an image.

1. If the Variations dialog box is open (which I would expect it still is), click Cancel to return to your image.
2. Use either the Magic Wand or the Lasso tool to select a portion of your image.

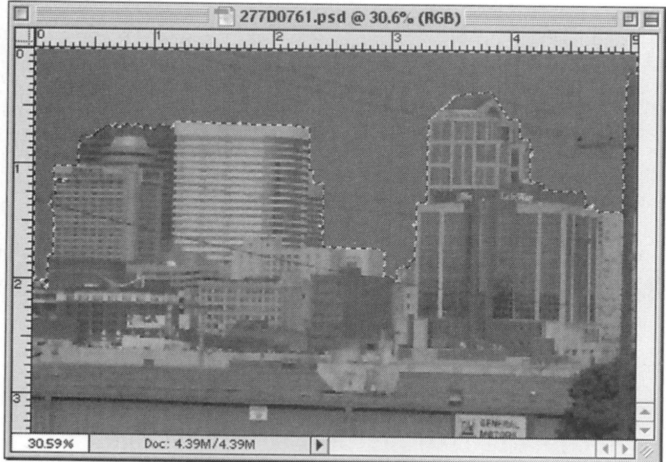

3. Select Image ➢ Adjust ➢ Variations to open the Variations dialog box.
4. Click a color selector that most closely matches the color you wish to affect. The only portion of the image that will be modified is the selected area.

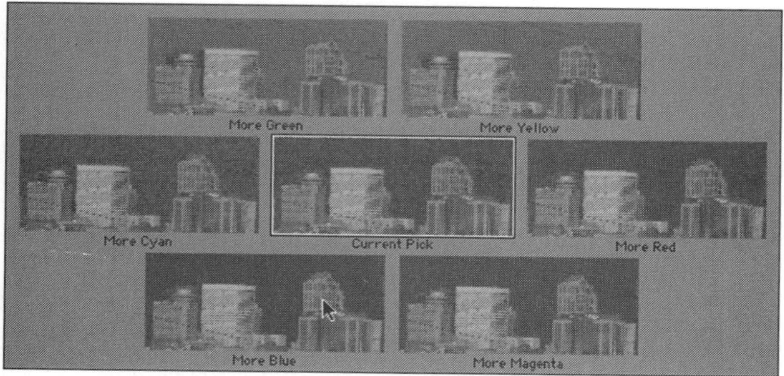

5. Click OK to accept the change and close the Variations dialog box.

6. Choose Select ➢ Inverse to invert your selection.

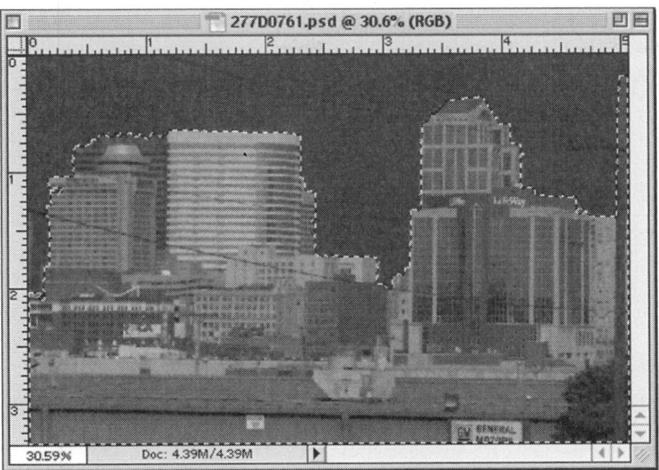

7. Select Image ➢ Adjust ➢ Variations to open the Variations dialog box again.

8. To deepen the dark areas of the image, click the Shadows radio button.

9. Click the Darker representation two or three times. Monitor the differences in the Current Pick representation.

10. Click OK to accept your changes and close the dialog box. Notice how much more vibrant your image is.

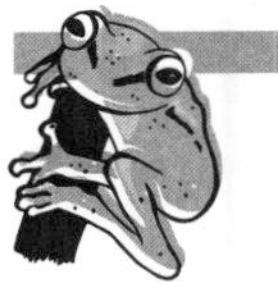

Tip

A good way to check the Variations effects and preserve your original image in case you don't like those effects is to select File ➢ Save As and save the modified image under a different name or in a different location. Then, with the modified image still on your screen, open the original file to see how they compare.

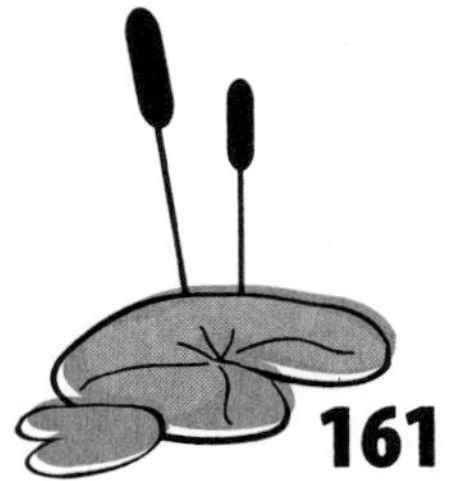

As you've seen, the Variations dialog box gives you some good, basic controls over image modifications. But there's a reason that Photoshop is the photo-manipulation software of choice for the majority of professional graphic artists: There are other image controls that give you more precise control over your work. Let's take a look at some of those.

Adjusting Levels

For more precise modification of light and dark areas, the Levels controls give you high-end tools that will help make your images pop off the screen or the printed page. You had a bit of experience using the Levels dialog box in Chapter 5, where you modified levels to make image text stand out. Now you will get more details about what the Levels controls can accomplish.

Introducing the Level Controls

When you select Image ➢ Adjust ➢ Levels with an image open, you see a histogram of the image, along with a batch of controls for modifying channels and image tones.

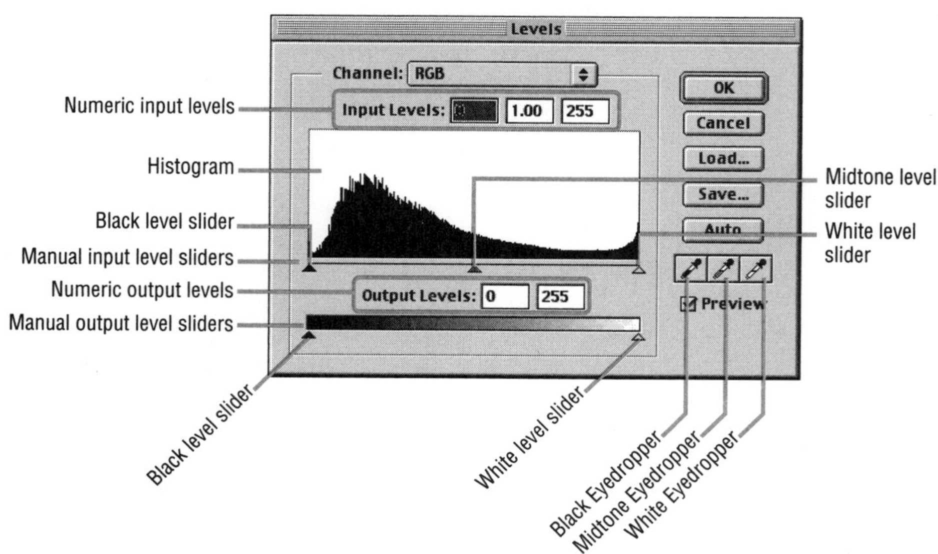

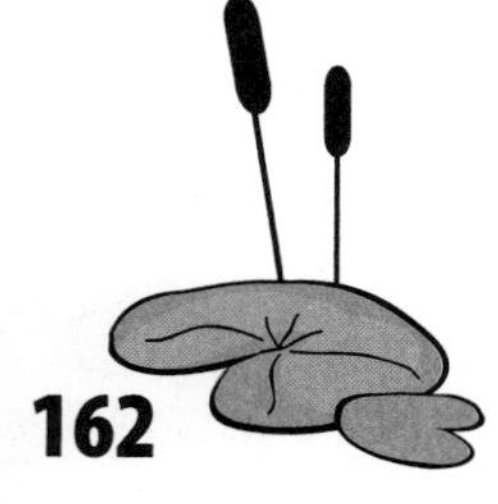

Note

As you learned in Chapter 5, a histogram is a graphical representation of the black, midtone, and white levels of your image.

Here is what you have to work with in the Levels dialog box:

- The Channel pop-up menu lets you choose whether your changes will affect all channels or a specific color channel.
- The Input Levels text boxes allow you to enter numeric values to affect the black, midtone, and white levels (from left to right) for your image.
- The sliders directly beneath the histogram let you manually adjust the black, midtone, and white input levels. Drag these triangular sliders to the left or right to change the levels.
- The Output Levels text boxes allow you enter numeric values to modify the output levels more precisely for printed output. (The appropriate adjustments are determined by the type of paper and the print process that will be used.)
- The sliders beneath the Output Levels text boxes let you manually adjust the image's output levels by dragging the sliders to the left or right.
- The OK, Cancel, and Save command buttons along the right side of the dialog box do what you would expect them to do. The Load button allows you to import histograms that you have saved, applying those modifications to your image. Click the Auto button to have Photoshop automatically determine the range between black and white, based on the selected image.

Note

When you hold down the Option (Alt) key, the Cancel button changes to a Reset button. Click Reset to return all of your modifications to their original settings.

- The three Eyedropper tools are for selecting black, midtone, and white areas (from left to right). You can use these to select the darkest and lightest areas of your image to use as a starting point in your input-level modifications.

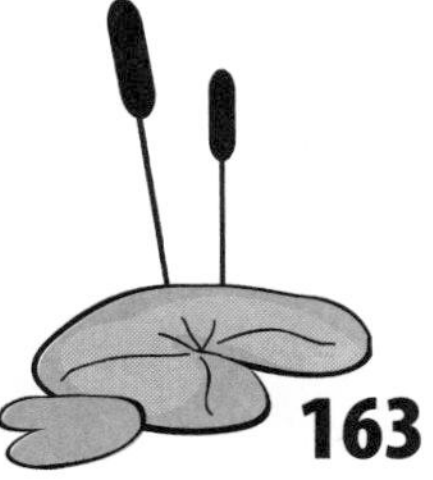

- The Preview check box, when selected, shows your image updates immediately, so you can see how your modifications are affecting the image.

Using the Levels Controls

You'll want to use the Levels dialog box when you wish to fine-tune the tone levels of an image.

1. Open the image you want to modify.
2. Select Image ➢ Adjust ➢ Levels to open the Levels dialog box.
3. Click the black Eyedropper tool.
4. Click the darkest part of the image to set the black level. Notice how the histogram changes as well.

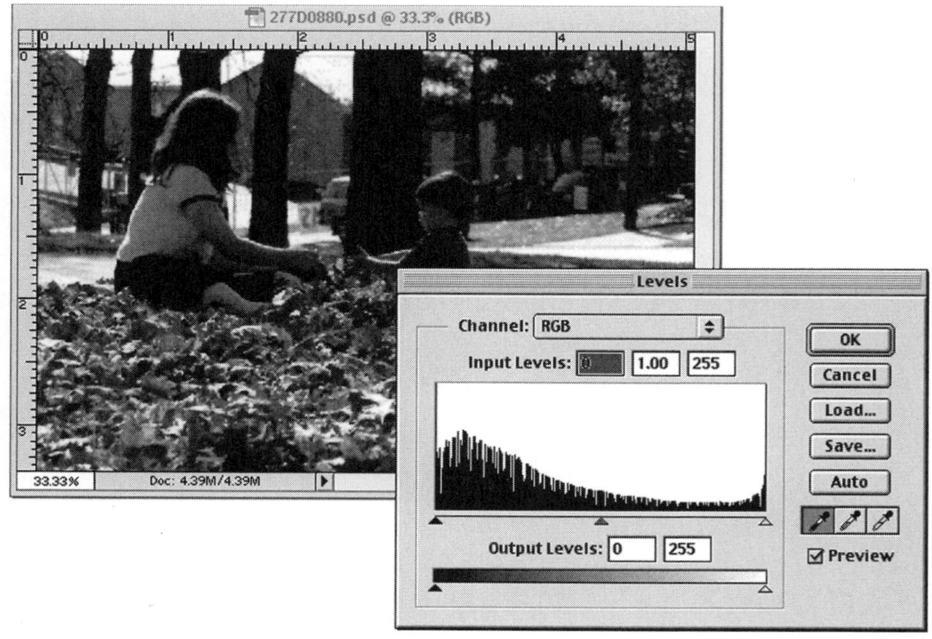

Note

If necessary, move the Levels dialog box to another portion of your screen so that you can see your image behind it and find the darkest and lightest parts.

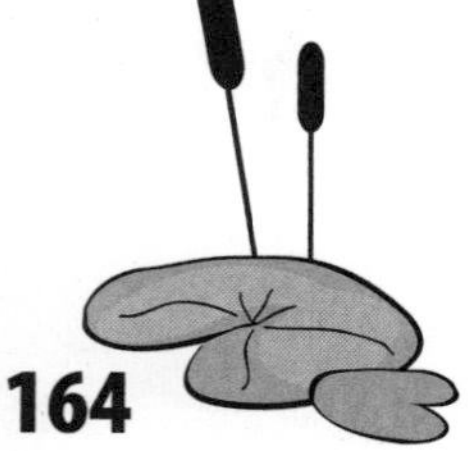

5. Select the white Eyedropper tool and click the lightest part of the image. Again, the histogram changes when you select the white point.

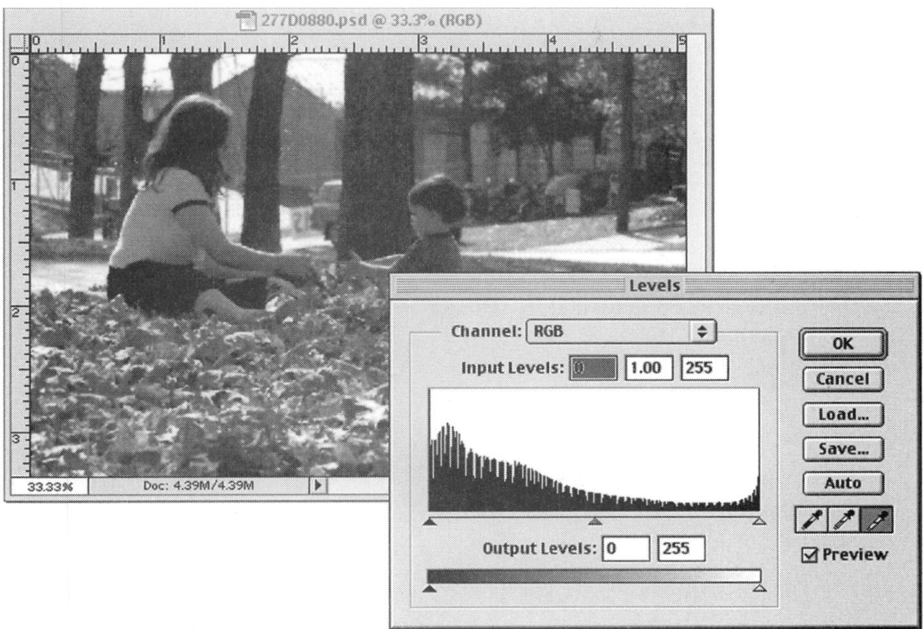

6. You will probably notice that the black level still overwhelms the image. To adjust it, drag the white slider beneath the histogram to the left until you're happy with the results. Both it and the midtone triangle will move.

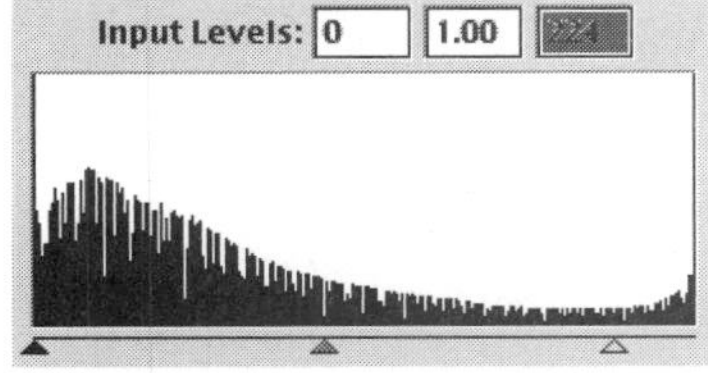

7. Drag the midtone slider under the histogram slightly to the left until the rest of the image brightens and you can see the details.

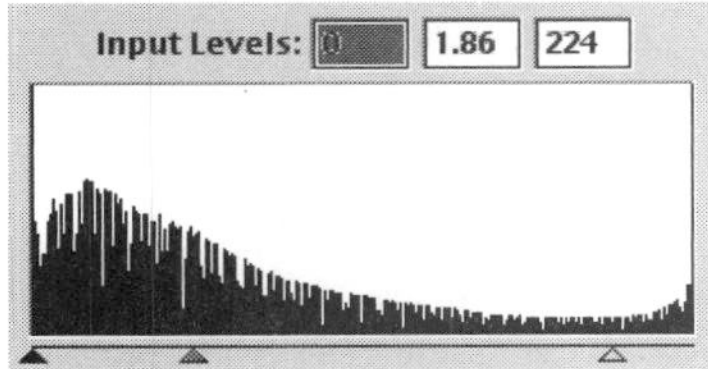

8. Drag the black slider slightly to the right, so that the shadows darken just a bit.

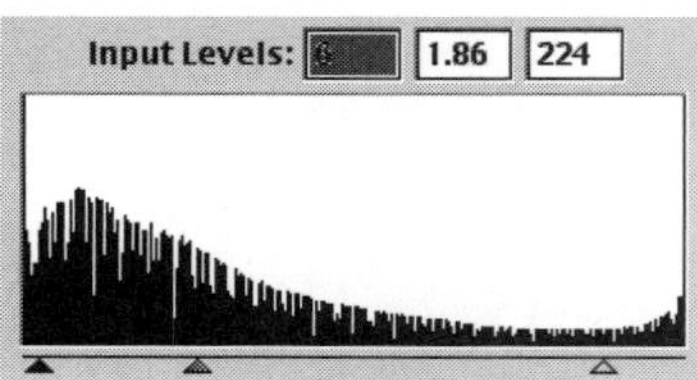

9. Notice that as you move these triangles, the numeric Input Levels text box values change to reflect the adjustments you have made.

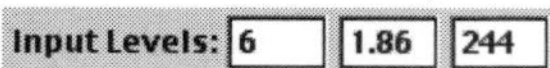

10. To see how you can retain these changes for use on other images, click the Save button. Photoshop displays the Save dialog box, in which you can give your level settings a name. Then you can create a new folder (in the main Photoshop folder or any of the other folders) to store your original Levels dialog box settings.

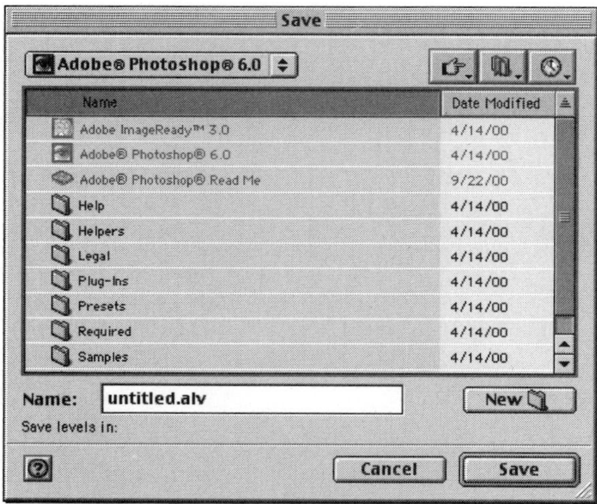

11. For now, just click Cancel to close the Save dialog box. Then click Cancel in the Levels dialog box to close it.

Controlling Brightness and Contrast

For some images, you will need precise control over the modifications of their brightness or contrast. Photoshop offers this type of control through the Brightness/Contrast dialog box. Although this is a fairly simple dialog box, don't let its appearance fool you. The two sliders give you a lot of power at your finger (or mouse) tips.

Let's experiment with the effects of adjusting the brightness and contrast in the practice image you used in the previous exercise.

1. Select Image ➢ Adjust ➢ Brightness/Contrast to open the Brightness/Contrast dialog box.
2. Position the dialog box on your screen so that you can see your image. Then move the Brightness slider all the way to the right.

3. Drag the Brightness slider all the way to the left. Notice how the image changes.

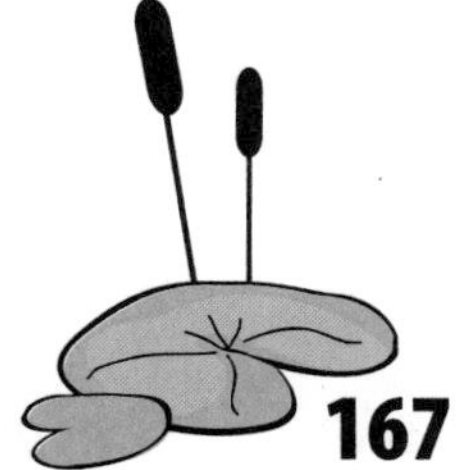

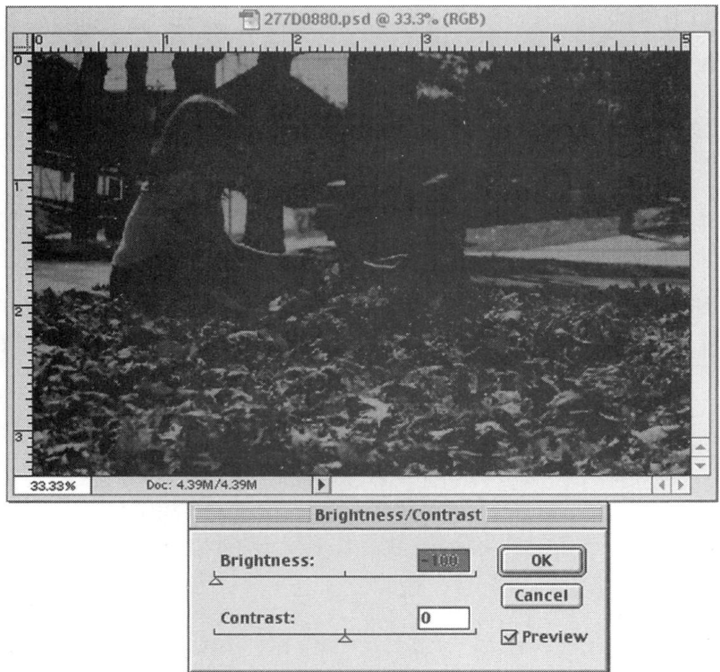

4. Reset the brightness to 0 by either moving the slider or clicking in the text box and typing **0**.
5. Drag the Contrast slider all the way to the right. Pretty psychedelic, huh?

6. Drag the Contrast slider all the way left. Rather gray, isn't it?

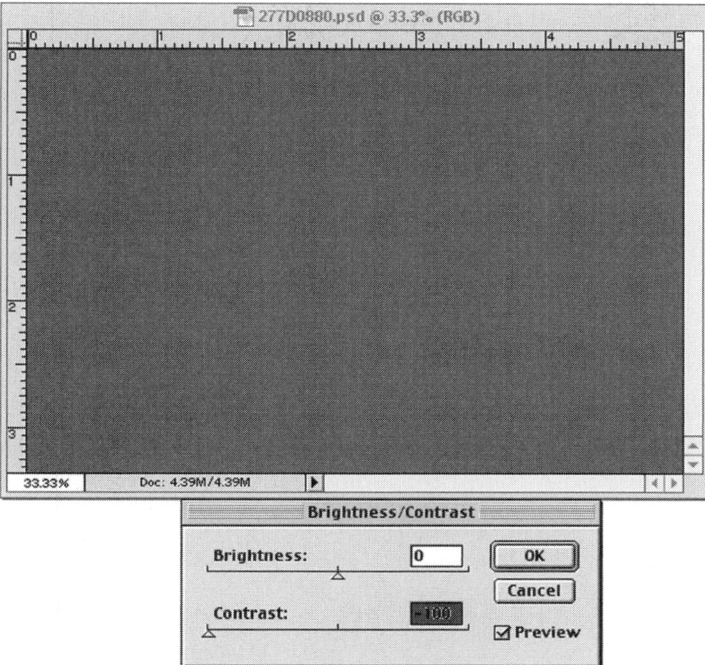

7. Experiment with the two sliders until you have the effect that you want. When you use the two controls in conjunction, just like the controls on a television set, you can make the image much brighter and more saturated.

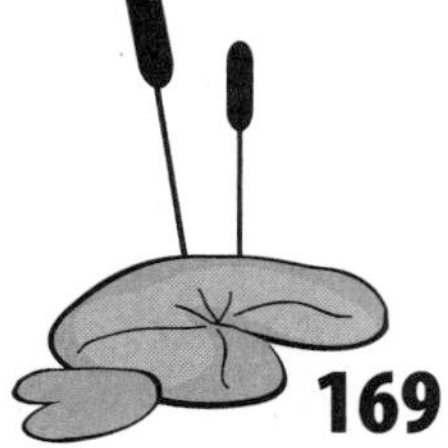

8. Click Cancel to close the dialog box and return your image to its original state.

Controlling Hue and Saturation

Hue and saturation affect the look of images by adding or removing color information. Adjusting hue and saturation through the Hue/Saturation dialog box can be time-consuming, but the effort is worth it, especially if you look beyond the normal photographic presentation. That's because you can create some extremely interesting looks when you use these controls on a selected portion of an image.

Introducing the Hue and Saturation Controls

One way of representing colors is through a color wheel, and that's what the Hue/Saturation dialog box works from. When you make changes to the hue or saturation, you are literally moving to another location around that wheel or across the radius of the wheel. When using these controls on a color image, you can adjust and change the overall colors, tune how brilliant the colors appear, and make the image lighter or darker.

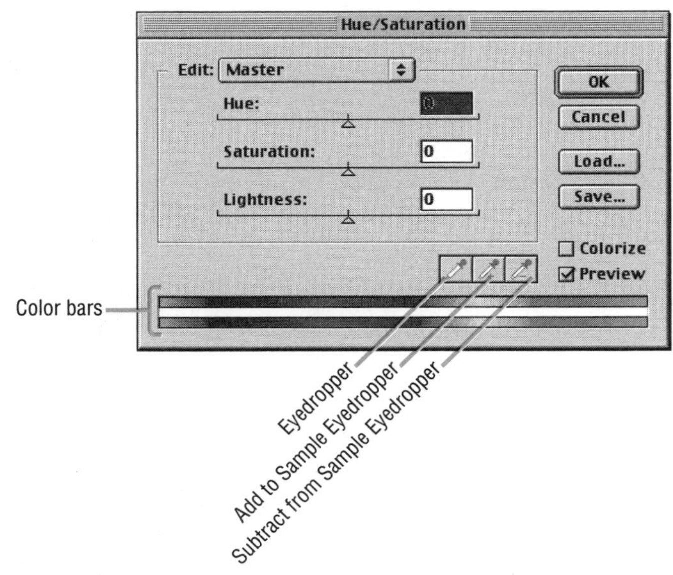

The Hue/Saturation controls work as follows:

- The Edit pop-up menu lets you select whether changes affect the overall image or various color groups within the image.
- The Hue slider adjusts the tonal quality of the color.
- The Saturation slider adjusts the color purity (or depth). You can use it to saturate and **desaturate** colors.
- The Lightness slider controls how washed out or brilliant a color is.
- The Colorize check box allows you to modify the color. You can use this feature to colorize a black-and-white image, selecting areas to colorize while leaving other areas unaffected.
- The Preview check box, when selected, shows your image updates immediately, so you can see how your modifications are affecting the image.
- The color bars at the bottom of the dialog box represent a flattened-out color wheel, with all the colors represented. The top bar shows the selected color, and the bottom shows the adjusted color.
- The main Eyedropper tool lets you select a color from the image and shows its range in the color bars.
- The Add to Sample Eyedropper tool expands the area of sampled colors that are displayed in the color bars.
- The Subtract from Sample Eyedropper tool removes color information you do not want included in the range displayed in the color bars.

desaturate
To reduce saturated color information to make a color more realistic or muted to achieve a specific effect.

Colorizing with the Hue and Saturation Controls

Let's experiment with the Hue/Saturation dialog box controls to get an idea of how you can use them to give your images some exciting looks.

1. Open an image to work on. When Photoshop asks if you want to discard the color information, click OK. This changes the image to a grayscale image.

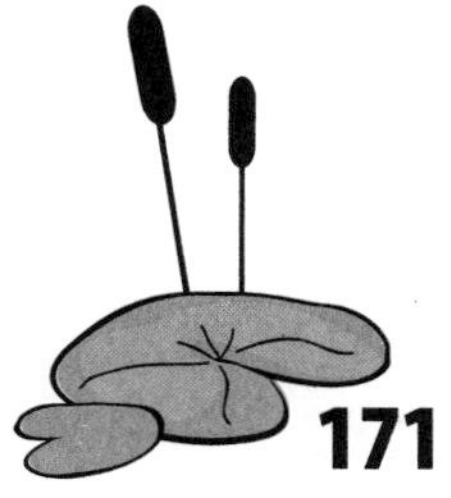

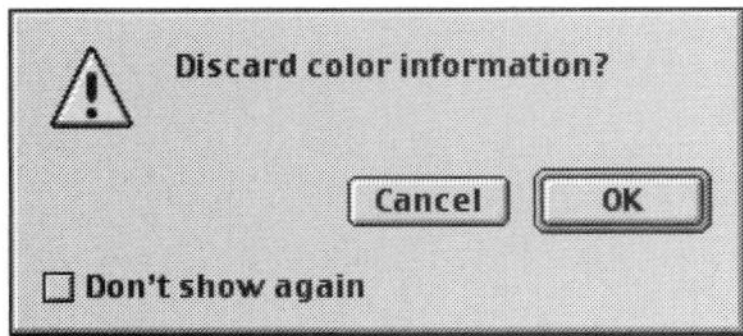

2. After your image opens on the screen, change it back into an RGB image by selecting Image ➢ Mode ➢ RGB Color.
3. Use the Lasso tool to outline an area that you want to modify.

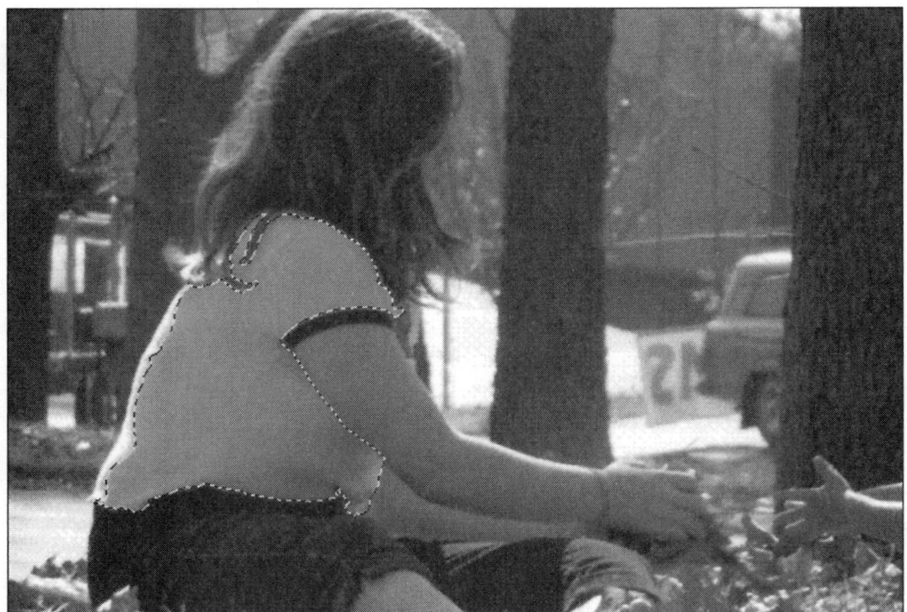

4. Select Image ➢ Adjust ➢ Hue/Saturation to open the Hue/Saturation dialog box.
5. Click the Colorize check box so that you can modify the color of the selected area.
6. Use the sliders or click in the text boxes and change the Hue setting to **63** and the Saturation setting to **50**. Leave the Lightness setting at 0. This will change the color of the selected area to yellow.

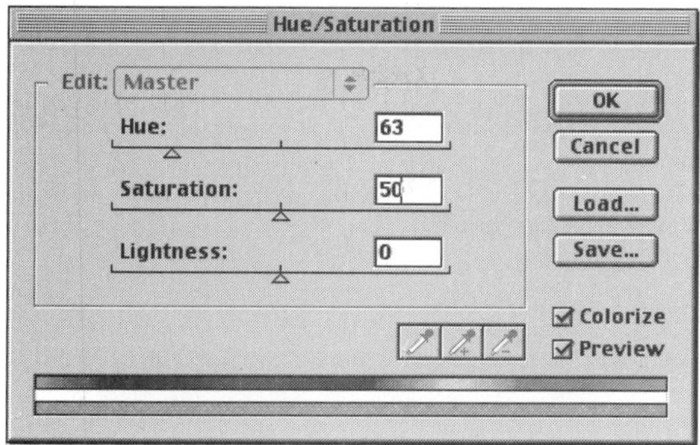

7. Click OK to close the Hue/Saturation dialog box.
8. Use the Lasso tool to select another area of the picture.
9. Select Image ➢ Adjust ➢ Hue/Saturation to open the Hue/Saturation dialog box again.
10. Set Hue to **234**, Saturation to **40**, and Lightness to **64**.

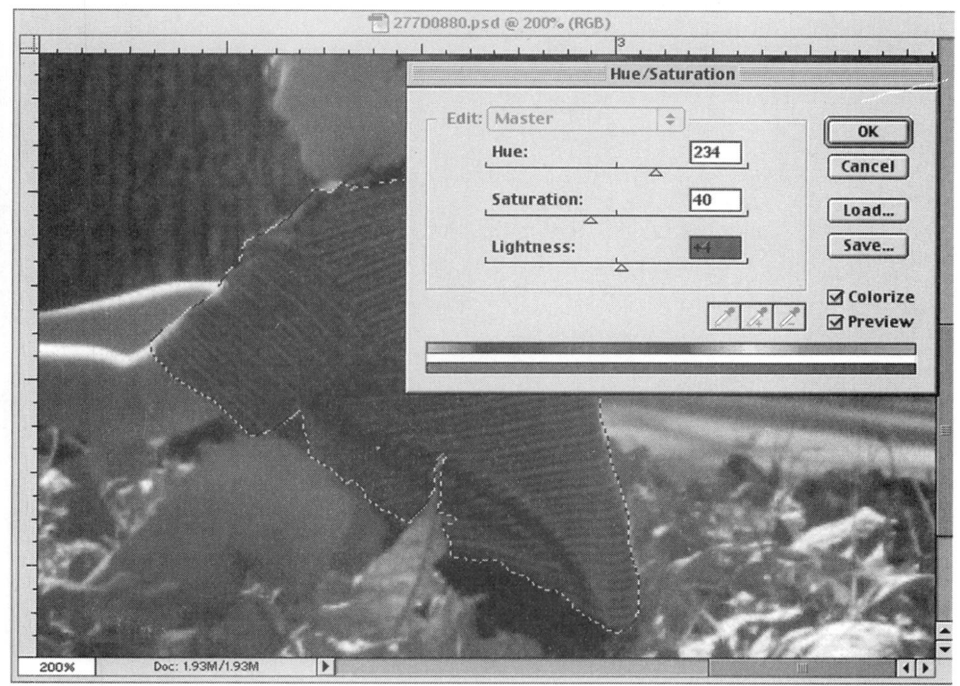

11. Click OK to close the Hue/Saturation dialog box.

Assigning Different Colors to an Area

You can also use the Hue/Saturation dialog box to assign different colors to an area. To do this, choose a section of your image, but select only a portion of it, creating some sort of pattern, such as flames.

Tip

Surround the subject and then use the Option (Alt) key to delete areas that don't need to be included in the colorization process.

Next, select a portion of the area you did not originally select and colorize that. Repeat the process until the flames (or whatever you're creating) are complete.

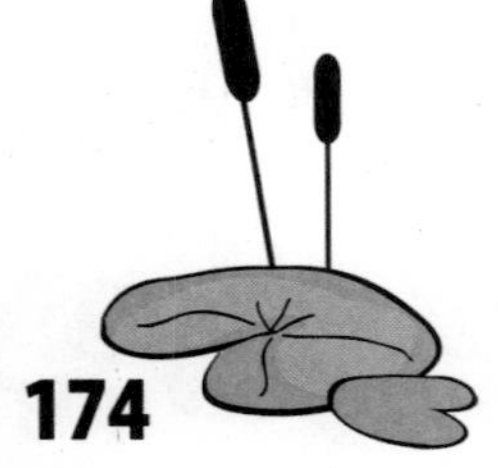

The finished image can look like those commercials for a popular sports drink, with certain areas colored while the rest is black and white. This technique can be used extremely effectively to create highly stylized black-and-white (grayscale) images. It can be used to draw attention to a specific area of a picture, for instance, to make eyes stand out.

Note

See the color section of this book for an example of a colorized image.

Changing the Image Size

You may need to change the size of an image for several reasons. One reason to make an image smaller is to create a thumbnail of the image for a Web page link to the larger version. Another reason is to turn a low-resolution image (72 dpi) into a high-resolution image fit for print (150 to 300 dpi).

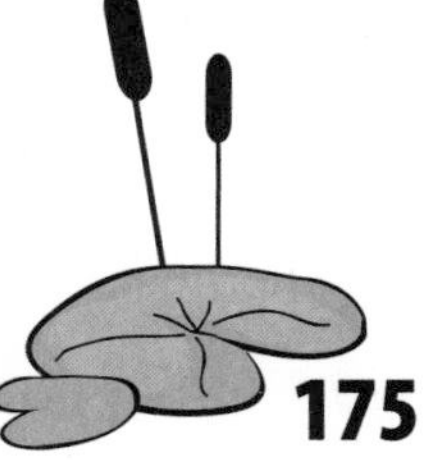

You can change image size through the Image Size dialog box, which is displayed when you select Image ➢ Image Size.

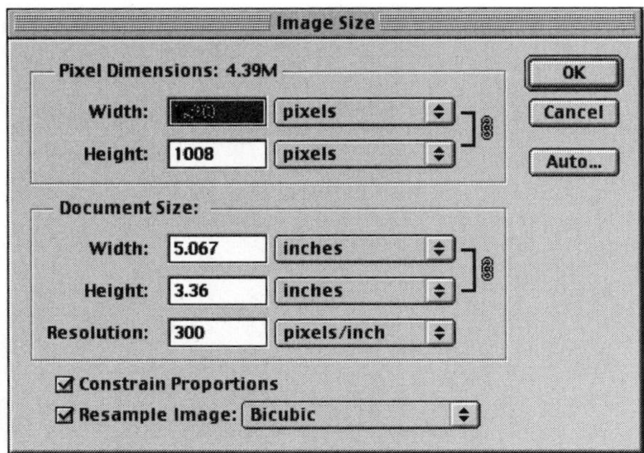

This dialog box gives you a lot of information about the size of your image:

- The Width and Height text boxes in the Pixel Dimensions section of the dialog box show numeric values for the width and height of your picture. The pop-up menu lets you choose between pixels and percent.
- The Width and Height text boxes in the Document Size section show the same information as those in the Pixel Dimensions section. However, the pop-up menu offers more selections: percent, inches, cm (centimeters), points, picas, and columns.
- The Resolution text box lets you set the **resolution** of an image in pixels per inch (ppi) or pixels per centimeters.

resolution

Refers to the number of pixels/dots per inch that make up the image. The more dots per inch, the higher the resolution and the larger the image file size. This is because there is more information stored in that file.

Creating an Image Thumbnail

Suppose that you have an image that you will use on a Web page. You want to create a link to it that shows the image, but in a smaller form. Usually, a 1-inch or 1.5-inch image width is a good size for a thumbnail. Here's how you can resize an image to create a thumbnail:

1. Open the image that you want to use for the thumbnail.
2. Select Image ➢ Image Size to open the Image Size dialog box.
3. Look at the Resolution field in the Document Size section of the dialog box. It should show 72 pixels/inch. Anything larger than that would

take a long time to download and would not improve the on-screen quality.

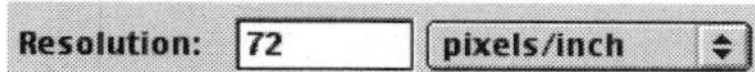

4. In the Width field in the Document Size section, enter **1.5** to change the width to 1.5 inches.

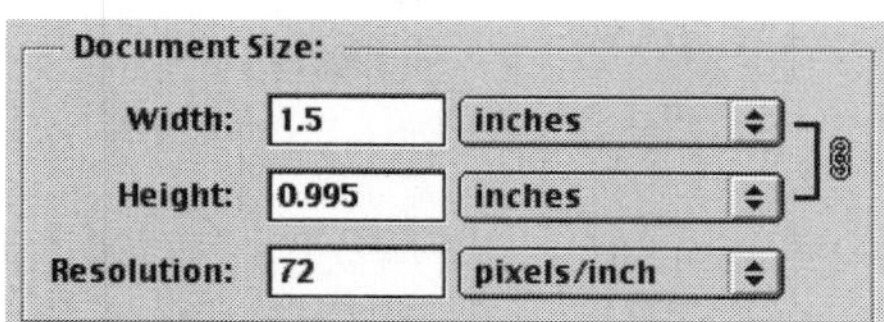

5. Notice the Height field value also changes to match the **aspect ratio** of the picture. This is because the Constrain Proportions check box at the bottom of the dialog box is selected. If you unchecked this option, you would need to mathematically determine the correct ratio for the other proportion.

aspect ratio
The height and width of the actual document. Changing the aspect ratio can make an image look too thin or too short.

☑ Constrain Proportions
☑ Resample Image: Bicubic

The image will be resized. Now you could save it in a format that is Web ready. We'll look at preparing images for Web applications in Chapters 9 and 10.

Tip

To make the thumbnail of an image easily identifiable, save it with a filename that includes the name of the original version and the word *Thumb*, as in *name*Thumb.

Making a Low-Resolution Image into a High-Resolution Image

You can easily change the resolution of an image from high to low without any loss of quality. It's more difficult to change a low-resolution image into an acceptable higher-resolution image, because fewer pixels are used to make up

a low-resolution image. A high-resolution image uses a pixel-blending technique that smoothes the edges of the content. When there are fewer pixels for Photoshop to work with (as with a low-resolution image), the program must guess (or interpolate) the colors for the new pixels. When Photoshop needs to do this, the results are not always pleasing.

Making a low-resolution image (say 72 dpi) into a high-resolution image (say 300 dpi) and retaining image quality takes some preparations.

downsample
Changing the resolution of an image, either from high to low resolution or vice versa.

1. When you scan your image into the computer, you need to do it at a higher pixel ratio. Scan the image in at a minimum of 1200 × 1200 pixels.
2. Select Image ➢ Image Size. You will see that you've created a very large 72 dpi (low-resolution) image. Because of this extremely large size, you can do what's called **downsampling**, creating a high-resolution image that is smaller without losing any quality.

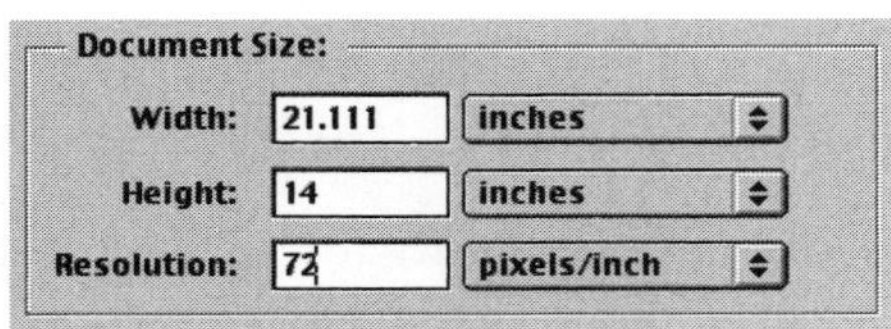

3. Deselect the Resample Image check box at the bottom of the Image Size dialog box.

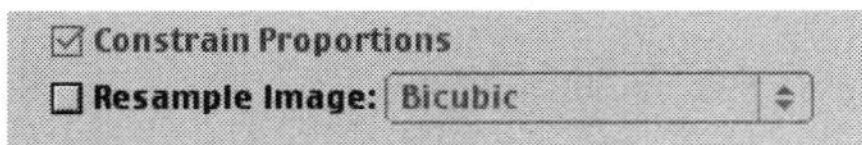

4. Change the Resolution to **300** dpi. Notice how the Width and Height ratios change to reflect the new resolution.

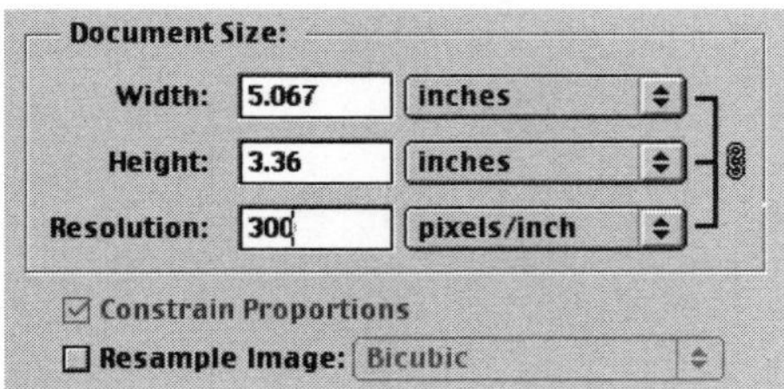

You now have a high-resolution image that can be used in any high-quality magazine, created using a low-resolution scan.

Moving On

You've learned some great tricks for modifying your images and creating some eye-catching graphics. Now you can look at some of the images in the color section with a more discerning eye, or look at images in magazines and have a better idea of how they were built.

In the next chapter, you'll get to use some of the skills that you've learned to design graphics that are suitable for the Web, as well as for other applications.

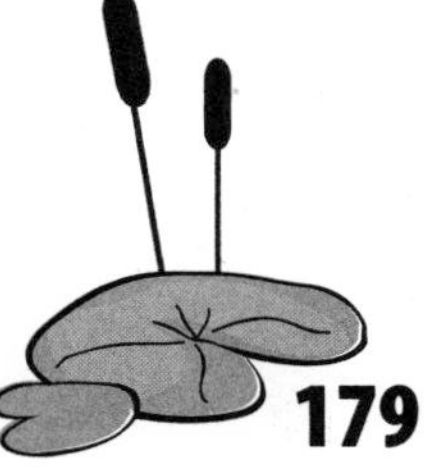

Part 3

Finishing Touches

If you want to create images for Web pages, you'll find plenty of help in Photoshop and ImageReady. Using Web-safe colors and effects that will make your images stand out on the Web page, you can design high-impact graphics in Photoshop. With a click of a button, you can move from Photoshop to ImageReady, where you can create Web-specific features like rollovers, image slices, and image maps. When your images are complete, you'll need to save them in the best format for how they will be viewed. Photoshop offers many file formats for on-screen and printed graphics.

Finishing Touches

Chapter 8

Designing Images for the Web

So far, you've learned a lot about the basic workings of Photoshop and are getting a good feel for what can be done. In this chapter, you'll learn how to apply the skills you learned to creating graphics that are appropriate for use on the Web. You'll work through several projects:

- A design for a rollover for a Web page
- A multilayered logo
- A montage of images

rollover
A button on a Web page that changes appearance when the on-screen cursor moves over it or it is clicked.

Designing Rollover Buttons

Rollovers are a staple of Web site design. Many Web sites use them in one form or another. Designing a rollover button entails creating at least two images, one slightly or totally different from the other. When these images are incorporated into a Web site and assigned the appropriate rollover information, one image is swapped out for the other when the user moves the cursor over it or clicks it.

Making the Base Button

For this example, you will create a Home rollover button that will look different when it has been selected. You will begin by opening a new document that is the size of the button that you want to create. Then you will assign a color and make layer copies of the document.

1. Select File ➢ New or press Ctrl+N (Cmd+N). In the New dialog box, select Inches from the Width and Height pop-up menus, and create a document that is 2 × 0.75 inches. In the Name field, type **RolloverButton**. Then click OK.

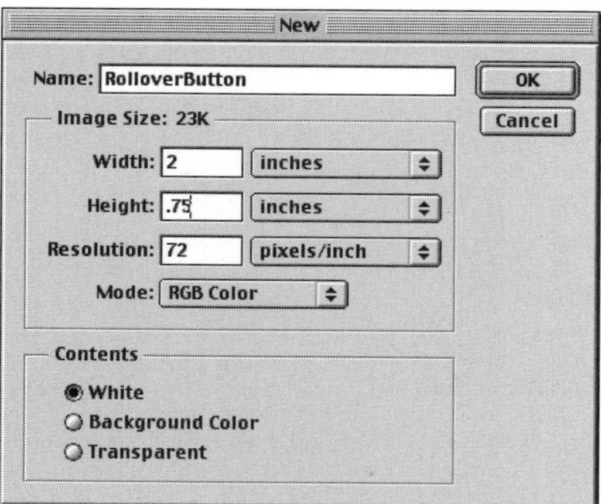

Note

The size of this rollover button is larger than what you would normally use for a Web page.

2. Select Window ➢ Show Swatches to open the Swatches palette. Open the palette's pop-up menu and select Web Safe Colors.aco. When the dialog box appears asking if you want to replace the old set with this new one, click OK.

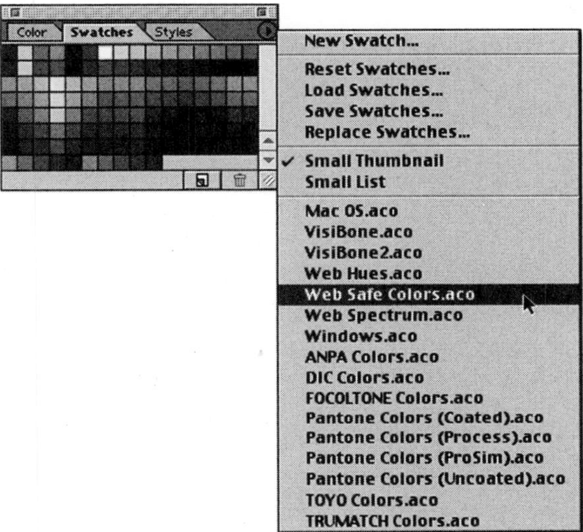

Tip

Use Web-safe colors when you are creating Web graphics such as buttons or background screens. These colors will look the same on any type of monitor.

3. Select a red color by clicking the appropriate swatch.

4. Select Edit ➢ Fill, select Foreground Color in the Fill dialog box's Use field, and click OK. The document fills with red.

5. In the Layers palette, drag the Background over the Create New Layer button to duplicate it.

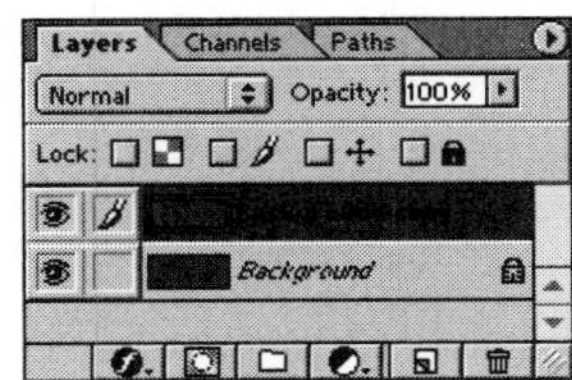

6. Delete the original Background.

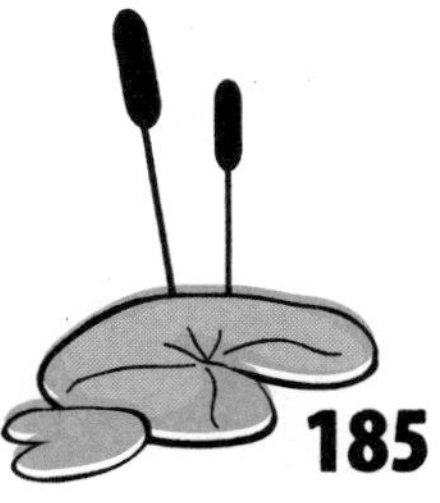

Note

As you learned in Chapter 3, the Background is locked, so numerous effects will not work on it. You can tell when a layer is locked by the lock icon that is displayed next to it in the Layers palette.

7. To rename the duplicated layer, select Layer Properties from the Layer palette's pop-up menu. In the dialog box, type a new name and click OK. A common convention is to name the base rollover image (the one first sent) **Main**.

Adding Button Effects

Now that you have a layer with the basic button size and color, you can add effects for the appearance of the button when it has not been selected, make another layer copy, and design the selected button's appearance.

1. Double-click the Main layer in the Layers palette to bring up the Layer Style dialog box. Select Bevel and Emboss in the Styles list. Change the Depth setting to **150** and click OK.

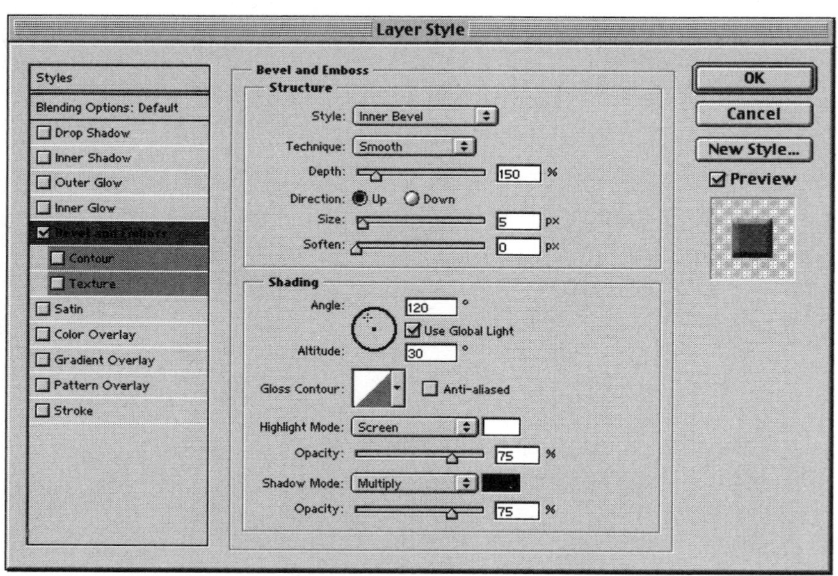

2. Duplicate this layer and rename it **Button_Down**.

3. Select Edit ➢ Transform ➢ Scale and reduce the size of this layer to fit inside the beveled area of the first layer. Click and drag the corners to resize the layer. Click twice anywhere inside the selection border to accept your size change.

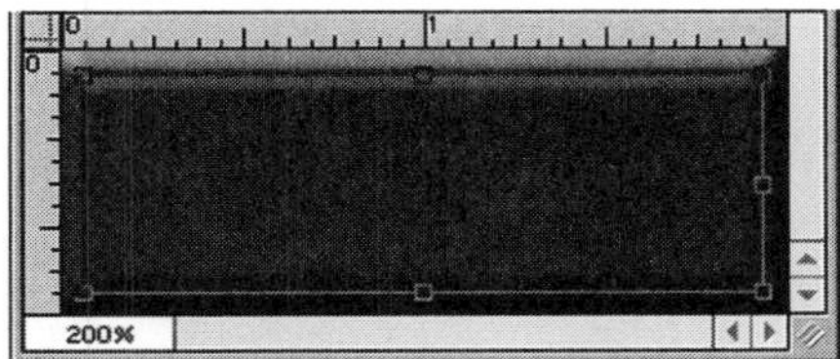

Tip

Zoom in on the image so it is easier to see what you are doing.

4. Double-click the Button_Down layer in the Layers palette. In the Layer Style dialog box, change the Bevel and Emboss settings as follows:

Depth: 200%

Direction: Down

Size: 4 px

Soften: 3 px

Angle: 130°

Altitude: 45°

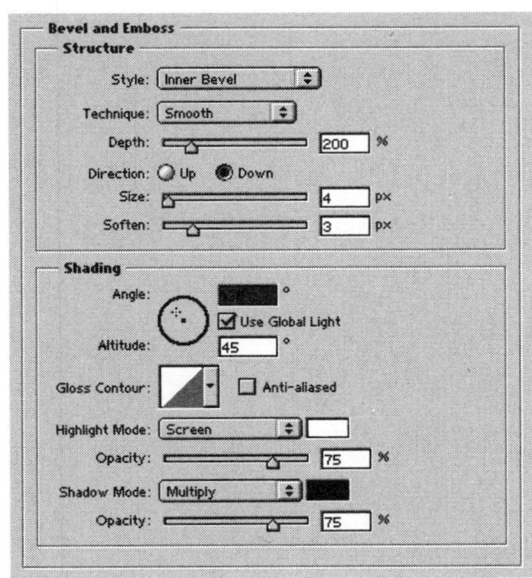

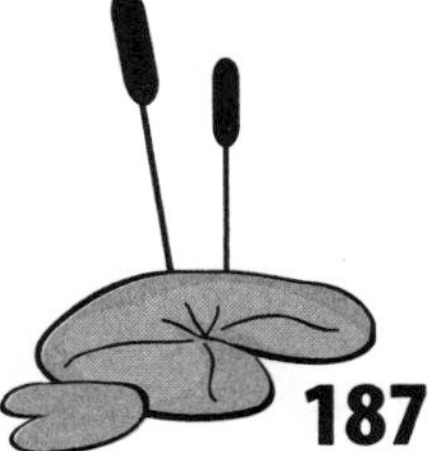

5. Click OK. The button now looks like it has an indentation, or as if that portion of the button has been pressed down.
6. Click the eye icon next to the Button_Down layer a couple times to turn it on and off. This will give you an idea of how your rollover will look when activated.

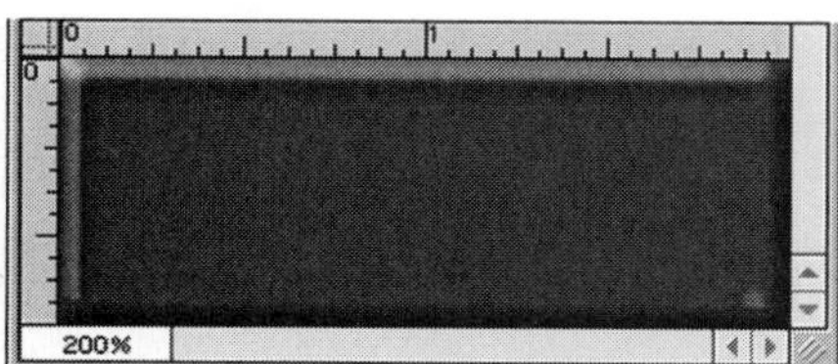

7. Now you can add some text to identify what this button will link to. Select the Type tool, choose any font you like (I used Impact), and type **Home**.

8. Scale the text so it's a tad wider, and then reposition it using the Move tool, so it sits more toward the bottom-right side of the indentation.

9. Duplicate the text layer, and then select Layer ➢ Rasterize ➢ Type to rasterize it.
10. Use the Eyedropper tool to select the interior color of the beveled background. Then select Edit ➢ Fill to change the color of the text layer.

11. Using the arrow keys on your keyboard, move the text up and to the left 3 pixels.

12. Select the first text layer and choose Filter ➢ Blur ➢ Gaussian Blur. Set Radius to **3** to create a drop shadow. Click OK when you're asked if you want to rasterize the layer.

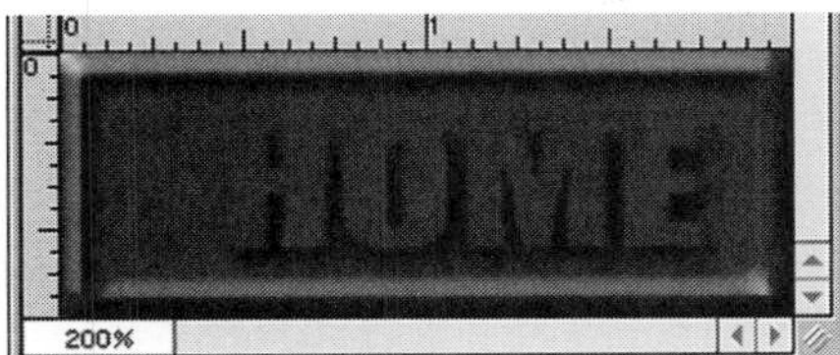

13. Keeping either of the text layers active, turn off the two other layers by clicking their eye icons. Then select Merge Visible from the Layer palette's pop-up menu to combine the text layers.

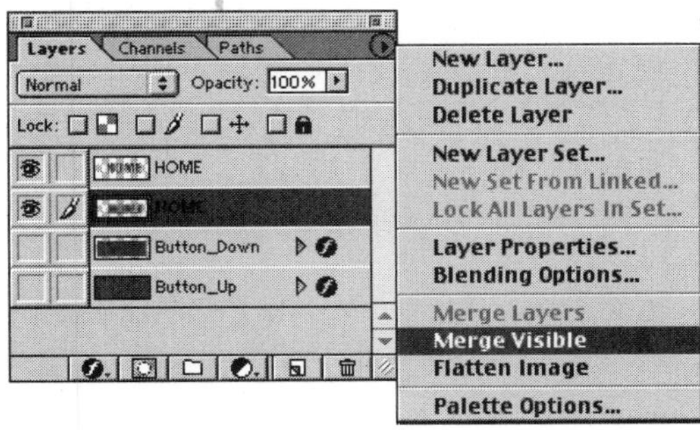

14. Reactivate the Button_Down layer. Reposition the text so that the red text is centered inside the button. Then select Merge Visible again to merge these two layers.

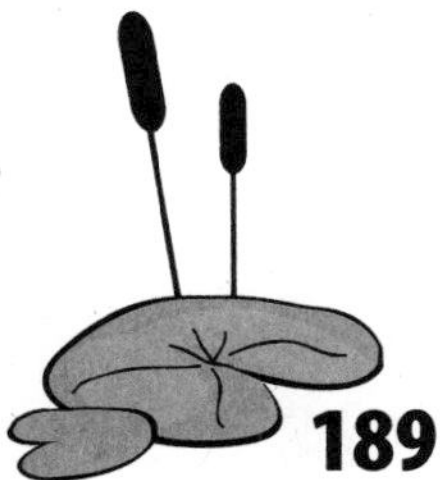

Tip

If you want to create more buttons using the same colors, do not merge the text and Button_Down layers. That way, you can create more text layers for your Web navigation buttons.

15. To see how the rollover button looks, activate the Main layer and turn the Button_Down layer on and off by clicking the layer's eye icon.

16. The rollover button design is finished. Select File ➢ Save or press Ctrl+S (Cmd+S). The file will be saved as a .psd file. This format retains all of the layer information.

You could also save each layer as a separate JPEG or GIF image, which can then be used as the Main and MouseOver images when brought into a program such as Adobe GoLive.

Note

For more information about how to use your Photoshop images in Web design, refer to *Mastering Adobe GoLive 4* and *Mastering Photoshop 6* (both published by Sybex).

Creating Logos

logo
An artistic or graphic representation of a name (such as a personal name or company name).

Logos are mainstay projects for many graphic designers and a great way to get started doing freelance work for friends and small businesses. (Yes, even your name can be turned into a logo.) Of course, logos often appear on Web pages.

Building a Company Logo

As an example, you will create a logo for a fictitious company called Rollicking Rollovers, Inc., which specializes in creating rollover buttons for Web sites.

1. Select File ➢ New or press Ctrl+N (Cmd+N). In the New dialog box, select Inches from the Width and Height pop-up menus, and create a document that is 4 × 2 inches. Then click OK.

2. If the Swatches palette isn't displayed, select Window ➢ Show Swatches to open it. Then select Web Safe Colors.aco from the palette's pop-up menu.
3. In the Layers palette, select New Layer from the palette's pop-up menu.
4. Select the Rectangular Marquee tool and draw a rectangle in the upper-left corner. Fill this with a bright color.

Note

When you're using the Rectangular Marquee tool in this manner to create filled shapes, make sure to turn off Preserve Transparency in the Fill dialog box.

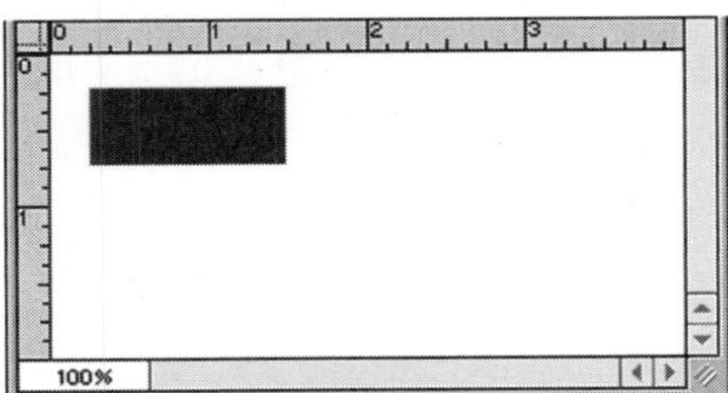

5. Use the Rectangular Marquee and Elliptical Marquee tool to create two more shapes on two more layers and position them so they overlap. Assign different Web-safe colors to these shapes.

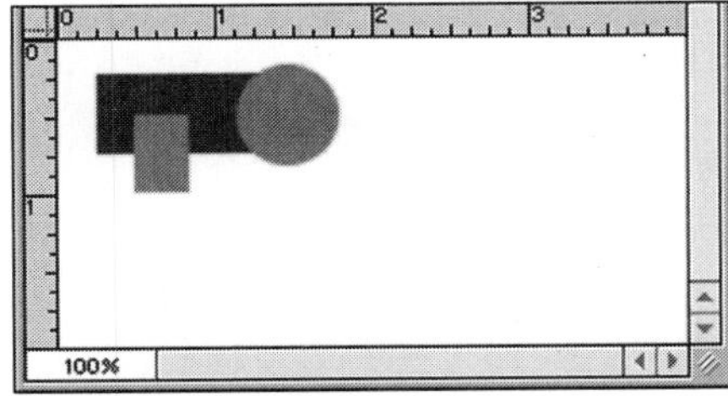

6. Select the Type tool and choose a font such as Helvetica or Arial. Type **ollovers**. No, that isn't a mistake. Do not add the *R* at this point.

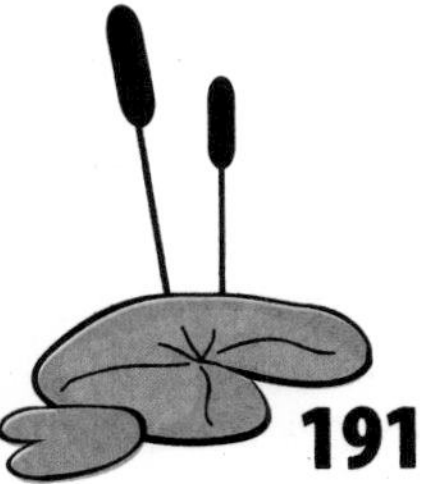

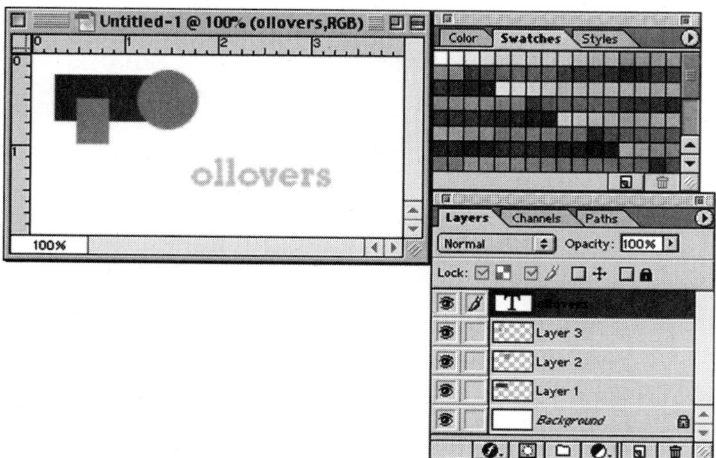

7. Create a new layer and type a capital **R**. Make this letter at least twice as large as the rest of the text (for example, 24 points if the rest of the text is 12 points).

8. Select Edit ➢ Transform ➢ Scale and expand the letter *R* manually until you are satisfied with its appearance.

9. Duplicate the layer with the *ollicking* text. Then click the Text Warp button on the options bar. Use the following settings in the Warp Text dialog box:

   Style: Twist

   Bend: –24%

   Horizontal Distortion: +34%

   Vertical Distortion: –56%

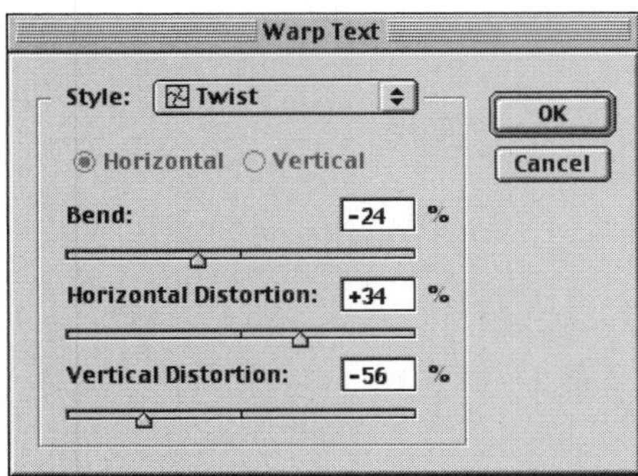

10. Double-click the layer with the warped text. In the Layer Style dialog box, select Pattern Overlay in the Styles list. Then select a pattern for your text.

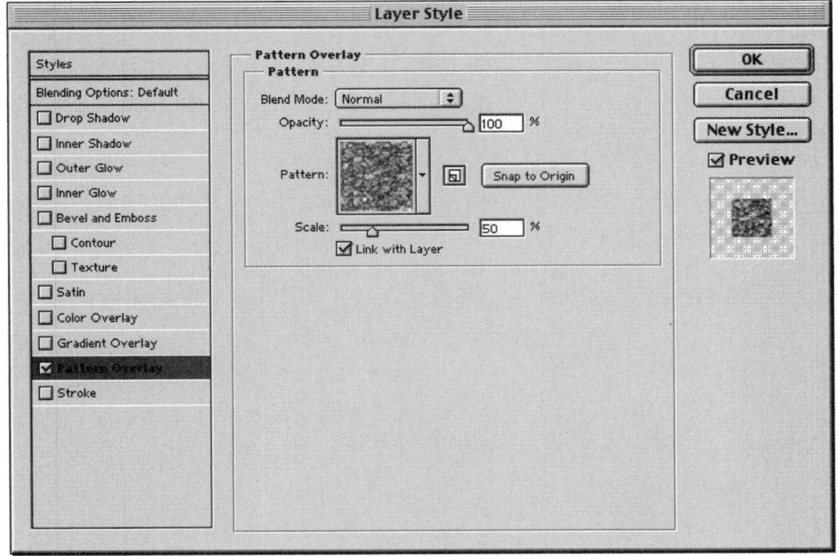

11. Select Bevel and Emboss in the Layer Style dialog box's Styles list. Experiment a bit with these settings to create your own interesting beveled look. For this example, I used the following settings:

Style: Inner Bevel

Technique: Smooth

Depth: 191%

Direction: Up

Size: 5 px

Soften: 1 px

Angle: 140°

Altitude: 45°

12. Duplicate the *R* layer. Double-click the new layer to open the Layer Style dialog box, select Bevel and Emboss, and choose Pillow Emboss from the Style pop-up menu.
13. In the Layers palette, click the Mode pop-up menu and select Dissolve.
14. Select Layer ➢ Layer Style ➢ Global Light. Set Angle to 130° and Altitude to 45°. This changes the look of the effect you assigned to the layer.

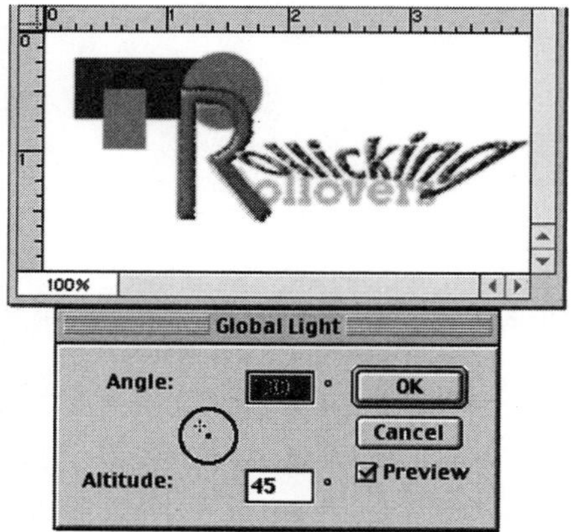

Creating the Logo Background

Now that you have designed the main logo elements, you're ready to create a background for it. You'll use some of Photoshop's filters to make the background interesting.

1. Activate the Background and duplicate it, and then click the eye icons for the other layers to hide them.
2. Click the foreground color swatch in the toolbox and select a deep-blue color.
3. Select Filter ➢ Render ➢ Clouds and click OK. This generates a random effect that looks like clouds.

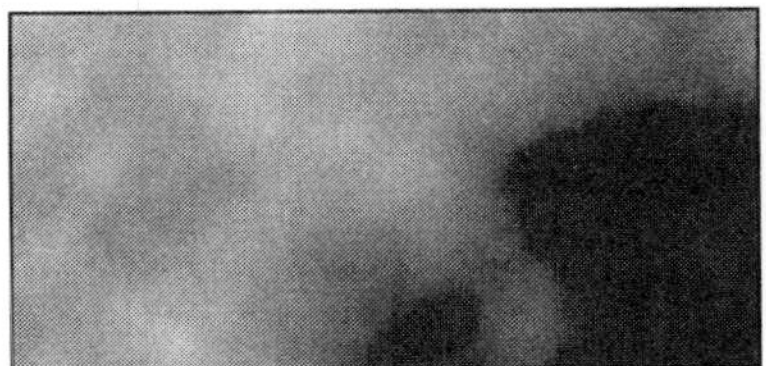

4. Select Filter ➢ Distort ➢ Twirl and change the Angle setting to 600°.

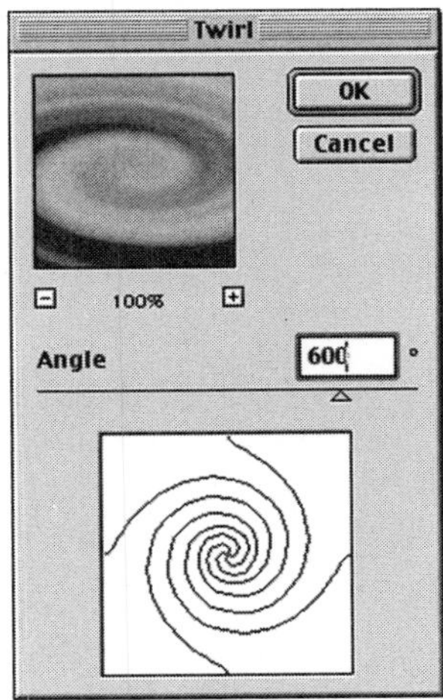

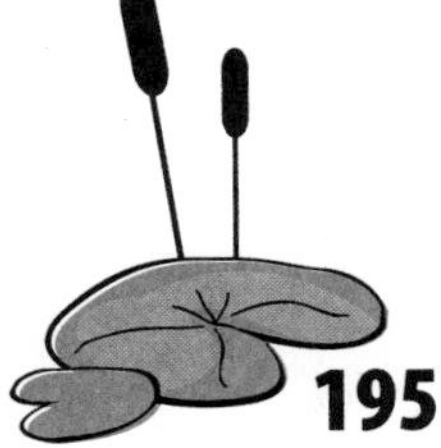

5. Select Filter ➢ Noise ➢ Add Noise. Set Amount to 12.5% and select the Monochromatic check box.

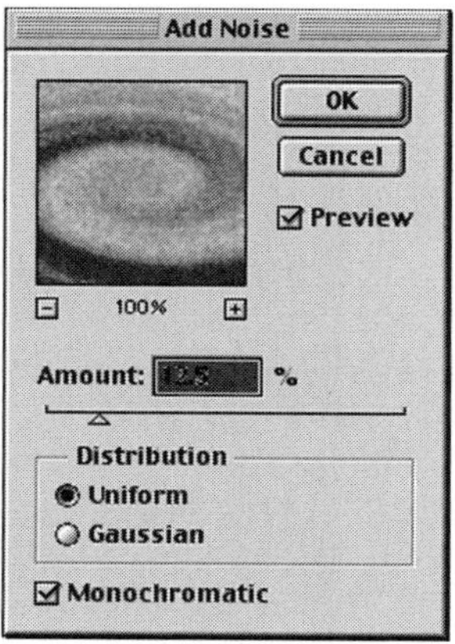

6. In the Layers palette, change the Opacity of this layer to 50%. Then make the other layers visible so you can see how your image looks so far.

7. Use the Elliptical Marquee to select an oval portion of the background, open the Actions palette (select Window ➢ Show Actions), click the vignette action (the one you created in Chapter 6), and then click the Play button.

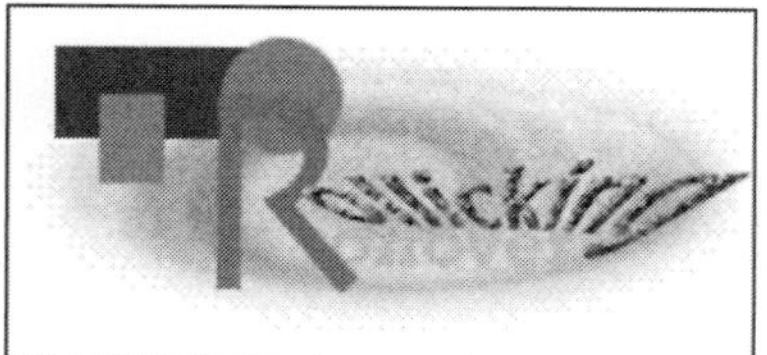

8. For the shapes you created earlier, use the Layer Style dialog box to assign different Bevel and Emboss effects to add interest to the shapes. For all of the elements, I used Inner Bevel and Smooth. For the horizontal rectangle, I left Direction set to Up. For the vertical rectangle, I

changed Direction to Down. And to create the globe-type look for the circle, I set Direction to Up and changed Size to 38 px, leaving Soften at 0.

9. Merge the three shape layers.
10. Use the Layer Style dialog box or select Layer ➢ Layer Style ➢ Drop Shadow to add a drop shadow to the *ollicking* layer. This will make it stand out from the background. Adjust the drop shadow's position and change the Opacity setting to 80%.

11. Move the shapes layer so that the circular portion is directly behind the *R*, and your logo is complete.

Creating Montages

Montages are fun projects, but you might want to build one for a more serious purpose, such as to use for a Web site's welcome page. It's probably safe to say that most of us experienced making montages for the first time during grade school. Instead of using paste and scissors, though, you'll use layers and various effects to build a montage in Photoshop.

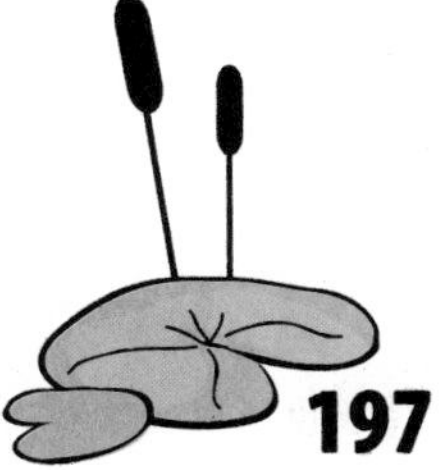

Building a Montage

For this example, you'll build a montage using portions of three different images. Find three images that you want to use, and let's get started. The first order of business is to decide how large you want your montage to be.

1. Choose your largest image and open it. Now here comes a great trick. Create a new document and, with the New dialog box open, open the Window menu and highlight the name of the image whose dimensions you want to duplicate.

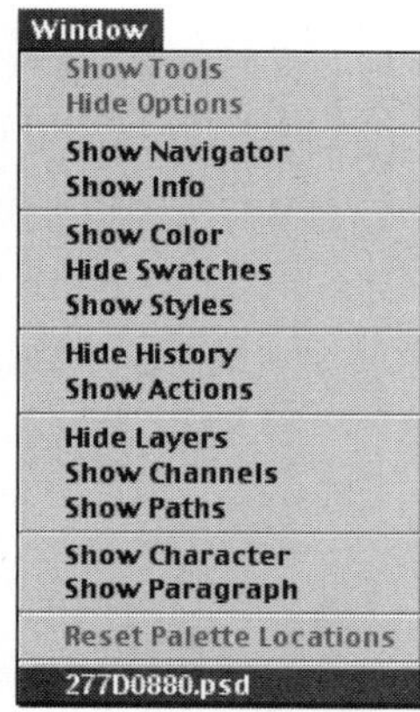

2. Use the Elliptical Marquee tool to select an area of the open image. Switch to the Move tool and drag your selection from there to the new document you just created. The selected area will be copied to the new file.

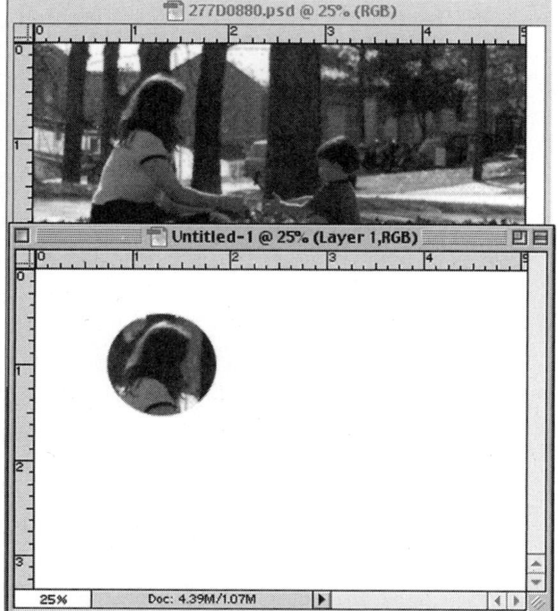

3. Select the Magic Wand tool and click outside this image to select everything except the image itself. Choose Select ➢ Modify ➢ Expand and expand your selection by **4** pixels.
4. Choose Select ➢ Feather and change the Feature Radius to **2**.
5. Press Delete from the document window to create the vignette.

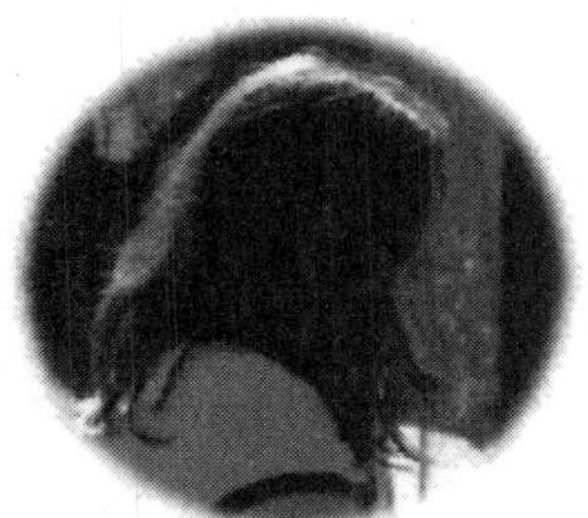

6. Choose Edit ➢ Transform ➢ Rotate and rotate your image on the layer. This will make your montage more interesting than having all of the different images set horizontally or vertically.

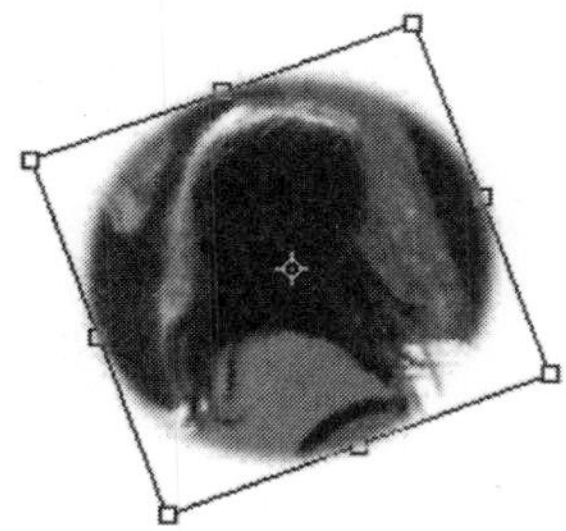

7. Switch back to your original picture by clicking the image's title bar to bring it to the front.
8. Select another portion of the original image. Repeat steps 4 through 6, and move this new vignette to another position on the workspace.

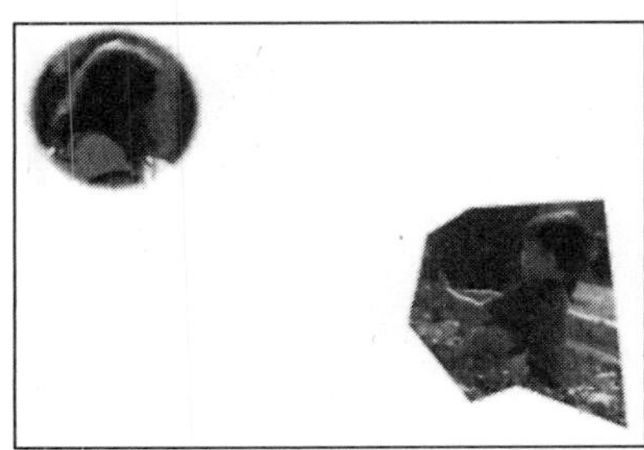

9. Use the Magic Wand to select the area outside the second image, but don't expand the selection this time. Choose Select ➢ Inverse to make the image the selection. Then choose Select ➢ Modify ➢ Border and create a 10-pixel border.

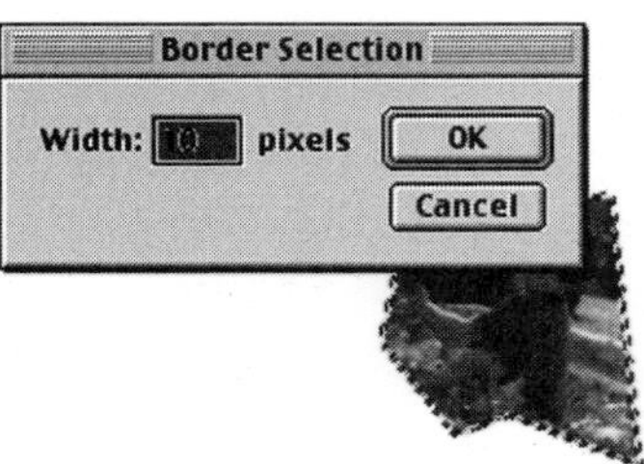

10. Select Edit ➢ Fill and fill this border with the color of your choice.

11. Repeat this process to select areas from the other two images you're using to add more layers to your montage. Make sure you create different sizes and shapes so the design isn't repetitive. As you place images, rearrange the layers by dragging the layer name above or below other layers to improve the layout.

Tip

Remember that you can create actions if you plan on duplicating effects on different layers. See Chapter 6 for details on recording and playing back actions.

Creating the Montage Background

Now that your images are in place, you can add some interest to the background. Let's use a Photoshop filter to make the photos look like they are placed on a sheet of paper.

1. Select the Background and choose Filter ➢ Sketch ➢ Note Paper. Use the sliders to set the appearance of the paper.

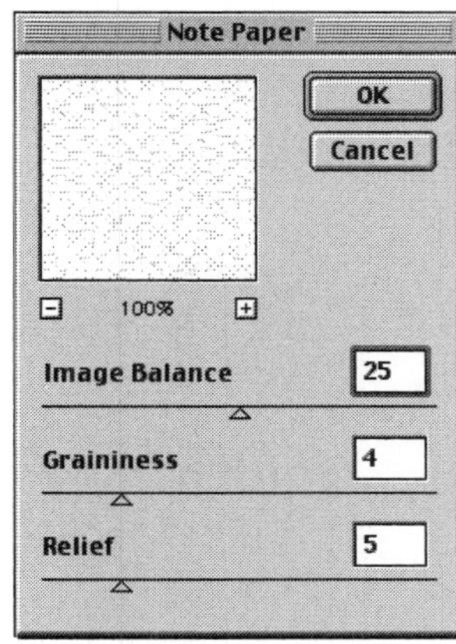

2. Merge the other layers and change their Opacity to 90% to give the impression that the images are pasted onto the page.

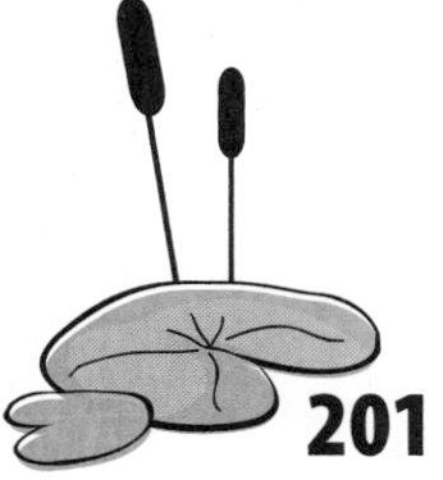

Moving On

In this chapter, you used some of the skills you learned in the other chapters, giving you the chance to see how what you've learned can be incorporated into realistic Web (and other) projects.

In the next chapter, you'll use the companion program that comes with Photoshop, ImageReady 3. You'll discover how you can build large format images and cut them up so they load quickly on your Web page and how to optimize your work for the Web.

Chapter 9

Using ImageReady

Along with Photoshop 6 comes a bonus program: ImageReady 3. ImageReady used to be a stand-alone application, but since Photoshop 5.5, it has been bundled as part of Photoshop's Web image arsenal. You can use ImageReady to optimize images for the Web, create slice files, produce image rollovers with links, and create animations. This chapter introduces you to the main ImageReady features:

- The ImageReady workspace and palettes
- Image optimization
- Image slices
- Rollover buttons with links

Introducing the ImageReady Workspace

ImageReady is so closely tied to Photoshop that you don't need to leave one program to access the other. Just click the Jump to ImageReady button at the bottom of the Photoshop toolbox, or press Ctrl+Shift+M (Cmd+Shift+M).

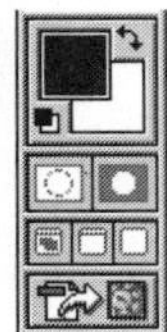

When you open ImageReady from Photoshop, the image you were working on in Photoshop is automatically opened.

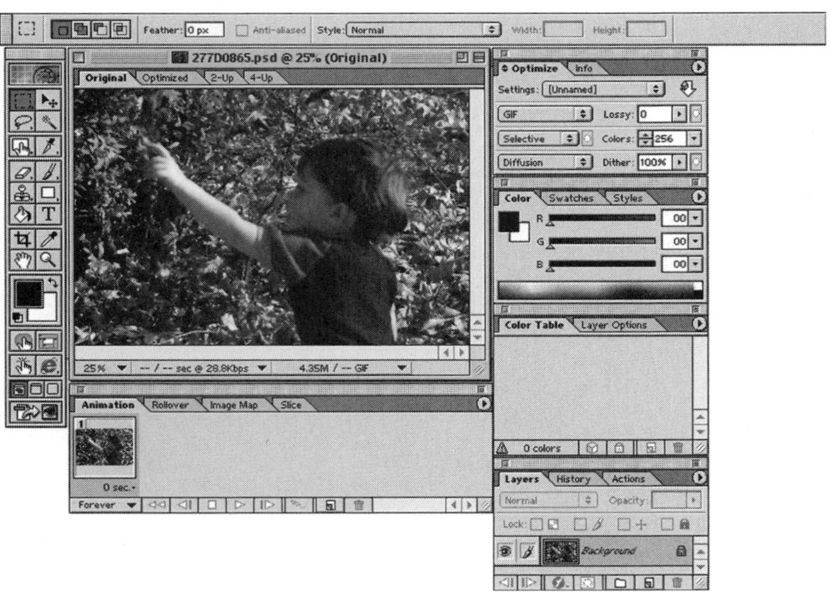

The first thing you'll notice is the difference between Photoshop's and Image-Ready's workspaces. The ImageReady window has four tabs across the top and an informational bar across the bottom. You'll also find that ImageReady has some different palettes than those in Photoshop.

Changing the View

Just above the image are four view tabs. These tabs let you view your image in—dare I say it—four different ways.

Click a tab to change the view displayed in ImageReady:

- The Original tab shows the image just the way it was imported.
- The Optimized tab shows the quality of the image based on the optimization settings you have assigned.
- The 2-Up tab shows a side-by-side comparison of the Original and Optimized views of the image.
- The 4-Up tab shows four different views of your image and different optimization settings and upload times.

Getting Information

In the 2-Up and 4-Up views, you can check the informational bar below the images to compare the size of the original file with the size of the optimized file.

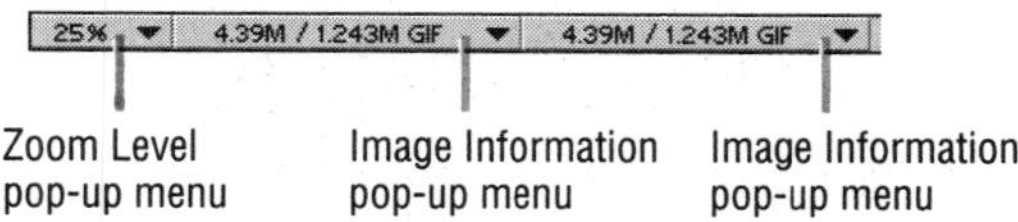

The Zoom Level display on the far left lets you set how much of the image you see. When an image is a higher-resolution file, you will need to zoom out farther to see the entire image.

Both of the Image Information displays (on the left and right sides) present the same information by default: The original file size in terms of space used on your disk and the file size based on the optimization settings you assign.

By clicking and holding down the mouse button on any of these pop-up menus, you can choose other view and informational options. For example,

you'll probably find it helpful to switch the Image Information display from showing original/optimized file sizes to showing the size/download time.

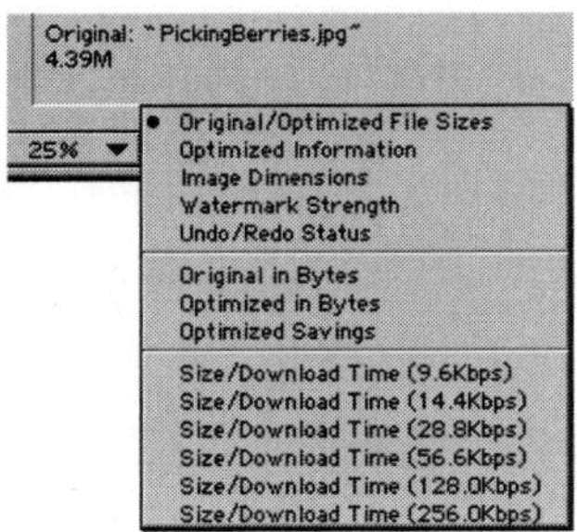

Working with the ImageReady Palettes

ImageReady's Optimize palette is where you assign optimization settings to your files. The settings on this palette control the image's file format and color treatment, as you'll learn in the next section.

Four other palettes that are dramatically different from Photoshop's are the Animation, Rollover, Image Map, and Slice palettes, which are grouped together.

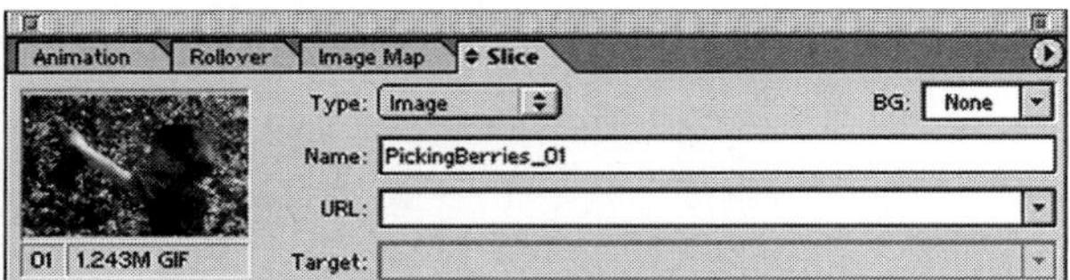

These palettes are used to add special effects for use on Web pages:

- The Animation palette gives you the ability to create animations, such as text moving into place or an image moving off the screen.
- The Rollover palette lets you assign rollover information to an entire image or a portion of the image.
- The Image Map palette gives you the ability to assign URLs to an image or a portion of an image. When Web page visitors click that portion of the graphic, it will take them to the assigned page or site.
- The Slice palette lets you assign a URL to a particular slice of an image.

Optimizing Images for the Web

After you import your file into ImageReady, via Photoshop or directly, the Optimize palette should be one of the first tools you use.

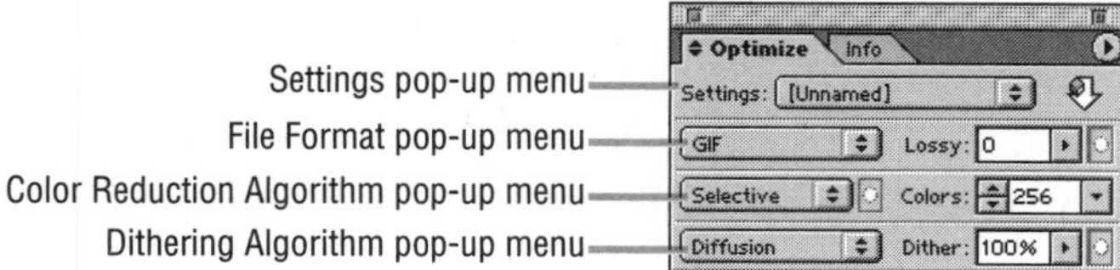

Introducing the Optimize Controls

The settings available on the Optimize palette depend on the file format you've selected. The Optimize palette for GIF files contains the following settings:

- The Settings pop-up menu lets you choose from a set of predefined settings.
- The File Format offers the GIF, JPEG, PNG-8, and PNG-24 file formats for your optimizations.
- The Lossy field applies to GIF images. The numeric value controls how much color information is lost when optimizing the files.
- The Color Reduction Algorithm pop-up menu lets you assign what type of color loss there will be by using different color modes (from system color palettes to Web-safe color palettes).
- The Colors field lets you choose how many colors will be allowed in the image, up to the maximum Web-safe amount of 256.
- The Dithering Algorithm pop-up menu assigns the type of color smoothing, or **dithering**, that will be used on the image.
- The Dither field controls the percentage of the dithering algorithm to be assigned to the image to alleviate **banding**.

dither
A method of distributing pixels to extend the visual range of color on the screen, such as producing the effect of shades of gray on a black-and-white display or more colors on an 8-bit color display. By making adjacent pixels different colors, dithering gives the illusion of a third color.

banding
A sharp differentiation between colors that makes them appear as if they were creating a separate band of color not associated with the ones surrounding it.

Changing the File Format

Now you'll see how the Optimize palette helps you pick the best format for your files.

1. Open a new file in ImageReady.
2. Choose Window ➢ Show Optimize to open the Optimize palette.
3. Click the 2-Up tab in the main ImageReady window to switch to that view.
4. Click the left Image Information pop-up menu and select Size/Download Time (56.6Kbps). Then select this display from the right Image Information pop-up menu. Notice how long it would take your image to download via a 56.6**Kbps** modem.

Kbps

Kilobauds per second, which is the measure for the amount of information that is transferred from the Internet to your computer via the modem. The maximum rate is based on the modem you use and the phone line itself.

Note

The average Internet connection speed is 33.6Kbps (kilobauds per second), with 56.6Kbps catching up quickly. High-speed connections such as ADSL and cable modems are still unavailable in too many areas to be widely used. So, it's best to check download times for 33.6Kbps and 56.6Kbps modems.

5. In the Optimize palette, click the File Format pop-up menu and select JPEG. The Optimize palette now has a Quality pop-up menu and text field for a numeric setting. Select Medium from the Quality pop-up

menu and change the value in the Quality field to 50. Now look at the download time; it should have decreased by a couple of seconds.

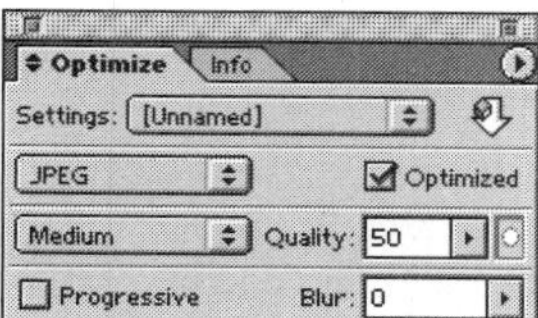

6. Click the File Format pop-up menu and select GIF. Set the Color Reduction Algorithm to Web. Set the Colors value to 256. From the Dithering Algorithm pop-up menu, select No Dither. Now check the download speeds for this optimization. It should increase slightly, but you'll notice the color transitions within the image have become rather harsh.

Note

To see all the available settings on the expanded palette, as shown in this example, select Show Options from the Optimize palette's pop-up menu (displayed by clicking the right-pointing arrow in the upper-right corner of the Optimize palette).

7. Change the Color Reduction Algorithm setting to Selective. This is a good setting for a photograph when saving it as a GIF file, because it creates a more natural blend between colors.

8. Change the File Format setting to PNG-24 (the highest quality PNG setting).

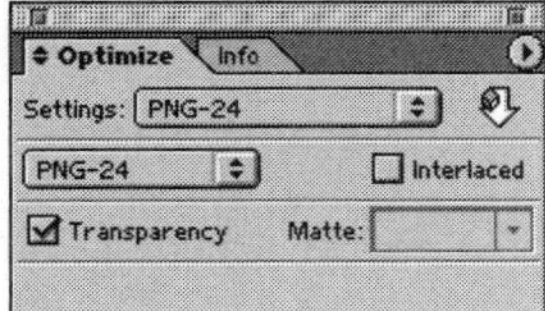

Tip

You should check the Image Information displays to compare file sizes and download times when using the JPEG, GIF, or PNG formats. These are important factors in determining which format to save in.

9. Notice how using the PNG-24 format affects your image. PNG creates an extremely crisp image that remains true to the original file.

You've seen that JPEG and PNG are the best formats for photographs because they reproduce the image much better. JPEG is currently pretty much the standard photographic image format for the Web. PNG actually produces better image quality, because it doesn't lose image information, but it isn't supported by as many browsers as JPEG is. This means that not as many people will be able to view images saved in the PNG format.

You should usually save line art and nonphotographic images in GIF format, because these files typically don't need a higher quality to reproduce correctly.

slice
A portion of an image. When using larger images for Web sites, designers often cut the image into different pieces (slices) to help speed up downloading times.

Creating Slices

What exactly is a **slice** and why would you want to slice an image? A sliced file is one that has been cut up into smaller images that, like a puzzle, make up the whole image when loaded in a Web page. When you're dealing with larger graphics, slicing a file into smaller elements helps speed up download time.

Now you'll create some slices to get an idea of how they work.

1. Open a large image file, either in Photoshop or directly in ImageReady. Make sure the file is 2.5 inches wide and/or tall or larger. If you opened the file in Photoshop, click the Jump to ImageReady button in the toolbox.

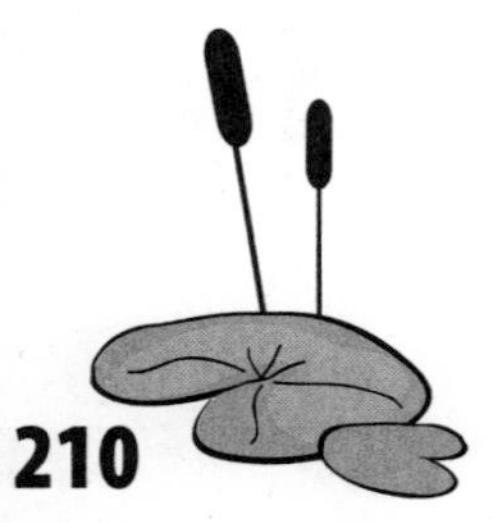

2. Select View ➢ Show Rulers to display the rulers. Then move your cursor over the horizontal and vertical rulers and drag into the image to create guides. The rulers and guides will help you cut your slices more accurately.

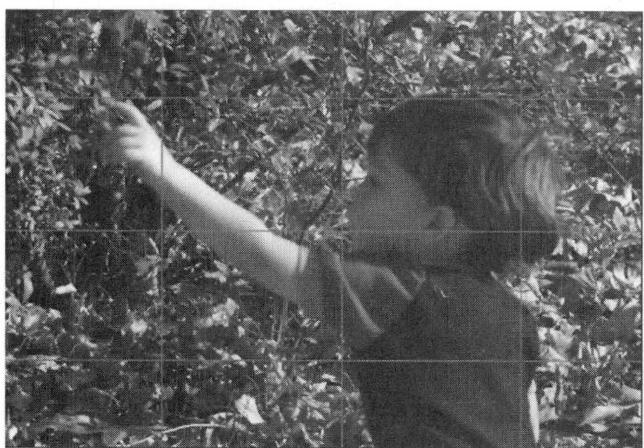

3. Select the Slice tool from ImageReady's toolbox.

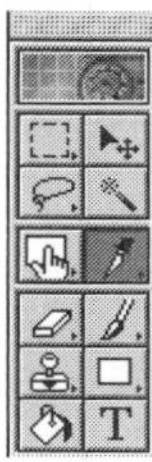

4. Click and drag the Slice tool from guide line to guide line to create different slices. Each slice will be assigned a number that is superimposed over the image.

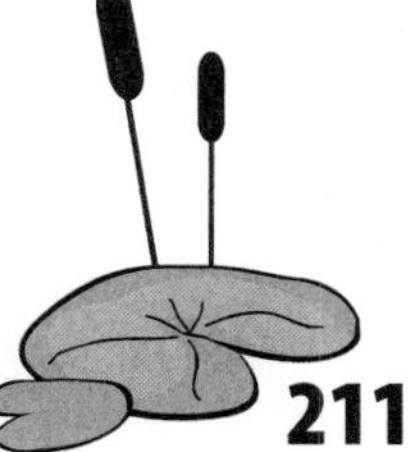

Note

If you don't see the slices and numbers, you need to activate slice visibility. Click the Toggle Slice Visibility button in the toolbox.

5. Click and hold down the mouse button on the Slice tool in the toolbox, and select Slice Select Tool in the pop-up list. Then click one of your slices to select it.

target
A destination for a URL link. A target can be a new, blank window that the page/window information will load into, the same page/window, or another portion of the same page.

6. Select Window ➢ Show Slice to open the Slice palette (or click the Slice tab if its palette group is already displayed). Here, you can give the slice a unique name, assign a URL, and specify a **target** for the link.

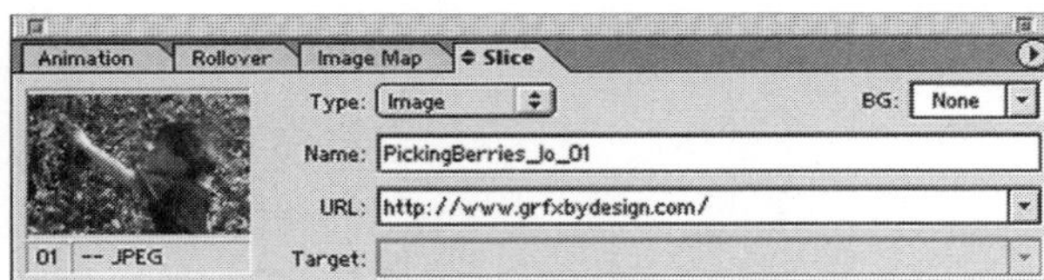

7. Type a URL in the second text field. The Target field becomes active, and you can use the pop-up menu to choose the target window:

   The _blank option opens a new, blank screen while leaving the original page open behind it.

   The _self option links to an assigned area on the same Web page.

   The _parent option makes the target the main link for all other links on your page.

   The _top option sends the viewer to the top of that Web page.

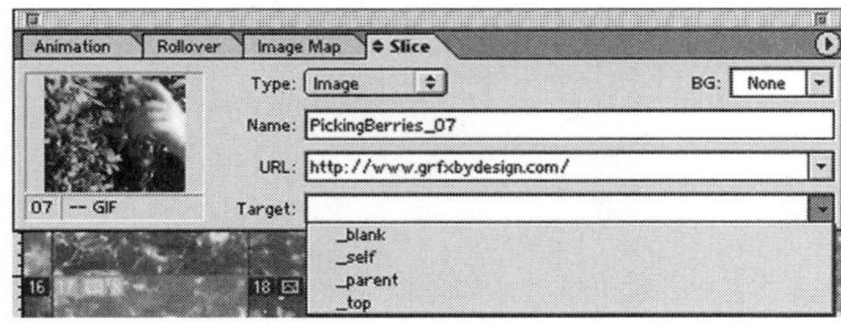

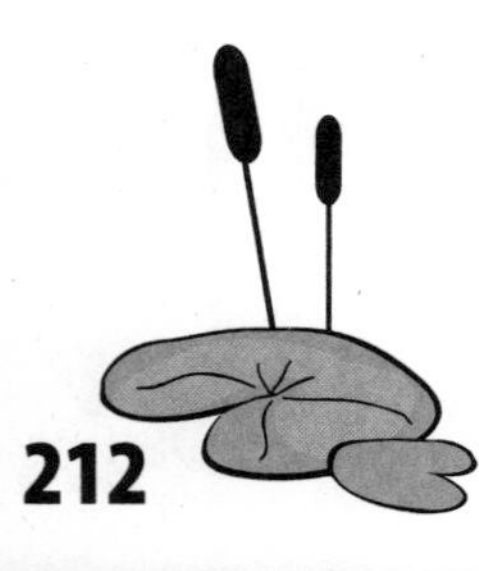

8. To return to Photoshop, click the Return to Photoshop button at the bottom of ImageReady's toolbox.

9. The slice information is transferred to Photoshop. Notice the guides superimposed on the image.

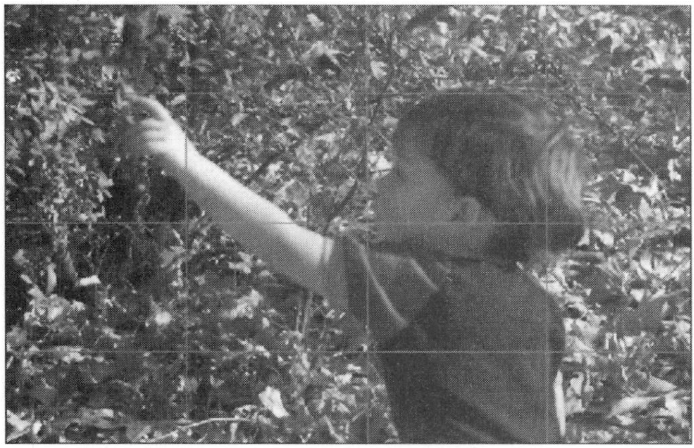

You'll learn how to work with an ImageReady file that has been imported into Photoshop in Chapter 10.

Building Rollover Buttons

As a practical example of working in ImageReady, you'll create a rollover button that includes text and a portion of an image. Rollover buttons can be any size, but they commonly are no more than 1 inch wide, so they don't take up a lot of room on a Web page. In this exercise, however, you'll make it larger, so that you can concentrate on building the button rather than magnifying it to see what you're doing.

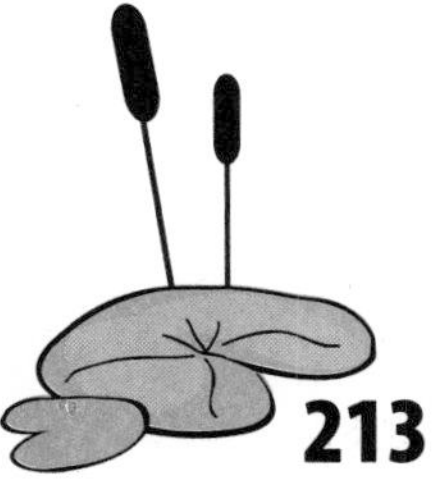

Note

Using ImageReady, you can turn portions of images into buttons and rollover buttons. This process is called creating an image map.

Creating the Button's Normal State

First, you'll create the base image for its normal state.

1. In ImageReady, select File ➢ New and create a document that is 340 × 240 pixels.
2. Select the Rounded Rectangle tool from the toolbox.

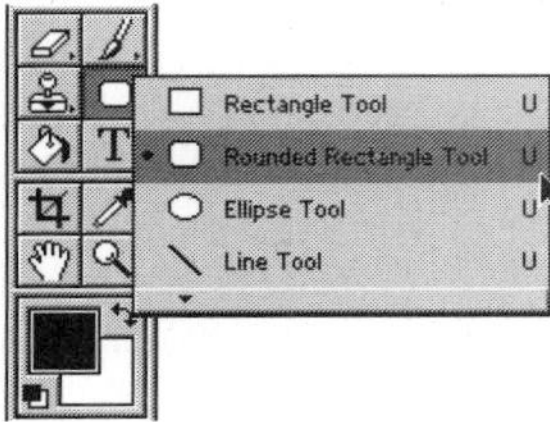

3. Make sure that black is selected as the foreground color, and draw a rectangle that fills most of the screen.
4. Change the foreground color to orange. Draw a second rectangle inside the first one.

5. Open Photoshop, and then load the PickingBerries.jpg file (which is available on this book's associated Web page).
6. Use the Lasso tool to surround the upper part of the boy in the picture, and then use the Polygonal Lasso tool to make a straight edge at the bottom of the selected area.

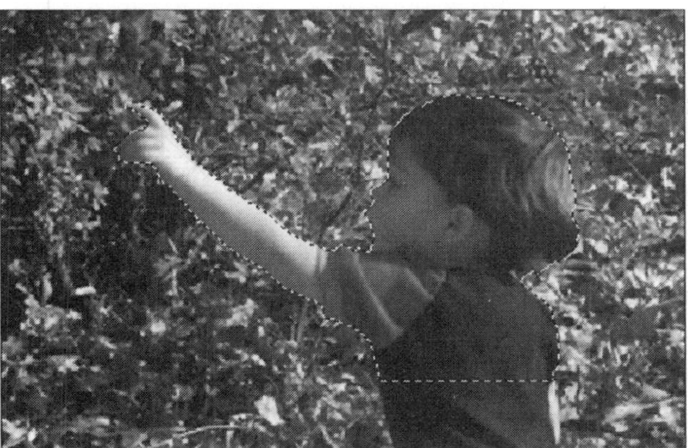

7. Press Ctrl+- (Cmd+-) to reduce the size of the image. Then arrange the windows until you can see both the Photoshop and ImageReady windows.
8. Select the Move tool and drag the boy onto the button window. Click the button window to bring ImageReady to the front. You'll notice the boy's image is too large for this button—there's not enough room to position him on the button and also add text.

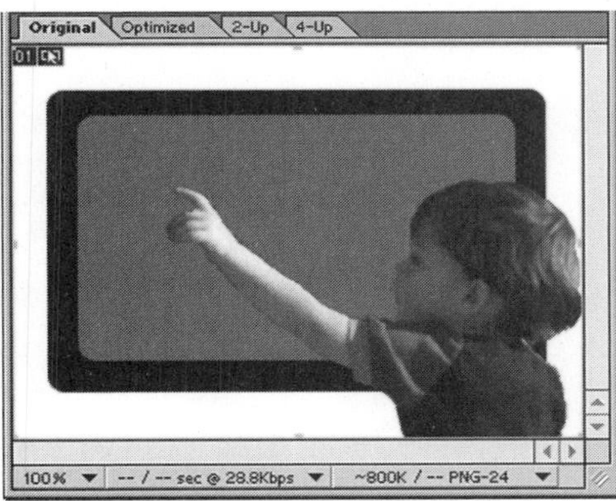

9. Move the boy into position so the bottom of his image is flush with the bottom edge of the black portion of the button.
10. Select Edit ➢ Transform ➢ Scale. Hold down the Shift key to constrain the image proportions, and scale the boy downward to fit nicely on the button.

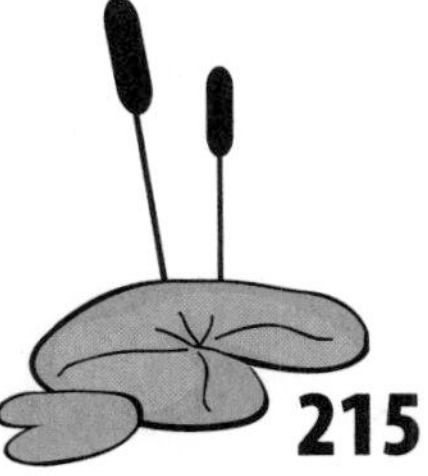

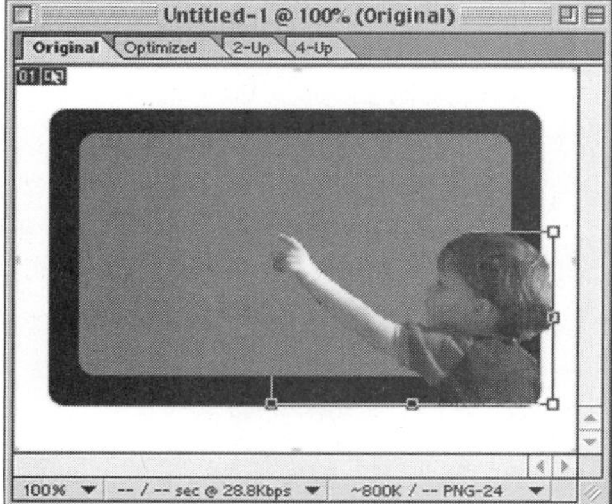

11. Select the Type tool and change the text color to black. Leave all of the other options at their default settings. Along the bottom edge of the orange interior, type **Pick Me**. Then choose Layer ➢ Rasterize ➢ Type.

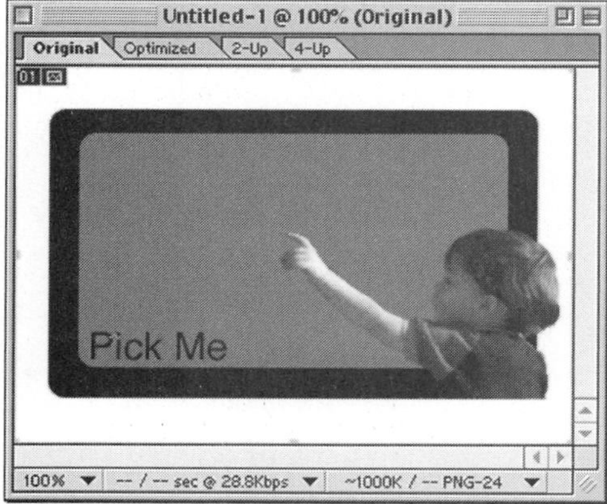

12. Save your file as **LargeButtonProject.psd**.

Creating the Button's Over State

Now that you have the base image completed, you need to build the over state. In this example, you will design the button so that when users move their cursor over the button, different text replaces *Pick Me*.

1. Open the Rollover, Layers, and Styles palettes (by selecting them from the Window menu).
2. Click the Create New Rollover State button at the bottom of the Rollover palette. ImageReady adds a copy of the button, ready for you to create the over state.

3. Click the Over image in the Rollover palette to activate it. Then select the Pick Me layer, activate the Move tool, and move *Pick Me* into the black border area until you can't see it.

4. To see what you have just done, select the Rollover Preview button in the ImageReady toolbox.

5. Move the cursor in and out of the workspace window. *Pick Me* should look as if it has vanished when the cursor is over the window.

6. To add the text that will appear in the button's over state, select the Type tool. Make sure that the same orange as you used for the interior rectangle is the selected color (it will be, unless you changed the foreground color swatch in the toolbox). Leave the default typeface and size, but select Centered for the alignment.

7. Before typing, select the layer representing the orange rectangle (it should be Layer 2), so that the text will be placed above the rectangle but beneath the image of the boy.

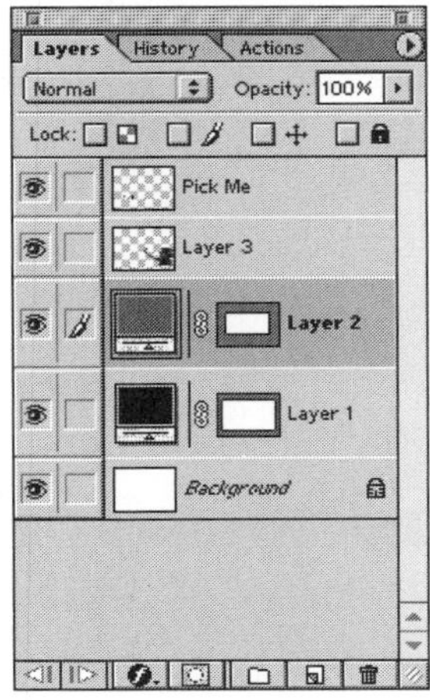

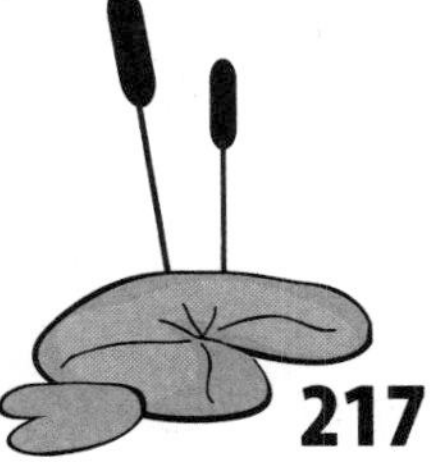

8. Click inside the orange rectangle and type **Photoshop Visual Jump-Start**. The text will appear to be invisible, because it blends perfectly with the rectangle, which is just what you want.

9. In the Styles palette, open the palette's pop-up menu and choose Text Effects. When prompted, choose Replace.

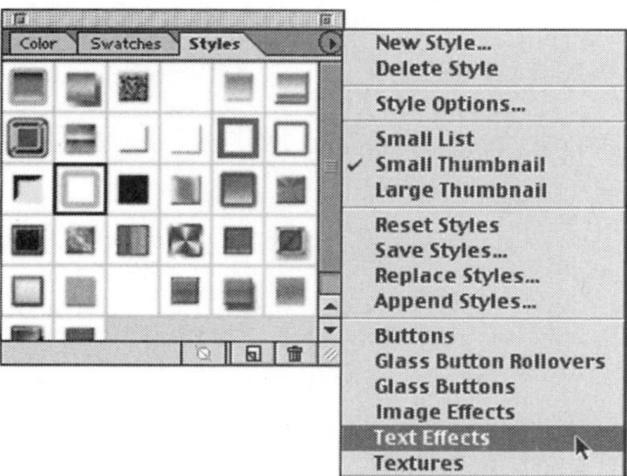

10. Click the Over image in the Rollover palette (but do not deselect the text). In the Styles palette, click the Frosted Glass style (third row, fourth from the left). You'll see the text pop out from the orange rectangle.

11. Select the Type tool and change the text size to 14 points. At the bottom of the orange rectangle, type **Click Here For Details**.

12. Select the Over image in the Rollover palette. In the Styles palette, choose the Clear Double Black Stroke style (third row, second from the left) for the text.

13. Click the Over image in the Rollover palette. From the Rollover palette's pop-up menu, select Copy Rollover State. Then select Create New Rollover State. ImageReady will name the new state Down. If you don't see the Over image duplicated for the Down image, open the pop-up menu and select Paste Rollover State.

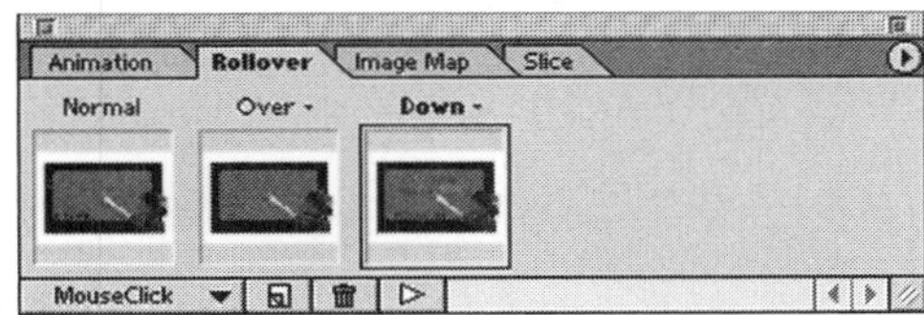

14. With the Down image selected, click the Slice tab at the top of the Rollover palette. In the Name field, change the name of the state to **MouseClick**. Type a URL in the URL field (be sure to include the **http://** in the URL). Then select _blank from the Target pop-up menu.

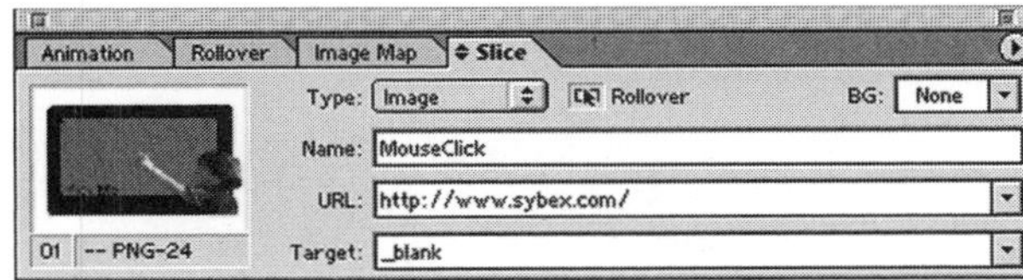

15. You can now preview the button to make sure the link works by clicking the Preview in Browser button in the toolbox. In the preview window, you'll also be able to see the HTML code that was generated as you built the rollover.

If everything works as it should, when you click the button you made, a new browser window will open, and you'll be taken to the URL you specified.

Moving On

This was a quick teaser of how ImageReady works. This program, like Photoshop, is very powerful. You'll want to review the *ImageReady 3.0 User Guide* to learn more about the intricacies of the program as you delve further into Web graphics preparation.

In the next chapter, you'll use what you have learned about ImageReady in combination with Photoshop to create Web-ready graphics. You'll also look at some of the other Photoshop features for sharing photographs.

Chapter 10

Saving Your Images

It may seem like a no-brainer—you tell the program to save your file and it's saved, right? Well, yes, that's correct in one sense.

You can just accept the defaults when you save a file and have it stored in Photoshop's native PSD file format. However, what if you want to use your image on a Web page? Then you need to decide the best format to use. Should it be JPEG, GIF, or PNG? If you are doing freelance professional work, you may need to save images in TIFF, PICT, or EPS format and pick a particular resolution.

This chapter covers the commands for saving images, as well as two very cool Photoshop features that automatically lay out your images for Web viewing or printing:

- The Save and Save As commands
- The Save for Web command
- The Web Photo Gallery feature
- The Picture Package feature

Using the Save and Save As Commands

At first glance, the Save and Save As commands might seem the same to you. Both save the files, but one gives you the ability to rename your file, change the folder it's stored in, and/or change its file format, without affecting the original.

Picking a File Format

When you save a file, you'll need to specify the format to save it in. The following are the most commonly used file formats:

Photoshop (.psd) The native Photoshop format. This format retains all layer information, including masks and paths.

JPEG (.jpg) The most common format for photographic Web graphics. Always save JPEG graphics at 72 dpi. This format is not suitable for print purposes because of its **lossy** nature.

GIF (.gif) The most common format for nonphotographic Web graphics. Although the GIF format is **lossless**, it can only hold 256 colors, so it is not suitable for photographic images.

lossy
A file-compression method that reduces the quality of the image when saved by removing information.

lossless
A file compression method that reduces the size of the file without any noticeable loss in image quality.

CMYK image
An image made up of cyan, magenta, yellow, and black. These four colors are combined to create all of the colors in an image. CMYK files are typically used in professional four-color printing.

Tip

GIF files can also be animated using GIF animation programs that can be found on the Web. Many of these programs are free.

PNG (.png) The newest of the photographic Web delivery formats. PNG files are much sharper than JPEG files and are lossless. The PNG format is becoming more popular on the Web, but it is still not used as often as JPEG, because older browsers do not support it.

EPS, TIFF, and PICT The formats most commonly used by professional printers. These files are saved at high resolutions (150 dpi or higher).

Photoshop DCS 1.0 and 2.0 A format that saves the file as a multipart document, including a full-color image as well as files for each of the colors. DCS format is used in conjunction with **CMYK** files.

Targa (.tga) An older format, which used to require a Targa video board installed in your computer. Some 3D programs, such as LightWave [6], require you to use this format for image maps on 3D models.

Saving Images with the Save Command

Although you've used the Save command throughout the exercises in this book (and probably for you own work as well), let's use it now and take a closer look at how it works.

1. Create a new file in Photoshop (at any size you prefer). Using the techniques you learned in the previous chapters, create some new layers and use the Marquee or Lasso tools to draw some designs. Alternatively, open an existing file and drag a portion of it onto the new image file. The main goal is to build a file with a few layers on it.
2. Select File ➢ Save or press Ctrl+S (Cmd+S) to open the Save As dialog box.

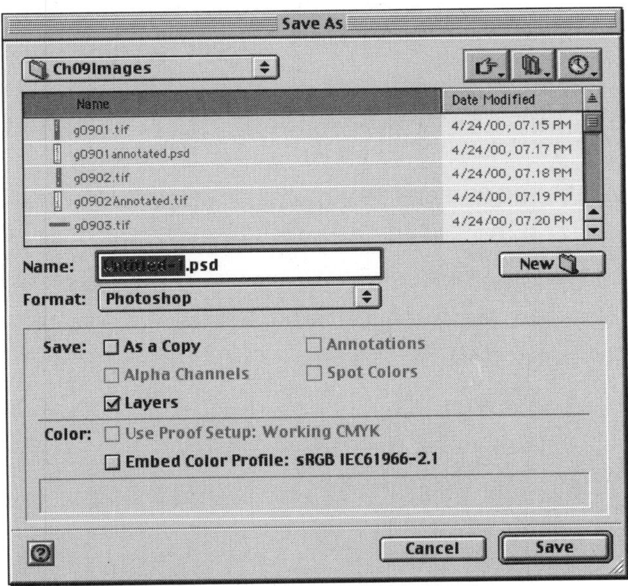

3. In the Folder pop-up menu at the top of the dialog box, navigate to the folder or area on your hard drive in which you want to save the file.
4. Enter a name for your file in the Name text box.

5. Click the Format pop-up menu to see all of your file format choices.

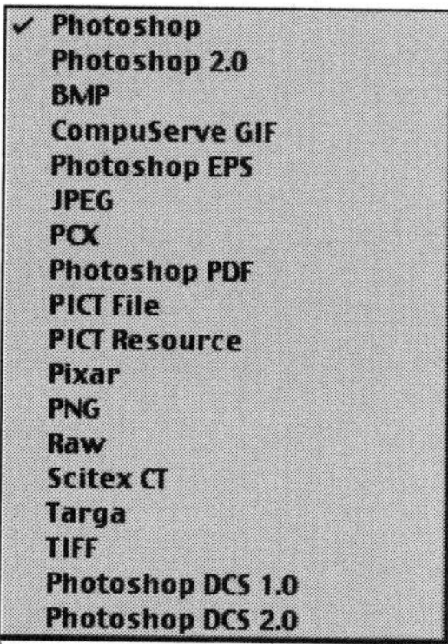

6. Leave the default Photoshop format or select any of the other formats from the Format pop-up menu. The extension—such as .psd, .jpg, .tif(f), or .pict—will be added to the image's filename automatically.

Note

In most cases, you should save at least one version of your image as a native Photoshop (.psd) file. This retains the layers, in case you want to modify them later.

7. Click the Save button to close the dialog box and save your image.

Once an image has been saved the first time, using the Save command to resave it (such as after you've reopened and modified it) saves the document with the same settings (location, name, format, and so on) as you set originally. You will not see the dialog box again. If you want to change any of the Save settings, use the Save As command, as described in the next section.

Changing Settings with the Save As Command

After you've saved a file, you can use Save As to assign a different file format, save the file under a different name, and/or choose a different storage location. For example, if you are working on a saved .psd file, you can use Save As to make a copy of the image in any other supported format.

To use Save As, open a previously saved file and select File ➢ Save As or press Shift+Ctrl+S (Shift+Cmd+S).

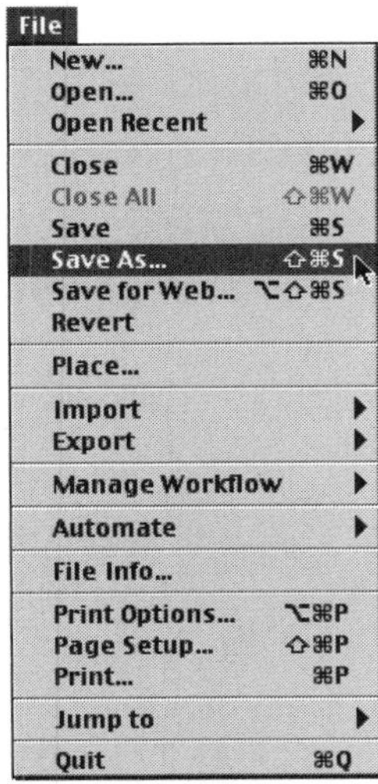

In the Save As dialog box, make any changes to the original settings. For example, you may want to save a copy as a JPEG (.jpg) file, because this format works well for most images that will be viewed on a computer. If the format change will have an effect on the file, Photoshop will display a message at the bottom of the dialog box. For example, when you change a file to JPEG format, you'll see the message "Some of the document's data will not be saved using the chosen format an options." This is because, as noted earlier, JPEG is a lossy format.

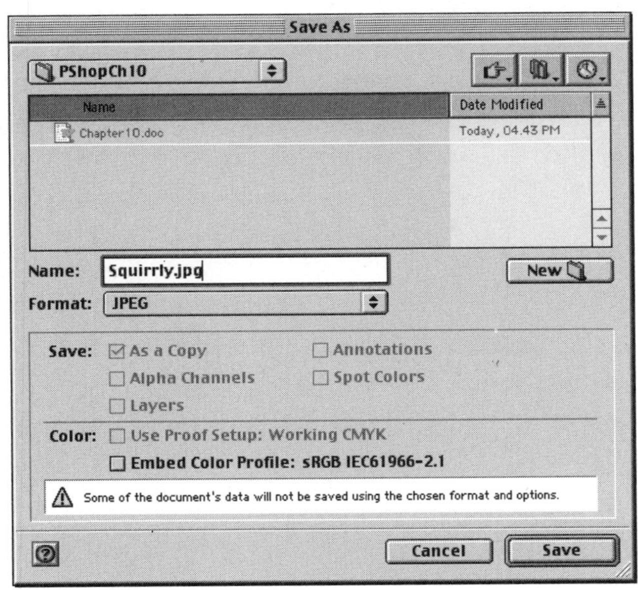

Using the Save for Web Command

If you are interested in using Photoshop to create images for your Web sites, you'll be using the Save for Web command a lot. This command not only lets you fine-tune all of the settings for images designed for the Web, but it also lets you save your settings for use with other images.

Introducing the Save for Web Controls

You can use the Save for Web command with any open file, because, when you're finished setting the Save for Web parameters, your file will be saved in the format you chose. Select File ➢ Save for Web to open the Save for Web dialog box.

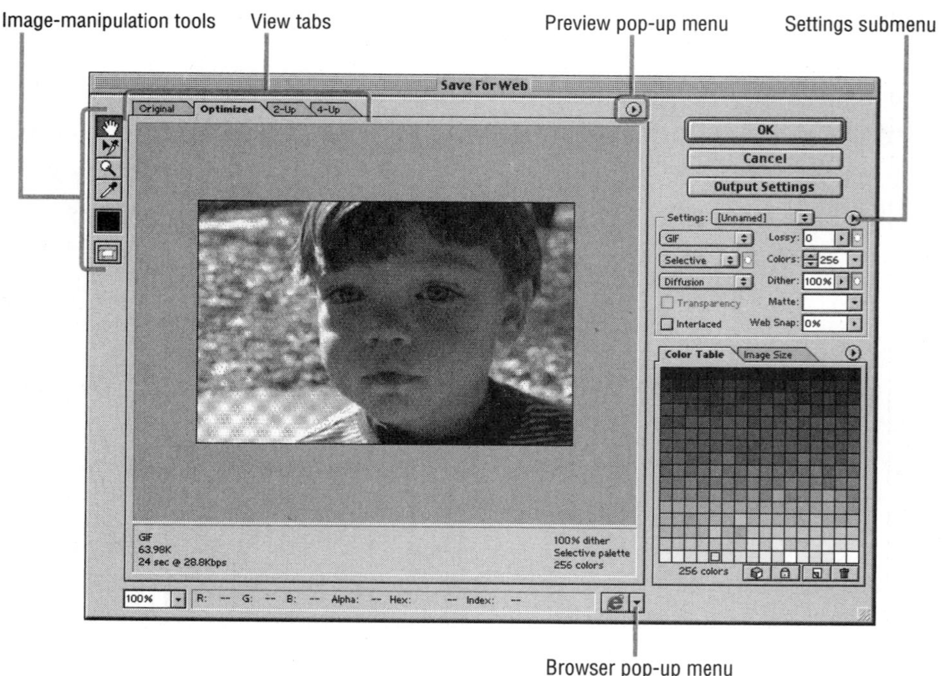

View Tabs

At the top of the dialog box, you'll see four tabs. The Original tab shows the current settings for the file. The Optimized tab shows the image with its optimizations.

When you click the 2-Up tab, you see two versions of your image. The one on the left shows the original file and its size. The one on the right shows the optimized file.

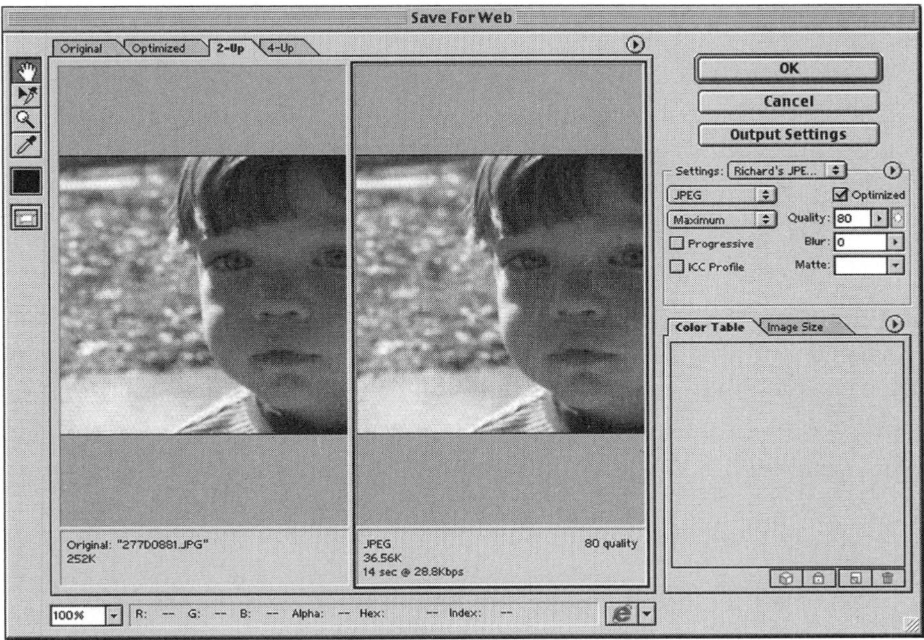

The 4-Up tab is probably the most useful of all of the Save or Web dialog box pages. It contains four image views, which each can be assigned an optimization setting. This allows you to compare the way the file will look and how quickly it will download with various optimizations.

Tip

Since the images in the 4-Up view are so small, you will rarely be able to see the entire picture. To reposition the image inside the window, select the Hand tool, place your cursor over the active image, and then click and drag it.

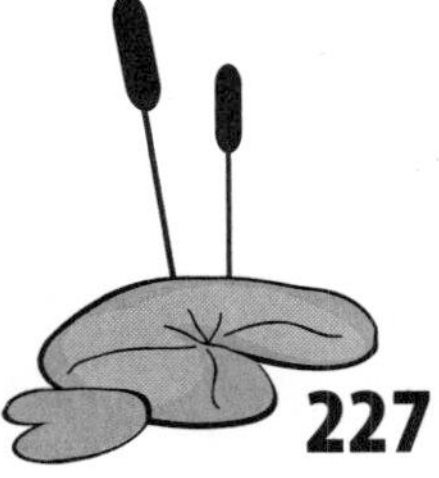

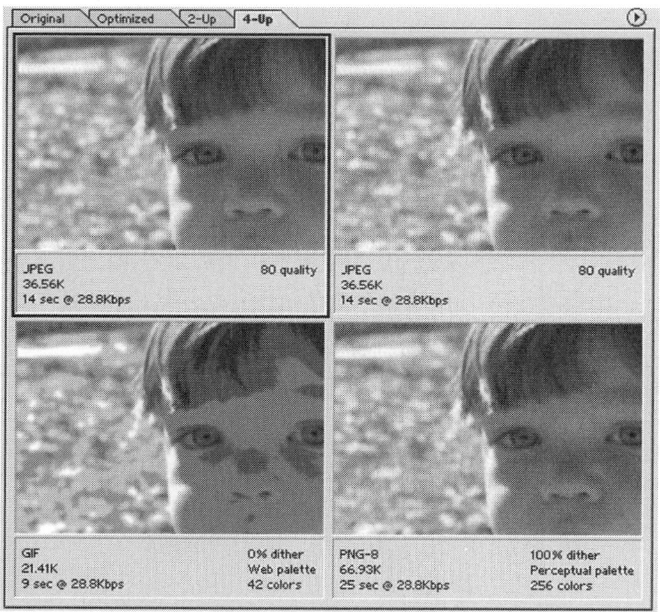

Under the images in the Optimized, 2-Up, and 4-Up tabs, you'll see some additional information based on the Save for Web settings. On the left side, you see the type of file format being used, the size (or modified size) of the file, and the image download speed based on the modem speed. The information on the right side includes the type of settings selected, the type of color palette selected, and the number of colors used in the optimized image.

The Settings Section

On the right side of the dialog box, the Settings section shows all of the current settings for the file. You can change any of these options. Clicking the circled arrow button immediately to the right of the Settings pop-up menu at the top of this section brings up the Settings submenu.

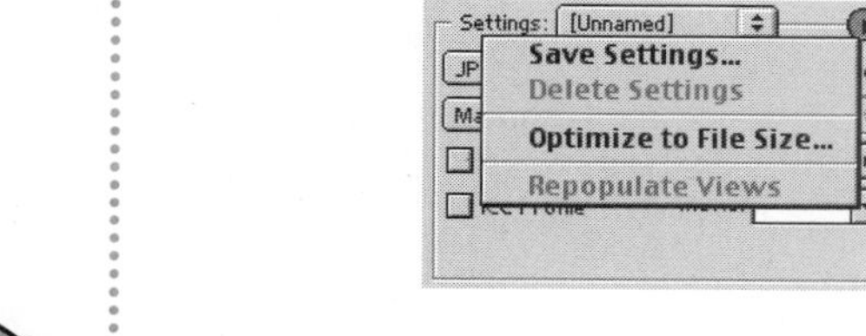

After you've adjusted the settings as you like, you can choose Save Settings to save them for reuse. The Delete Settings option becomes available after you've saved settings.

Choosing the Optimize to File Size option brings up a dialog box in which you can tell Photoshop that you want to limit the file to a maximum file size; for example, you might not want the file to be larger than 50KB. Enter that value in the Desired File Size text box. Then choose either Current Settings or Auto Select GIF/JPEG. Current Settings will use the settings assigned to the file and set the file size as close as it can. Auto Select GIF/JPEG will have Photoshop assign the best settings it can to meet your maximum file size, using the format that most closely matches that size.

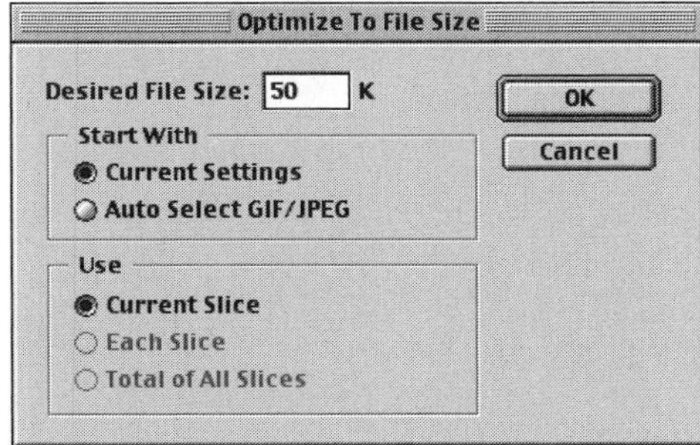

Note

The Each Slice and Total of All Slices options in the Optimize to File Size dialog box will be available only if you are using a file with slices assigned to it. See Chapter 9 for more information about slices.

Color, Size, and Browser Choices

On the lower-right section of the Save for Web dialog box, you see a palette with Color Table and Image Size tabs. Each tab has a pop-up menu associated with it. Color Table shows the available colors for your image's settings. (The Color Table tab will be empty if you are using a JPEG image.)

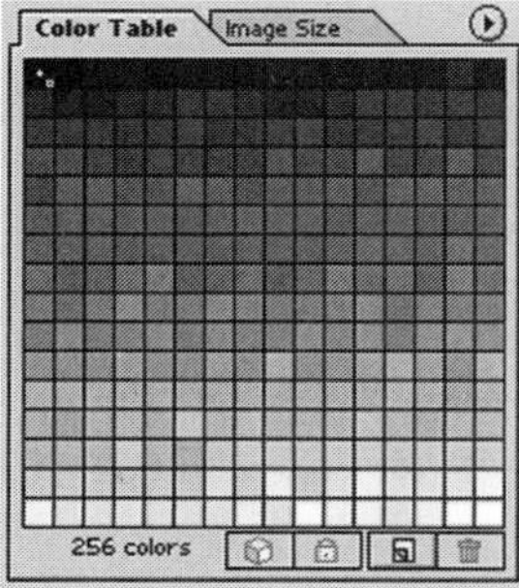

The Image Size tab shows size information for your image, such as its width and height. You can change these settings in the New Size section.

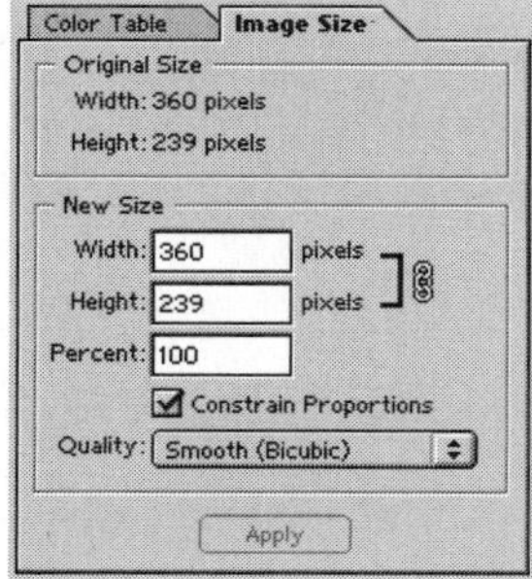

At the bottom of the Save for Web dialog box is the Browser pop-up menu. This allows you to select a Web browser, such as Netscape or Internet Explorer, to use to preview your images. Photoshop will launch the selected browser and open the image in the browser's window. You can pick any browser that is on your computer's hard drive.

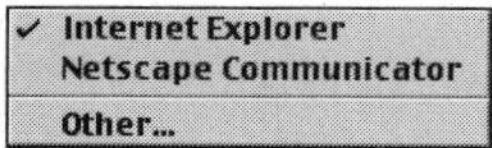

Image-Manipulation Tools

Along the top-left side of the Save for Web dialog box is a set of image-manipulation tools that you can use to work with the image shown in the dialog box.

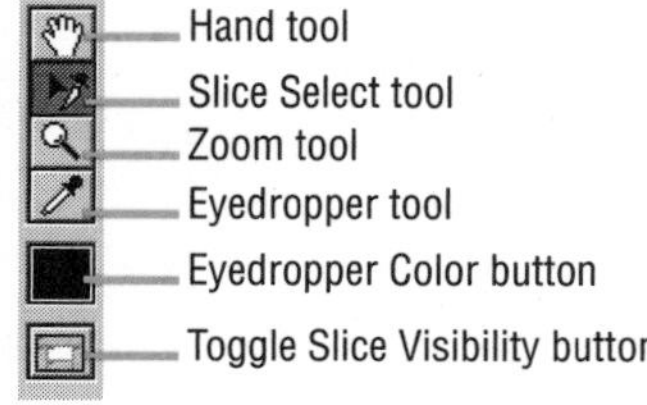

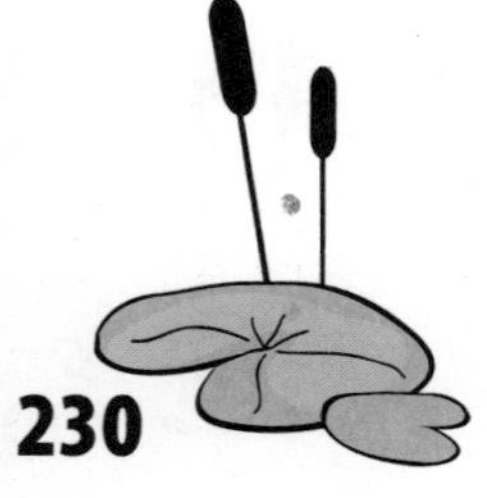

Hand tool Use this tool to move the image in the selected window into a more desirable position.

Slice Select tool If your image has slices assigned to it, this tool will select the slice you click. You can then assign optimization settings to that particular slice.

Zoom tool Use this tool to zoom in or out on an image. This affects all views. Press the Alt (Option) key while you click to zoom out.

Eyedropper tool This tool lets you select a particular color in the image and manipulate it via the Color Table palette.

Eyedropper Color button This color chip shows the color selected by the Eyedropper tool.

Toggle Slice Visibility button If slices are assigned to the image, clicking this button shows or hides the slices in the various view tabs.

Selecting Save for Web Settings

Now that you know about the parts of the Save for Web dialog box, let's see how you can use it to optimize an image for use on the Web.

1. Open an image in Photoshop and select File ➢ Save for Web.
2. If it isn't already chosen, click the Optimized tab at the top of the dialog box.
3. Click the Original tab and check the information below the image. Then click the Optimized tab and see how the file size compares with the original version.
4. Click the File Format pop-up menu in the Settings section on the right side of the dialog box and change from GIF (which is the default optimization setting) to JPEG.

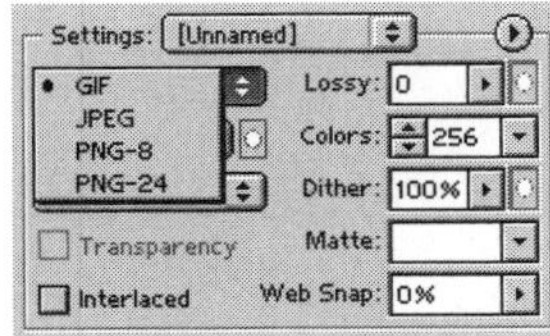

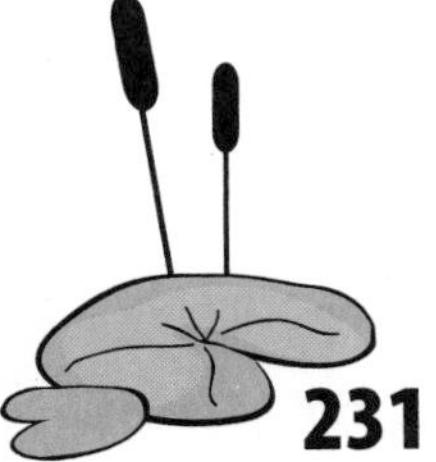

5. Notice that you now have an assigned setting in the Settings pop-up menu. Normally, when the file format is JPEG, the assigned setting will be JPEG High. You can use this pop-up menu to select other JPEG optimization settings. For now, leave JPEG High.

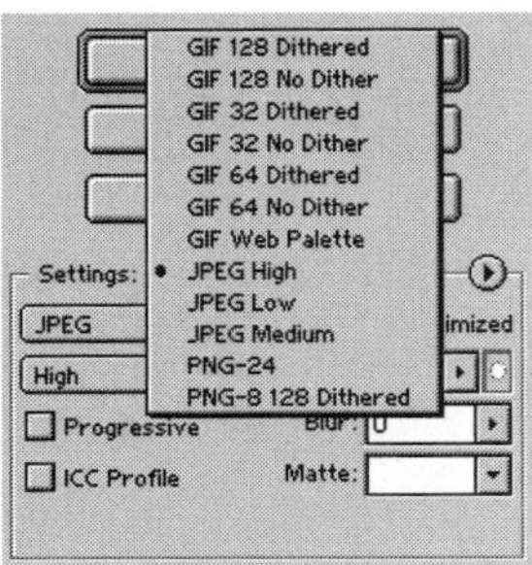

6. Change the Quality setting from 60 to 80. Notice that the setting in the Quality pop-up menu (immediately to the left of the Quality field) automatically changed to Maximum.

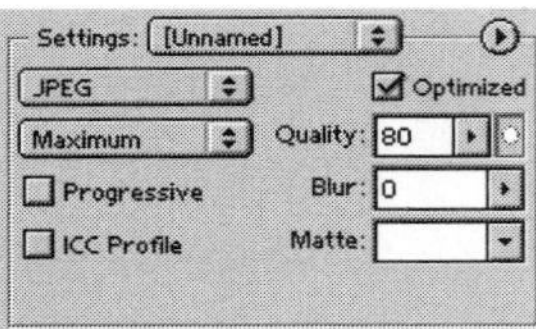

7. Click the circled arrow button immediately to the right of the Settings pop-up menu to bring up the submenu and select Save Settings. In the Save Optimized Settings dialog box, assign a name to your new setting and click Save.

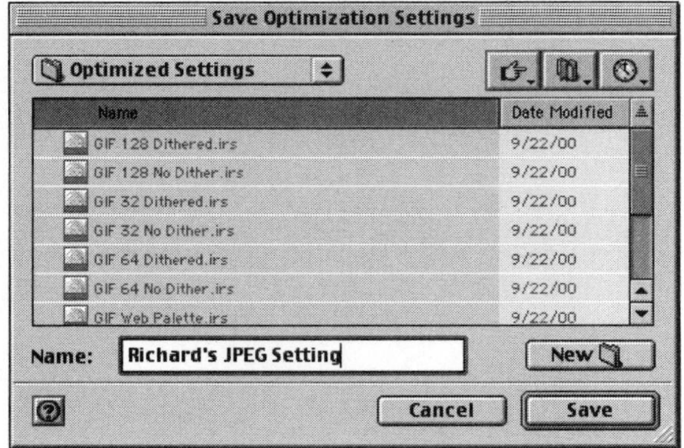

8. Click the Settings pop-up menu. You will see that your saved setting is now listed. You can assign your saved settings to all future images simply by selecting this option in the Settings pop-up menu.

9. Click the circled arrow button to bring up the Settings submenu again. You will see that after you have saved a setting, the Delete Settings selection becomes available in this menu. Select this option to remove your practice settings.

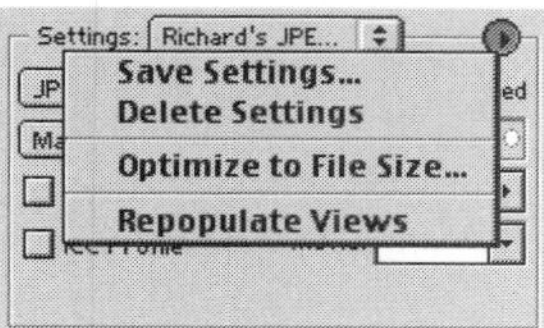

10. Click the 4-Up tab to see four views of your image. Notice that each image view shows a specific modem speed, such as 28.8Kbps.

11. To change the modem speed and other preview settings, click the circled arrow button in the upper-right corner of the 4-Up tab. Any changes you make in this menu will be applied in the current view tab.

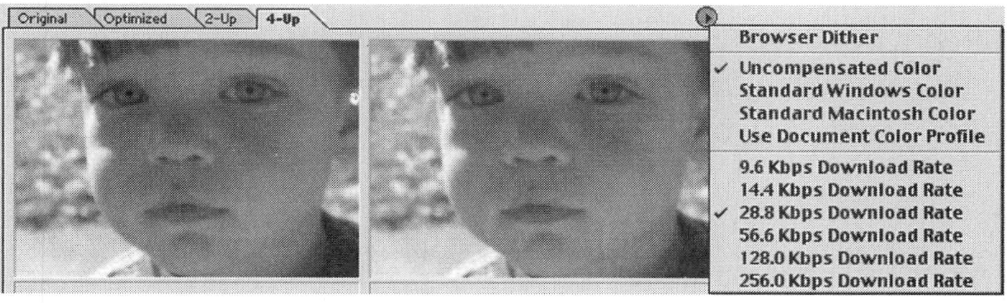

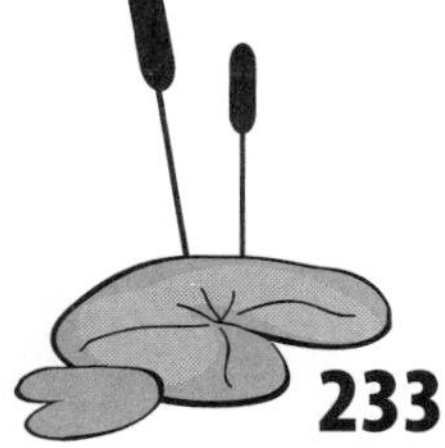

Tip

Press the Alt (Option) key at any time to turn the OK button in the Save for Web dialog box into a button titled Remember. Clicking this button saves parameters such as the scale of the image in the window. Then the next time you open that view, your optimization settings will be assigned automatically.

12. You can continue to experiment with the many options and tools in the Save for Web dialog box. When you're finished, click the Cancel button to close the Save for Web dialog box.

As you've seen, the Save for Web dialog box offers an extremely powerful set of tools. Use them to give your images the best appearance and quickest download times possible for the Web.

Using the Web Photo Gallery Feature

The Web Photo Gallery feature is a fantastic addition to Photoshop for everyone who wants to create an image gallery on a Web site. For most users, this is the perfect way to quickly and efficiently create Web pages that include thumbnails with links to larger images.

Suppose that you are creating a personal Web site where you can share pictures of your family with other family members and friends. If you were a professional Web designer, you would create two versions of each photo—a thumbnail and the full-size image—place them into a Web page layout via a Web production program, and then assign the links by hand. With Web Photo Gallery, all of this work is done for you.

Introducing the Web Photo Gallery Settings

To open the Web Photo Gallery dialog box, select File ➢ Automate ➢ Web Photo Gallery.

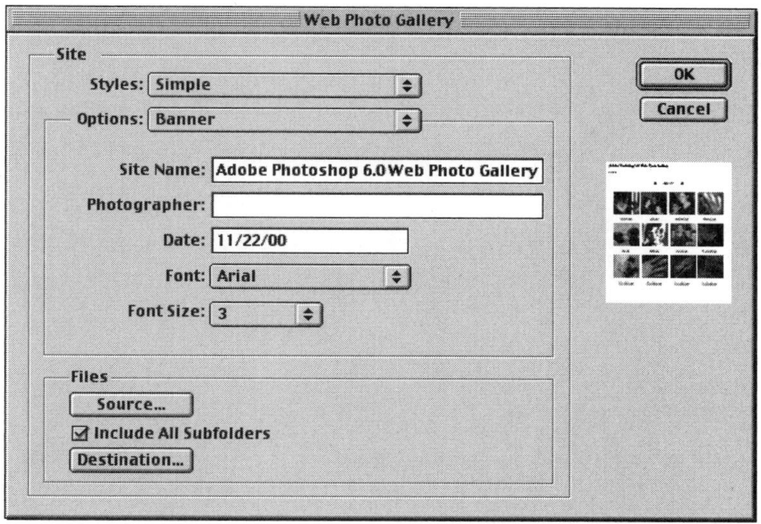

The Web Photo Gallery dialog box offers the following settings:

- The Styles pop-up menu lets you choose the way your thumbnail images will be displayed.
- The Options section offers choices for the way the image names, background, and informative text will be displayed.
- The Files section lets you tell Photoshop where your original image files (Source) are located and where you want your Web Photo Gallery page and files saved (Destination).

The preview display on the right side of the dialog box updates to let you see the layout of the style you select.

Building a Web Gallery Page

Now that you've discovered that you can create a Web page directly in Photoshop, let's go ahead and do just that.

1. Create a new folder and place a few images into it. The images to be included on your Web Photo Gallery page need to be in one location for Photoshop to include them on the page.

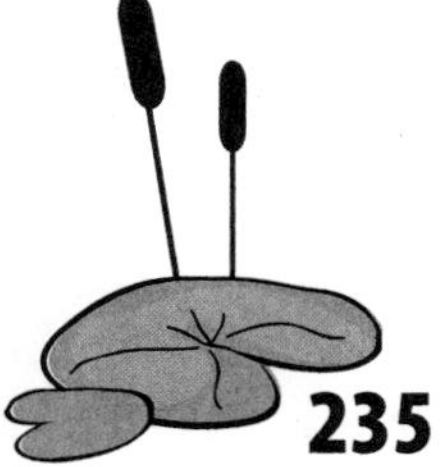

2. In Photoshop, select File ➢ Automate ➢ Web Photo Gallery.

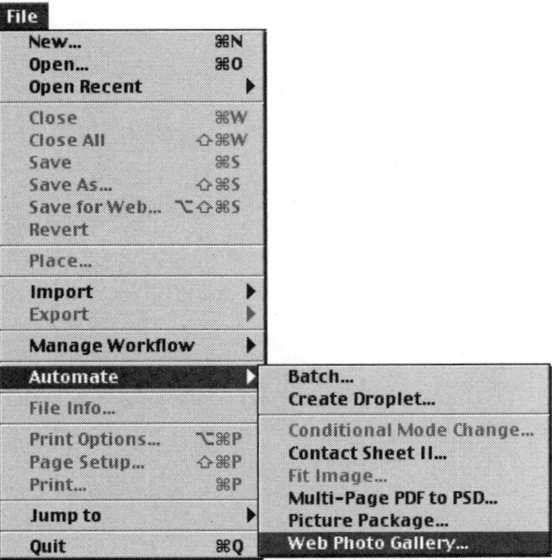

3. From the Styles pop-up menu in the Web Photo Gallery dialog box, select Vertical Frame.

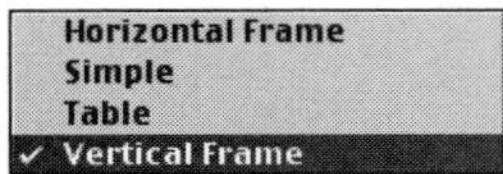

4. The Options pop-up menu shows Banner. In the Options section below, enter a name that will appear as the title of the page. Specify a photographer name, date, font, and font size as desired.

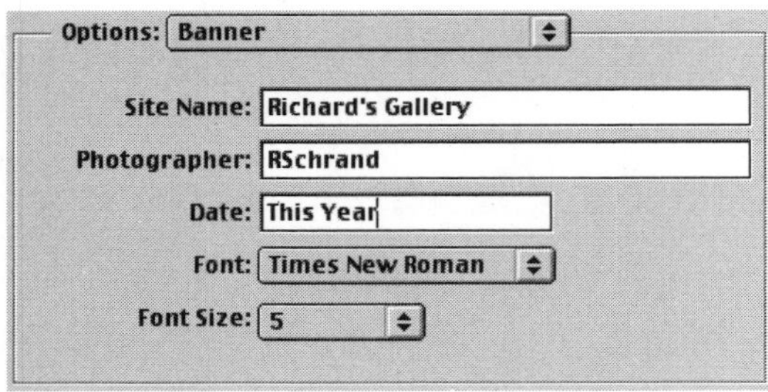

5. From the Options pop-up menu, choose Gallery Images. Set Border Size to 1 pixel and JPEG Quality to High.

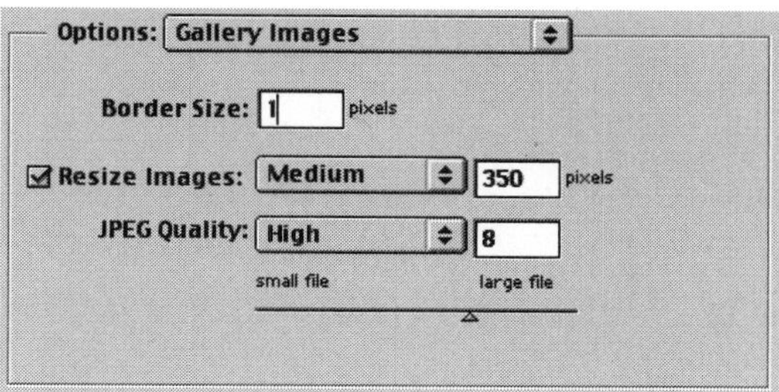

6. From the Options pop-up menu, choose Gallery Thumbnails. Here you can set options for the thumbnail captions and appearance. Leave the default settings for the thumbnails.

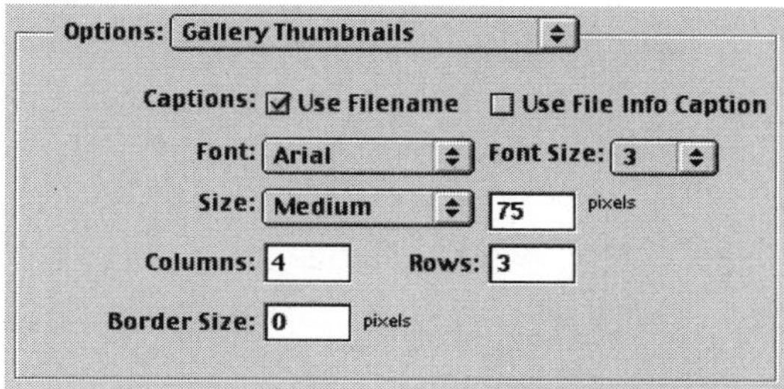

7. From the Options pop-up menu, select Custom Colors. You can choose colors for each area of the page, including link colors. For this example, leave the default settings.

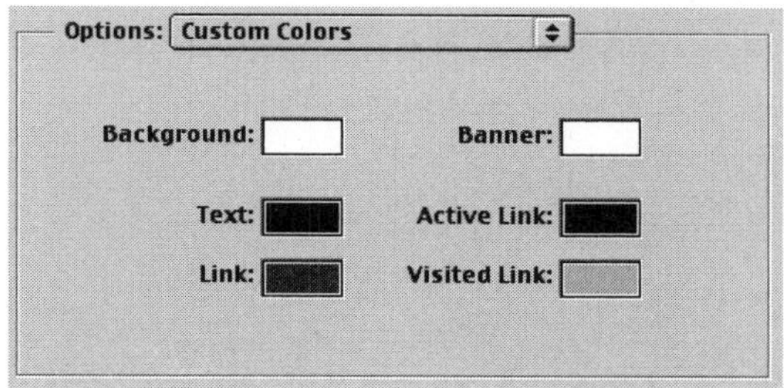

8. Click the Source button in the Files section. A basic navigation dialog box appears, asking you to find the folder where the images are stored. Navigate to the folder without opening it and click Choose. The path to

the folder is displayed in the Web Photo Gallery dialog box. If you have images stored in subfolders, select the Include All Subfolders option.

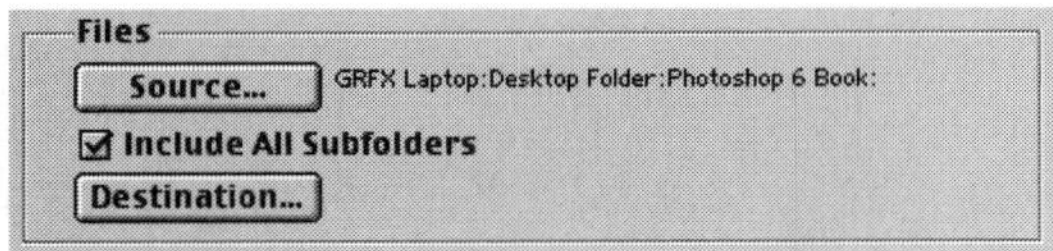

9. Click the Destination button. Photoshop asks you to create a folder or navigate to an existing folder where you want the Web Photo Gallery page to be stored. Click Choose to select a storage folder. The path is listed in the Web Photo Gallery dialog box.

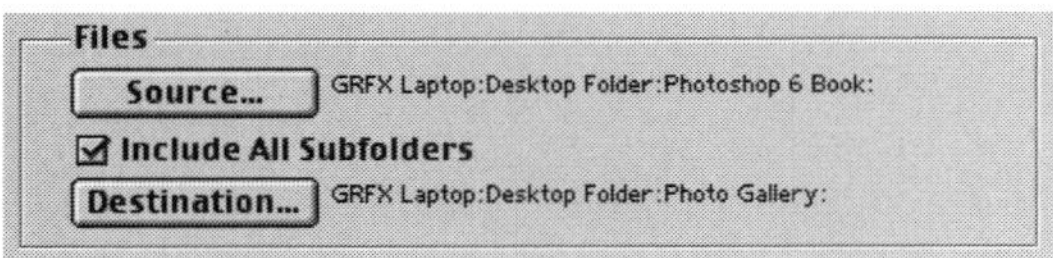

10. Click OK to create the page.

Photoshop now begins building the Web page, creating large images and thumbnails for the page. When it completes the page, Photoshop will open your main Web browser so you can see how the page looks and works.

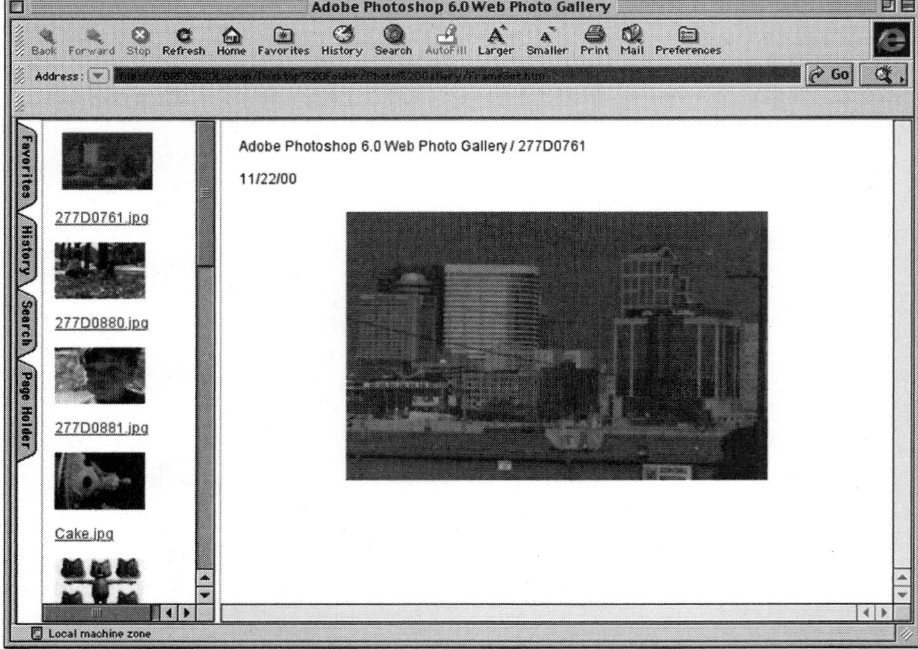

Note

You will need to consult your particular browser's manual or online help to determine how to open a file offline.

Using the Picture Package Feature

Contact sheets are a staple for photographers. If you've had a family photo taken by a professional photographer or your kids had their school picture taken, you've seen contact sheets. They're those photo pages that have copy after copy of the same picture on them. You just cut out the photos and hand them out to friends and family. Photoshop gives you the ability to make contact sheets quickly and easily.

Note

Photoshop also offers the Contact Sheet II option (on the File ➢ Automate submenu). This feature lets you place equally sized images on a page. See Chapter 1 for more information.

The Picture Package option offers a variety of layouts for your printed photos. To use the Picture Package option, select File ➢ Automate ➢ Picture Package. The Picture Package dialog box includes sections for specifying the image and laying out the page.

Picture Package
Source Image
Choose...
Use Frontmost Document
OK
Cancel
Document
Layout: (2)5x7
Resolution: pixels/inch
Mode: RGB Color

In the Source Image section, you can click Choose to open a dialog box where you can navigate to the image you want to use. Alternatively, if you have images open in Photoshop, you can select the Use Frontmost Document option to tell Photoshop to use whichever image is the top one on the screen.

In the Document section, you can use the Layout pop-up menu to select from a series of page styles. The Resolution setting specifies the quality of the image resolution, and the Mode pop-up menu offers color format choices (**RGB**, CMYK, or **Lab**).

RGB image
An image made up of red, green, and blue. These three colors are used to create the entire spectrum of colors in an image. File sizes are smaller when saved in this format.

Lab
A color mode that is device-independent. Lab color consists of lightness (L), a green–red component (a), and a blue–-yellow component (b). Lab can be used to adjust an image's luminance and color independently of each other.

pixelated
Describes an image that contains jagged edges. This term comes from the term *pixels*, which are squares of light that make up the on-screen image.

Warning

Do not specify a higher resolution than the resolution of the original document. If you are creating a Picture Package page using a 72 dpi image, don't make it 300 dpi. If you do use a higher-resolution, your picture will look very **pixelated**. On the other hand, you can, use a lower resolution, such as 72 dpi for a 300 dpi image.

When you pick a layout, make sure to check the document size. Some of the choices are not for the standard 8.5 × 11 inch paper size. For example, the layout shown below is 11 × 17. Before you print, you'll need to load your printer with the correct size paper. After you've made your selection, click OK to create the page.

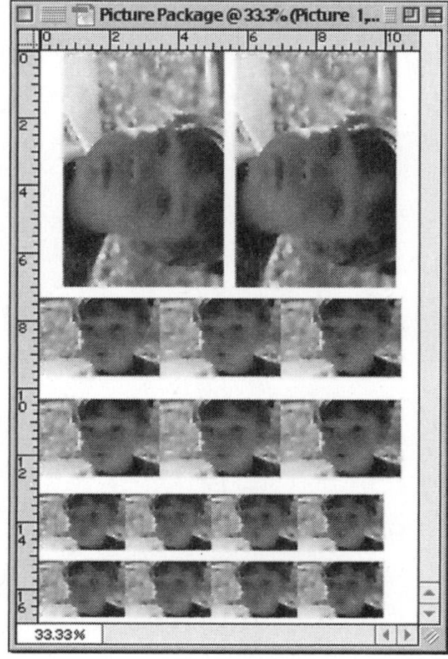

Closing Out

So there you have it—your start on the road to advanced image manipulation. I hope you've enjoyed this book and have a better understanding of what Photoshop can do and how to make it work. As mentioned at the beginning of the book, the study of Photoshop can be a lifelong endeavor because the program has so much to offer. By combining various tools and effects, you have an almost limitless ability to build exciting, original works of art.

Now it's time for you to delve into the depths of Photoshop. You may want to look into purchasing a book such as *Mastering Photoshop 6* (Sybex, 2001) to learn more advanced techniques. Whether you get another guide or experiment on your own, you will have a lot of fun creating fantastic images with Photoshop.

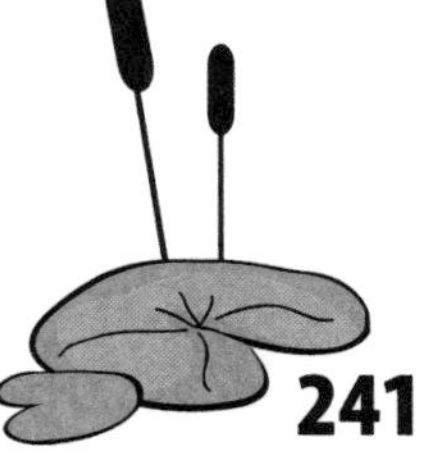

Glossary

action

Another term for command. An action is anything that makes a change to the file you are working on.

Alpha channel

A stored selection from an image. An Alpha channel is a grayscale representation. Black represents transparent areas; white is opaque.

anti-aliasing

Smoothing out of the pixels that make up the edges of the image. When you select the Anti-aliased option for a tool, Photoshop creates a subtle transition between pixels to make the edges appear smooth, rather than jagged.

aspect ratio

The height and width of the actual document. Changing the aspect ratio can make an image look too thin or too short.

Background

The bottom level of the workspace. The Background is locked and content cannot be modified like other layers (although you can fill the Background with a color). To modify the Background, make a copy of it and work with the new layer.

banding

A sharp differentiation between colors that makes them appear as if they were creating a separate band of color not associated with the ones surrounding it.

burn

In photographic terms, to darken an area of an image. Photoshop's Burn tool performs this operation.

busy

Refers to an image that has a lot of visual information.

channel

An area that stores information about an image's color. Channels include Red, Green, Blue, and Alpha when in RGB mode. In CMYK mode, the channels are Cyan, Magenta, Yellow, Black, and Alpha. By working with an image's color channel, you can create many different special effects, changing the entire appearance of the image.

CMYK image

An image made up of cyan, magenta, yellow, and black. These four colors are combined to create all of the colors in an image. CMYK files are typically used in professional four-color printing.

column
The vertical division of a page. Newspapers and many text books are printed using columns, so that more text can fit onto a page.

desaturate
To reduce saturated color information to make a color more realistic or muted to achieve a specific effect.

dither
A method of distributing pixels to extend the visual range of color on the screen, such as producing the effect of shades of gray on a black-and-white display or more colors on an 8-bit color display. By making adjacent pixels different colors, dithering gives the illusion of a third color.

dodge
In photographic terms, to lighten an area of a picture. Photoshop's Dodge tool performs this operation.

downsample
Changing the resolution of an image, either from high to low resolution or vice versa.

drag and drop
To move an image or selected area of an image from one workspace and place it onto another workspace. In the case of Adobe products, you can also drag and drop from one program to another, such as from Photoshop to Illustrator.

Duotone
A mode that uses two specified colors in your image for specialized effects. The other modes are Monotone (one color), Tritone (three colors), and Quadtone (four colors).

feathering
Blurring the edges of a selection, making the edges appear to fade out into the background.

gamut
The range of viewable and printable colors for a particular color model, such as RGB (used for monitors) or CMYK (used for printing). When a color cannot be displayed or printed, Photoshop can warn you that it is out of gamut.

gutter
The blank space separating columns.

histogram
A graphical representation of the color values in an image. The leftmost area is black, rightmost is white, and the area in between represents the midtones (the other colors or shades of gray that make up the image).

hue
The tonal quality of a color.

invert
Changing the area of the selection by reversing the area you selected.

Kbps

Kilobauds per second, which is the measure for the amount of information that is transferred from the Internet to your computer via the modem. The maximum rate is based on the modem you use and the phone line itself.

Lab

A color mode that is device-independent. Lab color consists of lightness (L), a green–red component (a), and a blue–yellow component (b). Lab can be used to adjust an image's luminance and color independently of each other.

layer

An additional level to your working file that allows you to place image information on it without affecting the layer beneath or above it. Think of a layer as a sheet of acetate through which you can see what is beneath it.

layer mask

An effect that removes a portion of an image to reveal the image behind (or underneath) it. In Photoshop, you can create layer masks using the Pen tool and the Paths palette.

logo

An artistic or graphic representation of a name (such as a personal name or company name).

lossless

A file compression method that reduces the size of the file without any noticeable loss in image quality.

lossy

A file-compression method that reduces the quality of the image when saved by removing information.

marching ants

Describes the movement of the outline created around an object when using a Photoshop selection tool such as the Magic Wand, Lasso, or Marquee tools.

midtones

The colors that fall in the middle of the overall range of colors in your image.

montage

An image made up of a number of separate images.

palette

A Photoshop window that contains controls or options for specific program areas.

path
An object composed of anchor points and line segments, created using the Pen tool. A path defines the outline of a shape. You can use a path to hide areas of an image or layer, define an area to become a selection, or create a clipping path that will show only the selected area when the image is brought into a page layout program such as InDesign or QuarkXPress.

PDF
The Portable Document Format, which was developed by Adobe as a way to share files no matter what type of computer you use. PDFs can be created in Photoshop, Illustrator, Acrobat, and other programs.

pixel
A tiny block of colored light, which is the smallest editable unit in a digital image.

pixelated
Describes an image that contains jagged edges. This term comes from the term *pixels*, which are squares of light that make up the on-screen image.

plug-in
Software that adds functionality to Photoshop. Plug-ins generally give you the ability to add special effects to your image.

rasterize
To convert vector information into pixel-based information. When you rasterize type, you can apply filters and other effects that do not work on vector-based type. However, after you rasterize type, you cannot edit the individual characters.

resolution
Refers to the number of pixels/dots per inch that make up the image. The more dots per inch, the higher the resolution and the larger the image file size. This is because there is more information stored in that file.

RGB image
An image made up of red, green, and blue. These three colors are used to create the entire spectrum of colors in an image. File sizes are smaller when saved in this format.

rollover
A button on a Web page that changes appearance when the on-screen cursor moves over it or it is clicked.

saturation
How intense or deep a color is.

scratch disk
A hard drive with unused space that Photoshop can turn into memory that it will use if necessary.

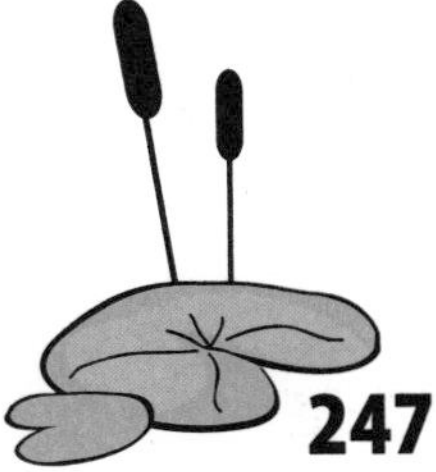

sepia-tone
A photograph that has a dark reddish-brown color (sepia) as the main color of the image.

slice
A portion of an image. When using larger images for Web sites, designers often cut the image into different pieces (slices) to help speed up downloading times.

snapshot
A saved version of an image. Using the History palette, you can save the current image to a snapshot to preserve that state of the image.

state
Adobe's terminology for the particular way an image appears at any given time. As you change the look of the image, you are changing the image's state.

system fonts
Fonts that come already installed on your computer when you buy it.

target
A destination for a URL link. A target can be a new, blank window that the page/window information will load into, the same page/window, or another portion of the same page.

thumbnail
A small graphic representation of a larger image.

vignette
A photograph without a defined edge or border. The image fades off gradually at the edges into the background.

work path
A temporary path you create using the Pen tool. The work path can be modified and edited.

zoom
To magnify an image or specific area of an image so you can see fine details better.

Index

Note to the Reader: Throughout this index **boldfaced** page numbers indicate primary discussions of a topic. *Italicized* page numbers indicate illustrations.

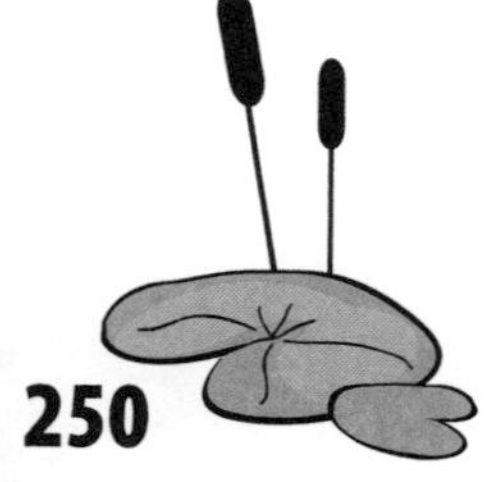

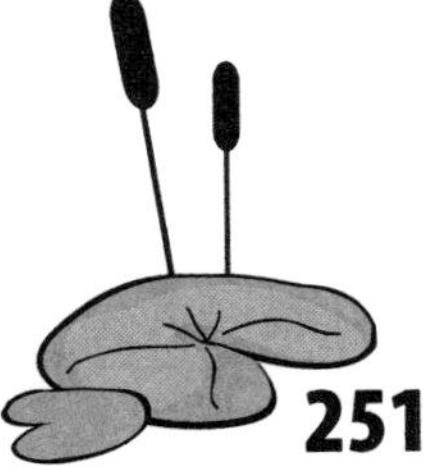

G

H

I

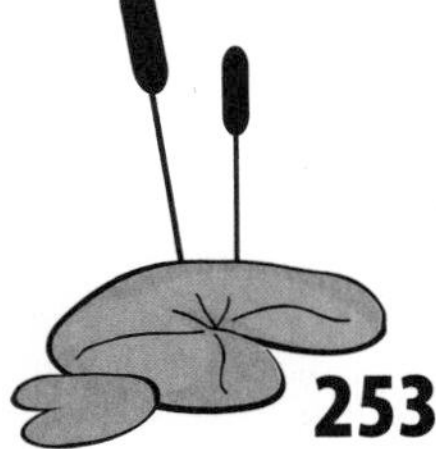

N

O

P

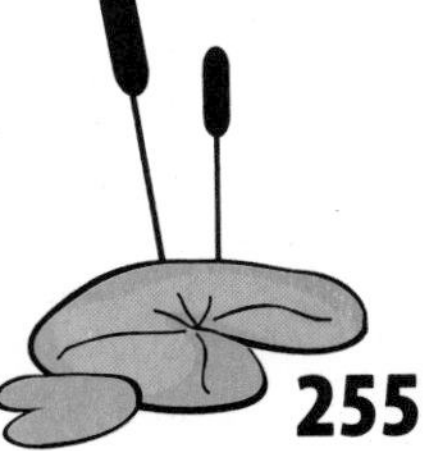

Q

R

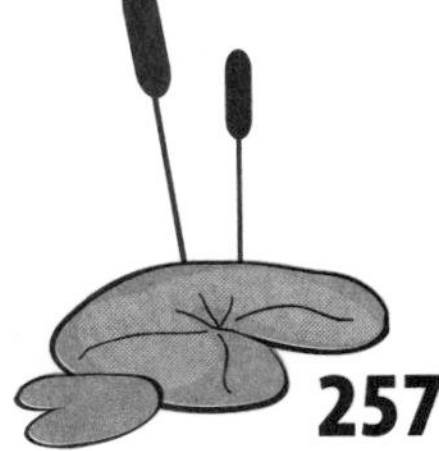

T

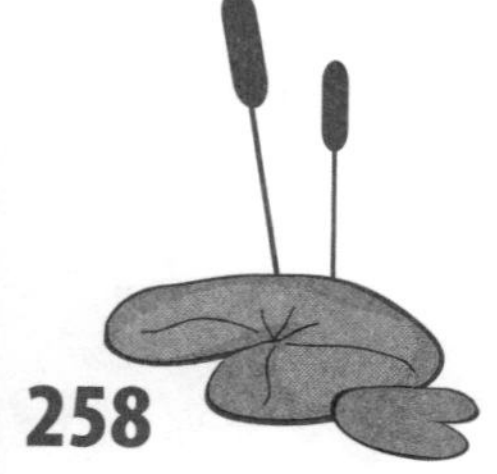

U

V

W

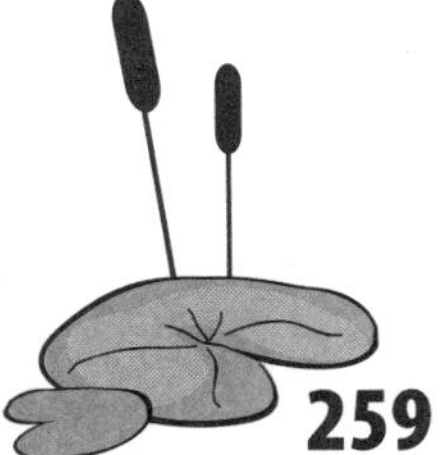

Notes

Notes

Notes

Notes

Notes